RAPE AND CRIMINAL JUSTICE
The Social Construction of
Sexual Assault

RAPE AND CRIMINAL JUSTICE
The Social Construction of Sexual Assault

Gary LaFree
University of New Mexico

Wadsworth Publishing Company
Belmont, California
A division of Wadsworth, Inc

Printed in the United States of America

1 2 3 4 5 6 7 8 9 10 — 93 92 91 90 89

LIBRARY OF CONGRESS
Library of Congress Cataloging-in-Publication Data

LaFree, Gary D.
   Rape and criminal justice : the social construction of sexual
assault / Gary LaFree.
          p.   cm.
   Bibliography: p.
   Includes index.
   ISBN 0-534-11055-X   ISBN 0-534-11056-8 (pbk.)
   1.Rape—United States. I. Title.
KF9329.L34   1989
345.73′02532—dc19
|347.3052532| 88–22882
                                       CIP

This book is dedicated to Shelly, Andy, and Kati

Preface

This book is a product of my experiences over the last 10 years observing trials, interviewing police officers, prosecutors, defense attorneys, and judges who process criminal cases, and working as a researcher in the felony section of a prosecutor's office. These experiences have led me to the conclusion that there is rarely such a thing as a definite truth in the legal system. Instead, the application of law to behavior is a task in which officials with imperfect vision are asked to measure outcomes (like determination of guilt or innocence and degree of culpability) that are obscure and constantly changing with a measuring stick (i.e., the law) that is itself malleable and inconstant. On the other hand, my experiences have made me feel just as strongly that violent personal crimes are all too real, oftentimes exacting an enormous cost on society, both directly through victimization and its aftermath and indirectly through the fear of victimization.

I want to make it clear at the outset that this book is more of an attempt to explain the application of law in rape cases than it is an attempt to understand the causes and consequences of rape. There are already a great many fine books and articles that deal exhaustively with the characteristics of rape victims and offenders, the consequences of rape for the victim, and the potential causes of rape. In contrast, this book examines the legal processing of rape cases in order to better understand the operation of the criminal justice system.

I have had a difficult time deciding what types of data analysis should be included in this book. In a discussion of the elements of good writing, William Strunk and E. B. White portray the reader as being "in serious trouble most of the time . . . floundering in a swamp" and argue that it is the duty of the writer "to drain this swamp and quickly get (the victim) on dry ground, or at least throw him a rope" (p. xii). The terminological "swamp" has gotten deeper and more difficult to traverse in criminology in recent years, in large part because of the explosive development of complex statistical methods. I want this book to be primarily one about ideas. However, much of the research related to these ideas is quantitative and of a type that may be unfamiliar to many readers. To reduce this problem, I have attempted to describe important results in everyday terms and to provide the interested reader with more complete information in technical appendixes. The nontechnical reader will be forgiven for skipping these appendixes entirely.

Rape is an ancient crime that has been poorly understood by criminologists and citizens alike. It warrants our serious attention.

Gary LaFree

Acknowledgments

Because this book is based on nearly 10 years of research, a great many people and institutions have contributed to it along the way. Part of Chapter 4 is a revision of an article that first appeared in *Social Forces* (volume 58, 1980); part of Chapter 5 is a revision of a *Social Problems* (volume 28, 1981) article; part of Chapter 6 is a revision of an *American Sociological Review* (volume 45, 1980) article; and part of Chapter 8 is a revision of an article with Barbara Reskin and Christy Visher, which originally appeared in *Social Problems* (volume 32, 1985). These revisions are all included here with the permission of the journals.

This book was made possible through the generous cooperation of the Indianapolis Police Department and the Marion County Prosecutor's Office and Criminal Courts. I want to thank the police officers, prosecuting attorneys, judges, defense attorneys, and jurors who freely contributed their time to this study. Special thanks to Sue Duffey who assisted me in the early phases of data collection. I am also indebted to the University of New Mexico, which helped in the preparation of the book by providing several grants-in-aid.

The research reported in Chapters 7 and 8 was supported by a National Institute of Mental Health grant awarded through the National Center for the Prevention and Control of Rape. Barbara Reskin was the coprincipal investigator of this grant and is largely responsible for the high quality of the data collected. Barbara also made very helpful suggestions on much of the research reported in earlier chapters. I want to thank Linda Copenhaver for her assistance with the juror interviews, Stephanie Sanford for her help in collecting the observational data and preparing the data for analysis, and Christy Visher for her very important contributions to the data collection and analysis. More than anyone else, Marie Matthews was responsible for the daily operation of the project and was indispensable in all phases of study design and data collection.

I especially want to thank several friends and colleagues who read the manuscript at various stages and provided very helpful comments, including Menachem Amir, Pauline Bart, Chris Birkbeck, Ron Farrell, Gil Geis, Doni Loseke, Martha Myers, Graham Tomlinson, Christy Visher, and Marjorie Zatz. Finally, special thanks to Paul and Kathy Douglas and Donna Watkins for their assistance with the preparation of the manuscript.

Contents

CHAPTER 1

Criminology and the Study of Rape

With ready-made opinions one cannot judge of crime. Its philosophy is a little more complicated than people think.

Fyodor Dostoevsky, *The House of the Dead.*

One summer evening in 1977, Lloyd Jeffries,* 32 years old, walked into a diner in downtown Indianapolis and ordered a cheeseburger. Martha Jones, 41 years old, took the order and began to prepare the food on a grill behind the counter. The customer and the cook were the only two people in the diner. After a few moments, Jeffries moved behind the counter, pulled a knife, grabbed Jones, and pushed her through the kitchen and out the back door of the diner. He then forced Jones into the trunk of his car and slammed the lid shut. After driving Jones to a location that she was later unable to identify, Jeffries bound her hands and raped and sodomized her at knifepoint. He then forced her back into the trunk and again began driving. When he stopped again they were in a wooded area. This time he forced Jones to have oral and anal sex, repeatedly threatened her with a knife, urinated on her, and sexually assaulted her with a stick. Jones begged Jeffries to release her. Instead, he began stabbing her in the back, neck, and arms. Later examination would reveal 25 stab wounds and a deep slash over her throat. Apparently con-

---

* All the names in these accounts are fictitious.

1

vinced that she was dead, Jeffries left Jones lying on the ground, naked except for a shirt, covered in blood. Miraculously, Jones managed to crawl out of the woods and back to the main road before collapsing unconscious near the highway. A passing motorist saw her beside the road and called the police. When Jones regained consciousness, she was in an Indianapolis hospital.

After she began to recover, Martha Jones remembered Lloyd Jeffries as the man who, two months earlier, had offered her $20 to go to bed with him. She identified Jeffries from police photographs, and he was arrested shortly afterward. Police detectives found part of the necklace Jones had been wearing on the night of the assault in the trunk of Jeffries's car.

The main defense offered at Jeffries's trial was that he was insane at the time of the incident. Evidence presented in court revealed that Jeffries had a history of mental problems, including several occasions when he threatened women with sexual assault. He was on medication for these problems at the time of the incident. In court, the defense argued that Jeffries's mother and siblings had all died in a tragic fire when he was a child and that he had had mental problems ever since. Jeffries's father eventually remarried a woman whom the defense claimed Jeffries hated—a woman who closely resembled Martha Jones. Nonetheless, two psychiatrists retained by the defense and two retained by the court all concluded that Jeffries was sane at the time of the incident. After deliberating for three hours, the jury convicted Lloyd Jeffries on multiple counts of aggravated rape, confinement, and attempted murder.

At about 1:00 in the morning on a summer evening in 1977, 19-year-old Cathy Marsh had just left a female friend and decided to try to find her boyfriend, Steve. Steve had told her earlier that he would be at a party that evening but had not given her the exact location. She stopped to talk with Paul Richards, a friend of Steve's, to get directions. Richards got into Marsh's car and they drove off together, ostensibly heading for the party and Marsh's boyfriend. On the way, Richards asked Marsh to stop at a tavern so he could buy beer. Richards then directed Marsh to drive to a wooded area near a gravel pit, claiming that Marsh's boyfriend would be there. However, once Marsh had stopped the car, Richards said to her, "I want to make love with you." Marsh refused. She claims that Richards then grabbed her and said that if she did not have sexual intercourse with him, he would "beat the hell out of" her. After forced intercourse, Marsh drove Richards home and then returned to the house that she shared with her boyfriend, Steve. When she told Steve what had happened, he immediately called the police. Shortly afterward Richards was arrested and charged with rape.

Richards maintained that Marsh had touched his leg just before they had intercourse and had told him that she wanted to "mess around." He further claimed that he had had a sexual affair with Marsh before the incident. When the case went to trial, the defense tried to show that Cathy Marsh was being pushed into prosecution by Steve, who wanted revenge. The defense challenged Marsh's credibility by pointing out that she was living with her boyfriend out of wedlock and asked the jury, "How many virtuous girls would go out looking for their drunken boyfriend at 1:00 in the morning and then leave with another boy for a gravel pit?" After deliberating for less than an hour, the jury acquitted Paul Richards.

On the morning of January 22, 1979, 15-year-old Sheila Davis was watching her younger sister and two younger brothers after her mother, Dorothy, was taken to a local hospital for an emergency operation. After breakfast, Sheila's stepfather, George Davis, left with her nine-year-old sister, Rachel, saying that he was going to take her to a grocery store to do some shopping. Instead, George Davis took Rachel to the home of Frank Davis, his father. On the way to Frank's house, George Davis forced Rachel to have oral sex with him. Once they arrived at Frank Davis's house, the girl was also forced to have oral sex with him. George then returned Rachel to their home. At 9:30 that evening Sheila Davis put her two brothers and her sister Rachel to bed and then went to bed herself. At about 1:00 in the morning, George Davis entered her bedroom and asked her to remove her clothing. She refused. He then removed her clothing, held her down, placed a pillow over her head to prevent her from screaming, and forced her to have sexual intercourse with him.

When Dorothy Davis, George's wife, returned from the hospital six days later, Sheila told her about her stepfather's actions. Dorothy took her daughters to the Indianapolis Police Department. George and Frank Davis were arrested and charged with rape for the January 22 incident. In later testimony, Sheila Davis revealed that similar attacks had been taking place two to three times a week for approximately eight years—ever since she had been legally adopted by George Davis in 1971. She testified that she had told her mother about it two years earlier. However, after her mother had confronted George Davis with the allegation, he had told Sheila that if she didn't change her story, he would kill her. Sheila testified that she had also told the family physician that her stepfather was forcing her to have sexual intercourse with him. However, both her stepfather and her mother had denied the charges, and Sheila had later told the physician that the charges had been false. Sheila further testified that on other occasions George had forced her to have intercourse with her 13-year-old brother, David. David confirmed this testimony and further claimed that on one occasion, his stepfather had forced him to have intercourse with a prostitute while Davis watched and took pictures.

Apart from the testimony of the children, the main evidence introduced in the trial of George and Frank Davis was a collection of pornographic magazines and pictures recovered from their homes. Much of the pornography had incest themes. The principal defense claim in the case was that the children had made up the story to punish their stepfather for leaving their mother. The defense also attempted to provide alibi witnesses to show that the two men were with other people when the alleged attacks occurred. After four hours of deliberation, the jury convicted both men on all charges.

Jennie Thorsten was 21 years old and lived with her boyfriend, Don, and her one-year-old son. On February 21, 1980, she got up at 5:00 A.M. to help Don get ready for work. Afterward, she returned to bed. At 7:00 A.M. she was awakened by a man holding a knife to her throat, who told her that if she moved, he would "cut her head off." She later said that she had gotten a clear view of the intruder's face and described him as about 6 feet tall, with dark, curly hair, wearing a teardrop necklace with a marijuana leaf on it and a silver watchband. She also remembered that the assailant had a tattoo on his arm. The intruder ordered Thorsten to remove her nightgown and then raped her. At one point, her baby began crying in the next room. The intruder told her "to go quiet the kid, or I will kill it." Thorsten went to the baby's room with the intruder, gave her son a bottle, and then returned with the intruder to the bedroom, where the assault continued. As the assailant left, he threatened Thorsten with violence if she went to the police. Thorsten took her baby to her cousin's house, where she called the police and her boyfriend, Don. She and Don then went to the police department, where she picked out Walter Milliken as the assailant from police photographs of recent arrestees. She had never seen him before.

The police eventually located and arrested Milliken. No fingerprints were recovered in the case, and the police laboratory did the examination for blood type of the assailant's sperm incorrectly, so the prosecution was unable to introduce it as evidence.

The defense agreed that a rape had occurred, but argued that Milliken was the wrong man. The defense attorney pointed out that while Milliken had a tattoo on his arm, he also had two large tattoos on his torso that Jennie Thorsten did not mention. Milliken's girlfriend testified that he never owned a necklace such as the one described by Thorsten. Several other witnesses testified that at the time of the incident, Milliken had a serious foot injury, which made walking difficult for him; Thorsten's testimony indicated that the assailant was walking normally. The defense also introduced alibi witnesses who claimed to have seen the defendant before 7:00 A.M. and after 8:15 A.M. on the morning of the rape. After deliberating for four hours, the jury convicted Walter Milliken of rape.

A common first reaction to accounts of rape like those just described is emotional: anger, shock, disgust, outrage, fear, disbelief. Perhaps you know someone who has been a rape victim. Perhaps you have been a rape victim. My most indelible impression from studying rape cases like these is the degree of sheer viciousness that often accompanies the crime. Several of the rape victims whose cases are described in this book were killed, hundreds were very seriously injured, and most required hospitalization. Apart from the physical injuries, there was a wide range of psychological and social consequences. Many of the rape victims included in this study changed homes and jobs. Many left the city in direct response to the crime. Although I have no way to calculate the effects precisely, it is clear that rape victimization often permanently changed the lives of the women who experienced it as well as the lives of their relatives and friends.

After your initial reactions to these cases, perhaps you also noticed just how different they are. Despite the fact that the defendants in all four of the cases summarized here were legally charged with the same crime, forcible rape, individual differences among the cases are nonetheless striking. Philosopher Michel Foucault (1970, p. xv) quotes a passage from Argentine writer Jorge Luis Borges, who describes "a certain Chinese encyclopedia" as dividing animals into the following categories:

> (a) belonging to the Emperor, (b) embalmed, (c) tame, (d) sucking pigs, (e) sirens, (f) fabulous, (g) stray dogs, (h) included in the present classification, (i) frenzied, (j) innumerable, (k) drawn with a very fine camelhair brush, (l) *et cetera*, (m) having just broken the water pitcher, (n) that from a long way off look like flies.

In a discussion of this extraordinary list, Foucault concludes (p. xvi) that what is impossible about it is not merely the things listed—which under the right circumstances are all ordinary—but rather the impossibility that such diverse elements should form some common basis for classification. Reading case descriptions such as those described may lead you to ask a similar question: Apart from the fact that all four cases involved the same criminal charge, how can they be included in the same field of study? Are there any similarities among them, and, where there are differences, can the differences be explained within some broader, theoretical framework? The main purpose of this book is to search for commonalities and patterns in official reactions to rape cases, to identify similar and dissimilar processes, and to try to make sense out of what might otherwise be interpreted as random, unexplainable, or idiosyncratic phenomena.

To do this, I intend to apply several criminological theories about how legal agents react to criminal cases to data on sexual assaults processed in Indianapolis, Indiana, during the 1970s and early 1980s. The results reported in this book are from two related studies. In the first, I used official police, prosecution, and court records to trace 881 rape cases reported to police in the years 1970, 1973, and 1975. In the second, my colleagues and I collected information on all sexual-assault cases tried by Indianapolis courts from July 1978 to September 1980. During the years in which these data were collected I also conducted dozens of interviews with the police, prosecutors, defense attorneys, and judges who processed the rape cases included in the study.

If you consider the four cases summarized somewhat more analytically, you may note that they raise two different types of questions. One question that may come to mind is, Why did the defendants in these cases do what they did? For example, what prompted Lloyd Jeffries to go on the rampage that resulted in the vicious rape and mutilation of Martha Jones? What led George Davis to sexually assault his own adopted children and to arrange for his father to assault them, too? A very different type of question that may arise is, How do the legal agents involved in these cases decide that a crime has occurred? For example, was Walter Milliken really guilty of raping Jennie Thorsten? Was Paul Richards really innocent of raping Cathy Marsh? How did the legal agents involved make these decisions? What facts did they rely on?

For the first half of this century, most criminologists in the United States concentrated on the first of these two general questions. However, beginning in the 1960s, a strong interest in the decision making of legal agents began to develop. In the next section, I explore these developments in greater detail.

THE STUDY OF CRIME AND LEGAL SYSTEMS IN THE UNITED STATES

The official processing of people suspected, charged, and convicted of crime in the United States encompasses a far-flung empire of officials whose decisions annually affect millions of Americans. The legal system employs more than 12 million people in 60,000 agencies, with a total annual budget of more than $10 billion (Hindelang, Gottfredson, and Flanagan, 1981). Included in the total are approximately 40,000 police agencies, nearly 17,000 courts, more than 8,000 prosecutors' offices, about 4,600 correctional institutions, and more than 3,200 probation and parole departments. Every year, police in the United States make nearly 11 million arrests (Brown, Flanagan, and McLeod, 1984, p. 415) and courts prosecute more than 2 million adult suspects (Hindelang, Gottfredson, and Flanagan, 1981, pp. 477–478) and another 1.3 million juveniles (Brown, Flanagan, and McLeod, 1984, p. 479). On a given day in 1984, an average of 328,000 persons were in the nation's prisons, 210,000 in its jails, and another 1,468,500 on probation or parole (Brown, Flanagan, and McLeod, 1984, p. 544). Indeed, the scope, expense, and size of the criminal-justice system in contemporary America seems to confirm a somewhat cynical observation made by Karl Marx more than 150 years ago: "The criminal appears as one of those natural 'equilibrating forces' which establish a just balance and opens up a whole perspective of 'useful' occupations" (Marx, 1981, p. 53).

Although volumes have been written about the specialized decision making that occurs at each stage of the criminal-justice system, the basic elements involved in these decisions are straightforward: *legal agents applying law to behavior.* This simple formulation underscores a fundamental distinction in criminology between research on legal agents and law, generally called "the sociology of law," and research on the nature and determinants of criminal behavior, referred to as "criminal etiology." The subject matter of *the sociology of law*, like the legal institutions it studies, can be divided into two parts. The first reflects a concern with how law is *created*—how social groups determine what types of behavior should receive formal, public attention. The second is concerned with how law is *applied*—how police arrest, prosecutors prosecute, jurors judge, judges sentence, and prison guards guard. *Criminal etiology* is the study of the causes of crime. More generally, it reflects a concern with crime rates and how they change, and with the characteristics of individuals and groups that violate criminal laws.

Since the beginning of academic criminology in the United States in the early 1900s, most research has focused on criminal etiology—on what Travis Hirschi and David Rudisill (1976) call "the great American search" for causes of crime. Indeed, most of what social researchers regard as mainstream North American criminology is in this tradition, including such influential classics as Clifford Shaw and Henry McKay's research on social disorganization, Edwin Sutherland's theory of differential association, and Robert Merton's theory of anomie. The hallmarks of this research are the assumptions that crime is an objective social fact and that criminology can (and should) focus on criminal behavior apart from the study of criminal justice and the sociology of law. These assumptions are part of a much broader set of assumptions collectively known in the social sciences as "positivism."

In criminology, *positivism* has generally referred to the belief that human behavior, including crime, is determined by a variety of biological and social forces, over which the individual criminal may have little or no control. Positivists assume that crime is an objectively given feature of reality. Hence, it can be counted and studied just like any other phenomenon: planets, trees, people under 45 years of age, and so on. However, when applied specifically to the study of crime, positivism includes several additional assumptions. One of the most consequential of these centers on the observation that in order to study criminal behavior as an objective fact, researchers are often forced to take someone else's word for who is criminal and who is not.

Those who study criminal behavior have generally relied on official police or court records to distinguish criminals from noncriminals. However, for this to be a meaningful comparison, a chain of three assumptions is required: first, that people in society generally agree on what constitutes legal and illegal behavior; second, that this agreement is reflected in the creation of criminal law; and third, that legal agents correctly apply criminal law in individual cases and thereby separate the guilty from the innocent. Taken together, these assumptions suggest a self-reinforcing system in which offenders break laws that are based on well-established and widely shared societal rules and values, they are apprehended and punished for their acts, and their punishment reaffirms the rules and values that underlie the criminal law. From this perspective, the role of criminology is to identify the causes of crime and, perhaps, ultimately to eliminate them.

CHALLENGES TO MAINSTREAM CRIMINOLOGY

Beginning in the 1960s, the traditional emphasis in criminology on explaining the causes of crime was challenged on several theoretical fronts. Although there are many important individual differences among these challenges, all of them share at least one characteristic: *in contrast to positivist theories concerned primarily with criminal etiology, they all assume that criminology cannot ignore the creation and application of law.*

One of the earliest and most influential of the new challenges to mainstream criminology was first enunciated in a 1963 book by sociologist Howard Becker about marijuana users and society's efforts to control their behavior. *Outsiders* made some startling and original assertions about crime and its control. Perhaps the most basic of these was the idea that deviance and crime are not objective properties of certain actions or behavior, but rather definitions constructed through social interaction. In Becker's words (1963, p. 9), "Deviance is *not* a quality of the act the person commits, but rather a consequence of the application by others of rules and sanctions to an 'offender.'" This assertion, which may seem relatively harmless, was in fact a serious challenge to the then-popular positivist assumptions about crime and the legal system. It suggested, for example, that legal sanctions are not always or even usually applied when the law is broken, that many and perhaps most people who break the law are never identified, that other people who do not break the law are nonetheless treated as criminals, and, in general, that there are fewer differences between criminals and noncriminals than most of us usually assume.

If the law is not applied to people because of their criminal behavior, the obvious question becomes, "How *is* it applied?" Becker offered an answer to this question for each of the two components of the law: the written law, which provides the rules that define criminal behavior, and the legal system, which actually applies these rules. In both cases, the answer to the question is similar: the law is written and applied to maintain the social power of dominant groups. Becker writes that "Differences in the ability to make rules and apply them to other people are essentially power differentials" (p. 17) and notes that "rules tend to be applied more to some persons than others" (p. 12).

Becker's study of marijuana smokers and the articles and books that immediately followed it—the first formulations of what is most often referred to as *labeling theory*—turned most of what was then mainstream North American criminology on its head. Instead of assuming that criminal laws are generally objective and uniformly applied, we should assume that they are generally subjective and inconsistently applied. Instead of studying why people commit crime, we should be more concerned with the general processes by which legal agents decide that a given act should be defined as criminal and the ways in which they conclude in specific cases that a crime has been committed. Instead of trying to determine what should be done to criminal offenders, we should be more concerned with how criminal processing affects those who are processed.

The publication of Becker's book was followed by a cascade of research that applied, extended, modified, and critiqued labeling theory. For the first time in North American criminology, many researchers were devoting more time to the study of society's reaction to crime than to the characteristics of arrested or convicted offenders. Labeling theory also had important effects on criminal-justice policy. For example, the labeling theorists' claim that official reactions to crime often make matters worse resulted in, or at least was used to justify, programs to keep offenders out of institutions as much as possible and movements to eliminate laws against activities that many people did not consider deviant.

As the 1970s began, challenges to mainstream criminology became even more direct. Early versions of labeling theory such as Becker's had suggested revisions in the way we look at crime and the legal system. But by the mid-1970s, a variety of emerging *conflict theories* offered a more thorough critique of the legal system. Most strands of conflict theory stressed the need to study crime and official reactions to crime in the larger context of social class, economic systems, and power. Other conflict theorists argued that crime problems could not be solved by working within the existing framework of capitalist society and advocated a socialist revolution as the only solution to crime problems in the United States.

In this book I concentrate on two propositions from labeling theory and conflict theory that I believe have special relevance to the study of rape and that remain among the most basic and influential of the contributions made to criminology by the two theories:

1. *Crime is not an objective property of certain behavior, but rather a definition constructed through social interaction.*
2. *The law is applied to control the behavior of individuals who threaten the power of dominant groups.*

CRIMINOLOGY AND RAPE

This book explores these two themes through a study of official reactions to cases of forcible rape. Rape has several strategic characteristics for an application like the one proposed here. First, labeling and conflict theories pose a fundamental challenge to the idea that law is based on the consensus of those governed by it. But obviously some crimes are likely to bring more universal condemnation than others. In general, people agree more about the importance of *mala in se* crimes (wrong in and of themselves) like murder and rape than *mala prohibita* crimes (wrong because they are prohibited by law) like prostitution, gambling, and drug use. This fact no doubt explains why many of the best known labeling and conflict studies focus on crimes about which society seems to have a good deal of ambivalence, including Becker's (1963) study of marijuana users, William Chambliss's study of vagrancy (1964), Mary Owen Cameron's (1964) study of shoplifters, Joseph Gusfield's (1967) research on the prohibition of alcohol, Thomas Scheff's (1974) research on mental patients, and Anthony Platt's (1969) research on juvenile delinquency. In contrast, rape is a mala in se crime, universally condemned by societies, whose prohibition can be traced back several thousand years. In this sense rape provides a less common type of application than has usually been the case in tests of labeling and conflict theories.

Second, rape is the only crime in which men are almost universally the offenders and women, the victims (the major exception being male–male rape, which occurs primarily in prisons). Because of this fact, social reactions to rape are also, in part, general reactions to men, women, and their behavior. My assumption is that reactions to rape in a society provide a theoretical "window" into underlying assumptions about the sexes and gender relations. If, as labeling theory asserts, deviance and crime are not objective properties of behavior but definitions constructed through social interaction, in the case of rape these constructions should tell us something unique about the way society perceives women, men, and the proper role of each.

Finally, rape is a strategic topic because it provides a natural laboratory for the study of how law, crime, and social-control bureaucracies change over time in the face of shifting social conditions. It is hard to think of a single aspect of the official processing of rape cases in the United States that has not been challenged, and in most cases changed, in recent years (see Largen, 1976; Rose, 1977; Galvin, 1985; Gornick, Burt, and Pittman, 1985). Rape law has been extensively modified, many communities have initiated special counseling and medical services for rape victims, police departments have added rape investigation units, and many prosecutors' offices have developed rape prosecution teams. In 1975 the federal government created a National Center for the Prevention and Control of Rape under the auspices of the National Institute of Mental Health, which has funded hundreds of research projects on the causes and prevention of rape. In short, then, rape provides a strategic topic for considering the evolution of the law and its enforcement.

THE PROPER ROLE OF CRIMINOLOGY

The implications of accepting either the view that crime statistics represent actual behavior or the view that they reflect the reactions of legal agents are potentially far-reaching. For criminologists who believe that statistics generally represent criminal behavior, the task of criminology is to examine those statistics and try to determine why people commit crime. They assume that crime exists as an objective fact that can be studied like any other object. By contrast, for criminologists who believe that crime statistics generally represent the vicissitudes of official decision making, the task of criminology is to determine how the legal system operates and what consequences its operation has for those being processed as criminals. They assume that criminal labels are based on the subjective judgments of legal agents.

An underlying theme of this book is that criminology has now grown large and diverse enough to proceed simultaneously along both of the research fronts suggested by these two views of crime. I am convinced that the men who were arrested and convicted of rape in Indianapolis during the years of our study bear only a faint relationship to all men who committed rape there. At the same time, it is nonsense to claim that there is no objective reality in the legal system— that none of the men found guilty of rape in the trials we observed were really guilty. In fact, the maddening quality of social reality is that it is neither totally objective nor totally subjective. If it were totally objective, criminologists could be more like physicists. If it were totally subjective, criminologists could concentrate on being artists. But, alas, criminologists are stuck somewhere in the middle, in a limbo between objectivity and subjectivity.

Such reasoning has led me to conclude that the proper path for criminology must lie somewhere between the extreme positivist view that the law represents a widely shared system in which offenders are arrested, prosecuted, convicted, and punished for their acts and the extreme labeling-conflict view that those accused and punished for criminal behavior bear no relationship to those who have actually committed it. The difficulty of this "middle path" was aptly summarized in another context by the British social historian R. H. Tawney, who once warned policymakers against the tendency to assert "the impossibility of absolute cleanliness as a pretext for rolling in a manure heap" (1971, p. 56). That is, we may never actually reach objectivity, but it is possible for us to move closer to or farther away from it.

The two propositions from labeling and conflict theory introduced above will provide the theoretical framework for the
chapters which follow. The most fundamental contribution of
labeling and conflict theories—like many other new ideas
in science—was not that they provided new answers to old
questions but, more basically, that they suggested the importance of asking new questions. In Chapters 2 and 3 I consider
the ways in which labeling and conflict theories challenged
mainstream criminology's assumptions about the proper
subject matter of the field. I develop the theoretical connections between labeling theory and official reactions to rape in
Chapter 2 and between conflict theory and reactions to rape
in Chapter 3. Chapters 4 to 8 then apply the labeling and conflict propositions to data on the official processing of rape
cases. Chapters 4 and 5 explore the idea—most closely associated with labeling theory—that criminal sanctions are based
less on objective properties of behavior than on definitions
constructed through social interaction. Chapter 4 applies this
idea to the decision making of the rape victim and the police,
and Chapter 5 applies it to the decision making of the prosecution and courts. In Chapters 6 to 8 I turn to the conflict-
theory argument that law is applied in a discriminatory
manner to control the behavior of individuals who threaten
the power of dominant social groups. In Chapter 6 I consider
this argument in terms of the race of victims and defendants,
and in Chapters 7 and 8 I consider it in terms of women who
appear to have broken gender-role norms. Finally, in Chapter
9 I discuss the implications of the results for criminology and
social policy and offer some conclusions.

The Labeling Perspective and Official Reactions to Rape

We see that the actors themselves often disagree about what is deviant, and often doubt the deviant character of an act. The courts disagree; the police have reservations even when the law is clear; those engaged in the proscribed activity disagree with official definitions.

Howard Becker, *Outsiders.*

What seems necessary is to . . . challenge the sentimental notion that social behavior is inherently meaningful. . . . Meaning becomes, instead, something that each man tries to impose on the world.

Randall Collins, *Conflict Sociology.*

Images of violent crime are so prevalent on television and in the movies that most adults have seen hundreds of police and court dramas involving the processing of defendants charged with violent offenses. Differences between these media portrayals and real cases are instructive. For example, in television portrayals of trials, the audience often becomes a kind of mass jury as the facts of the case are painstakingly laid out by each side. If the story is told well, the feeling of suspense builds gradually from witness to witness, as new evidence is revealed. When the dramatic dénouement finally comes, we know who the guilty party is. The defendant, under intense cross-examination by a skillful attorney, confesses, or perhaps the victim tearfully admits that her entire story was a fabrication. This leads to catharsis, to the feeling that justice has once again been done. Thus, television portrayals of police work and trials are often morality plays in which good ultimately triumphs over evil. This is rarely the situation with real cases. In the years that I spent collecting and analyzing the data reported in this book, I never saw a rape defendant break down on the stand and confess. Nor did I witness a single victim who, under the pressure of a surprise defense witness or the skillful harangues of a Perry Mason, publicly admit that she had lied.

This raises a fundamental difference between the actual functioning of legal systems and Hollywood portrayals of them. In television dramas, the story gradually becomes one and the same with the "real event." There is no distinction between "what really happened" outside the drama and what we gradually learn happened during the drama. Although it may take an hour or more, we gradually learn, through investigation, evidence, interviews, and testimony, what really happened. But with real rape cases we seldom know. Instead, participants and observers develop "theories" of what happened. As a spectator, my theories of what happened in individual cases sometimes changed from witness to witness, or even from statement to statement. In real cases, there is never absolute certainty, but only probabilities. It is, of course, in recognition of this basic fact that the law must include probabilistic statements like "guilt beyond a reasonable doubt," "probable cause," and "preponderance of the evidence."

In some respects, mainstream criminology in the United States has accepted a view of crime similar to that commonly adopted by television and movies. Thus, like the media, many criminologists have assumed that the law represents a widely shared system in which offenders are arrested, prosecuted, convicted, and punished for their acts. The guilty are correctly separated from the innocent, and the question of why they committed the crimes they did can then be addressed. Beginning in the 1960s, labeling and conflict theorists criticized these assumptions and raised the possibility that legal-processing decisions may tell us more about the characteristics of the participants and legal bureaucracies than about actual criminal behavior. Labeling and conflict theorists argued that the main task of criminology is not to explain why people commit crime but to determine how the legal system operates and what consequences its operation has for those being processed as criminals. In the next section I briefly consider the theoretical roots of labeling-theory challenges to mainstream criminology and some of its implications for the study of the legal processing of rape cases.

THE EMERGENCE OF LABELING THEORY IN CRIMINOLOGY

To understand labeling theory, we need to return to some of the basic premises of *symbolic interaction theory*, especially as developed in the 1920s and 1930s by sociologists Charles Cooley, W. I. Thomas, and George Herbert Mead. Because symbolic interactionism is a social-psychological theory, it emphasizes microlevel explanations of behavior such as face-to-face encounters and group pressures on the individual. Symbolic interactionists contend that people develop images of themselves early in life through their interaction and communication with others. *Symbols*—words or gestures that signify ideas, persons, or things—are crucial in this process because they form the basis of human interaction. Language is the most important system of symbols. Symbolic interactionists argue that through language and other types of communication, people constantly change and reconstruct their images of themselves and others.

Symbolic interaction theory has important implications for both the study of criminal etiology and the sociology of law. In terms of criminal etiology, the theory suggests that criminal behavior is not caused by fixed biological attributes, deep psychological drives, or rigidly structured social organization, but instead is a product of social interaction. This perspective was fully developed in Edwin Sutherland's theory of differential association, first published in 1939. Sutherland's theory emphasized the interaction between the accomplished criminal and the novice in order to explain how people learn to commit criminal behavior. In contrast, the main contribution of labeling theory is that it applies the insights of symbolic interactionism to the study of law and social control by focusing on the social interaction between the alleged criminal and the official agents making the allegations. Thus, it is primarily a theory of how people come to be identified as criminal or deviant and the consequences of these processes for those so labeled.

From its base in the 1960s, labeling theory moved not only forward in time but also backward by incorporating the ideas of earlier theorists into an emerging theoretical perspective. For example, many labeling theorists interpreted the work of historian Frank Tannenbaum as an important precursor to labeling theory. Tannenbaum is probably best known for his concept of *the dramatization of evil*. By this, Tannenbaum referred to social processes through which an individual's bad or evil acts are "dramatized" by being associated with an image of the individual deviant. Thus the tendency to see specific *behavior* as evil is transformed into a tendency to see specific *individuals* as evil. Tannenbaum believed that this process had a self-fulfilling character:

> The process of making the criminal . . . is a process of tagging, identifying, segregating, describing, emphasizing, making conscious and self-conscious; it becomes a way of stimulating, suggesting, emphasizing, and evoking the very traits that are complained of. . . . The person becomes the thing he is described as being (1938, p. 19).

Sociologist Edwin Lemert made this point even more directly in 1951, in his discussion of primary and secondary deviance (pp. 75–76). *Primary deviance* refers to acts that are never identified or punished by anyone in authority. Labeling theorists maintain that a great deal of deviant and criminal behavior never results in a deviant or criminal label. However, in some cases—and it would be a major task of labeling theory to identify these—officials discover and react to primary deviance. Once people are labeled deviant, the community begins to treat them differently. They are expected to adhere to additional rules that apply only to them. As they interact with community members who see them as deviant, they begin to develop a deviant identity. If an individual so labeled now commits a deviant or criminal act, it is called *secondary deviance* because the person commits it as "a means of defense, attack, or adjustment to the overt and covert problems created by the consequent societal reactions to him" (Lemert, 1951, p. 76).

Labeling-theory ideas such as these created a new interest in the sociology of law by asserting that official criminal labels cannot be taken at face value. Legal processing is not simple, automatic, or inevitable, as positivist criminology would have it. Hence, criminal behavior, as measured by police or court statistics, is of less interest than the *processes* by which these statistics are created.

LABELING THEORY AND RAPE RESEARCH

Research on rape in North America, like criminological research in general, has been primarily concerned with criminal etiology. Psychological explanations were most common up to the 1950s, while sociological explanations have been more common since the 1960s. Researchers in the psychological tradition (e.g., Guttmacher and Weihofen, 1952; Karpman, 1954) assume that to understand rape, it is most important to study the rapist. In actual practice, this has generally meant that psychological research on the causes of rape has been limited to the study of incarcerated offenders. Much of this literature has concluded that rape is perpetrated by a few deeply disturbed men. Thus, Benjamin Karpman (1954, p. 477) writes: "Rapists are victims of a disease from which many . . . suffer more than their victims." A major assumption of this type of research is that other aspects of rape— features of the setting, actions of the victim, societal norms and regulations, laws and their enforcement—are of less importance for understanding rape than the convicted rapist's psychological attributes.

Although social explanations of rape have become more popular in recent years, psychological perspectives have continued to generate new research up to the present (e.g., Groth, 1979; Koss and Leonard, 1984). It is easy to see why. People are generally concerned and fearful about rape. Next to murder, it is the street crime that carries the harshest penalties. A valid theory of why rapists commit rape would therefore have enormous value. Moreover, there is the ongoing practical problem of how to "rehabilitate" or otherwise deal with the thousands of men convicted of rape each year. Beyond this, psychological explanations are likely to be more palatable to the public because they portray rape not as a widespread social problem but as an isolated act of a few sick individuals. No basic changes in society, but only the incarceration and treatment of a handful of serious offenders, would be required. However, despite the tremendous appeal of psychological theories, their contribution to our understanding of rape has been limited by their failure to isolate any personality traits that distinguish rapists from nonrapists and the overwhelming evidence that men institutionalized for committing rape represent only a fraction of all rapists.

Early Social Theories of Rape

As with psychologically oriented research, most social research on rape has sought to identify its causes. In the 1960s and early 1970s, researchers linked rape to the characteristics of defendants (Svalastoga, 1962; Amir, 1967; *University of Pennsylvania Law Review,* 1968; Chappell et al., 1971); the characteristics of victims (Svalastoga, 1962; Amir, 1967; *University of Pennsylvania Law Review,* 1968); ecological patterns (Chappell et al., 1971); subgroup processes (Blanchard, 1959); and male–female sex ratios (Svalastoga, 1962). Criminologist Menachem Amir's (1971) study is the most comprehensive of the early social approaches.

Amir's theory of rape is generally based on Marvin Wolfgang's (1958) *subculture-of-violence theory* (see also Wolfgang and Ferracuti, 1967), which asserts that socially disadvantaged persons form a subculture with a set of values different from those of the dominant culture. Because they are powerless, members of this subculture resort to violence—including rape—to fulfill their needs. Amir's research shows that 77 percent of rapes reported to Philadelphia police during the years of his study were committed by offenders whom he classified as low-status and poor. For Amir, this supports the theory that rape is an integral part of a lower-class subculture of violence in which aggression and exploitation of women are commonplace.

Amir's research is typical of criminological research that concentrates more on causes of crime than on the processes by which alleged offenders come to be treated as criminals. Thus, while Amir's study includes detailed information on victim and offender characteristics, it excludes information on the official processing of the cases in his sample. Without such information, it is impossible to study how the characteristics of the rape cases in the sample are related to case outcomes. This has the effect of focusing attention on characteristics of individuals and ignoring the system that processes these individuals and brings them to the attention of researchers. For example, rather than considering the overrepresentation of young blacks in the sample as possible evidence of differential treatment by processing agents, Amir interprets it as evidence for the subculture-of-violence theory. Similarly, rather than considering the destination of cases in which the victim uses "indecency in language and gestures" (p. 495) in terms of differential system processing, Amir interprets it as evidence of "victim precipitation" of the crime.

Amir's study of rape is a pioneering effort in that it provides a comprehensive portrait of the characteristics of men charged with rape and women who report rape. However, it excludes much of the broader social significance of rape by failing to consider the system of social control that defines rape and applies its definitions to actual cases. Thus, like the psychological theories that preceded it, Amir's subculture-of-violence theory places rape at a comfortable distance from most of society by assuming that rape is committed primarily by a few violent, lower-class men.

Rape and Social Structure

Anthropologists were probably the first academic group to explicitly associate rape more generally with the structure of society. For example, anthropologist Robert LeVine (1959, p. 987) links the high rate of rape among the Gusii of southwestern Kenya to intersexual conflict, supported by a social structure that encourages men to subdue women forcibly in sexual encounters. Similarly, anthropological studies of the Cheyenne Indians by E. Adamson Hoebel (1954) and the Mangia of Oceania by Donald Marshall and Robert Suggs (1971) conclude that males sometimes use group rape as a sanction against unfaithful wives. A more recent example is Peggy Sanday's (1981) research on rape in tribal societies. Sanday distinguishes between societies that are relatively "rape-prone" and those that are "rape-free" and concludes that in rape-prone societies women have little power and do not participate in public decision making.

Although an appreciation of the social significance of rape can be found in anthropological literature before the 1970s, the feminist movement, which gathered strength during that decade, is chiefly responsible for focusing and spreading these ideas (for reviews, see Brownmiller, 1975; Bart, 1975; Clark and Lewis, 1977; Chappell, Geis, and Geis, 1977; Rose, 1977; Schwendinger and Schwendinger, 1980, 1983; Deming and Eppy, 1981; Bart and O'Brien, 1985; MacKinnon, 1987; Estrich, 1987). The central assumption of the feminist perspective on rape is that rape results from institutionalized sexism rather than psychopathology, violent subcultures, or victim precipitation. Feminists claim that rape and the threat of rape have traditionally served as mechanisms by which men maintain women's subordination in an inequitable social system. For example, in *Against Our Will,* Susan Brownmiller's influential book on rape, she characterizes it as "nothing more or less than a conscious process of intimidation by which all men keep all women in a state of fear" (1975, p. 5). Thus, like the anthropologists, feminists have emphasized connections between rape and more general relationships between men and women. For example, much of Brownmiller's book is an account of the meaning of rape in diverse social settings, including warfare, gang violence, and race-related power struggles.

With the resurgence of the feminist movement in the early 1970s, research on rape expanded dramatically, gained methodological and theoretical sophistication, and began to encompass a broader range of research questions, which included a concern with rape laws and how they are applied, as well as criminal etiology.

LABELING THEORY AND CONSTRUCTING RAPE

The rise of the modern feminist movement, with its reconceptualization of rape, generally coincided with the increasing popularity of conflict theory in criminology. Indeed, it seems likely that many of the same social forces produced both events: earlier participation in civil rights and antiwar movements, opposition to racism and sexism, and discontent over evidence of widespread inequality, injustice, and corruption. Many conflict criminologists have also been active in the feminist movement.

By contrast, the development of labeling theory largely preceded the feminist movement and a corresponding research interest in the social significance of rape. Moreover, because labeling theory was originally applied most often to those charged with crime rather than to crime victims, its application to rape was less obvious than it was to other types of crime. However, the rationale behind the perspective—the idea that legal classification decisions are not necessarily the direct result of actual behavior, but represent stereotypes resulting from social interaction—is equally applicable to victims and offenders. In fact, the common criticism that the victim's credibility in rape cases is as much an issue as that of the offender (Robin, 1977; Holmstrom and Burgess, 1978; Schwendinger and Schwendinger, 1983) suggests that labeling-theory insights may be applied to victims as appropriately as to defendants in rape cases.

Criticisms of Labeling Theory

Perhaps the single most important contribution of labeling theory to criminology is its insistence that the relationship between the crimes that are committed and the crimes that lead to official sanctions is far more tenuous than mainstream criminology assumes. This thinking can be summarized in three propositions:

1. Definitions of crime change over time and from place to place.

2. There is little societal consensus about rules and laws.

3. The application of law is not infallible, so that some innocent persons are found guilty and some guilty persons are never apprehended and punished.

It is difficult to argue with the first and third of these propositions. Even a cursory inspection of laws will convince us that definitions of crime do change over time, and it seems unlikely that any criminologist would seriously argue that the legal system correctly identifies *all* wrongdoers or that no innocent person is ever convicted of a crime. Thus, one of the most persistent challenges to labeling theory has been to address adequately the issue of whether people agree about what types of behavior constitute crime and how serious different types of crime are.

Critics (Wellford, 1975; Greenberg, 1976; Nettler, 1984, p. 200) have noted repeatedly that the labeling-theory assertion that no acts are intrinsically criminal is incorrect, because acts like murder, rape, and robbery are consistently prohibited by all societies. In fact, this point is also made by some labeling theorists. For example, sociologist Kai Erikson (1966, p. 8) seems to have this distinction in mind when he observes that "it is undoubtedly true that no culture would last long if its members engaged in murder or arson among themselves on any large scale, but there is no real evidence that many of the other activities considered deviant throughout the world . . . have any relationship to the group's survival."

Critics further contend that, contrary to labeling-theory claims, the degree of popular consensus about the seriousness of various crimes is very high. In fact, there is empirical support for this criticism. For example, criminologists Thorsten Sellin and Marvin Wolfgang (1964) presented descriptions of a wide range of offenses to groups of university students, police officers, juvenile division officers, and juvenile court judges and asked them to evaluate the relative seriousness of the offenses described. In general, these different groups showed a high degree of consensus about the seriousness of different acts of deviance and crime. Similar conclusions have been found by other researchers (e.g., Velez-Diaz and Megargee, 1970; Rossi et al., 1974; Chilton and DeAmicis, 1975). One of the most comprehensive examinations of attitudes toward the seriousness of various crimes was carried out by Graeme Newman (1976) in a study of India, Indonesia, Iran, Italy (Sardinia), Yugoslavia, and New York City. Newman reports (p. 153) a "universal (i.e., cross-cultural) consensus" concerning the disapproval of most crime and deviance.

Labeling Theory and Rape

Thus, prior research would seem to permit two conclusions with important implications for the labeling proposition about the relativity of criminal sanctions. First, that mala in se crimes like murder and rape are universally condemned and, second, that there is imperfect but widespread agreement about the seriousness of such crimes. Given that rape is a mala in se crime, it is necessary to consider these conclusions seriously. Their limitations may become apparent if we distinguish between asking people how they *would react* to someone found guilty of a crime, like rape, and observing how people *actually react* to rape cases. That is, people may express a fair amount of agreement about how serious rape and other mala in se crimes are in the abstract, but they may exhibit little agreement in their actual reactions to these crimes. This line of reasoning is supported in a case study included by anthropologist Bronislaw Malinowski in his classic study of the Trobriand Islanders (1926).

Malinowski describes (pp. 77–80) a case in which a young man broke the rules of exogamy by having sexual relations with his maternal cousin, the daughter of his mother's sister. Malinowski observes that, if someone were to inquire into the matter among the Trobrianders, they would find that the natives show horror at the idea of violating this exogamy rule. But when it comes to the actual application of morality and ideals to real life, things take on a much different complexion. In the case described, Malinowski found that despite clear evidence of the crime, the villagers were not outraged by the knowledge, nor was there a direct public reaction.

I encountered similar gaps between widely shared attitudes toward crime and actual processing decisions in field work I conducted in the late 1970s on police treatment of rape cases. In the initial phases of field work I interviewed police officers who processed rape cases, and I observed the operation of a recently created rape investigation unit. I found that when the police talked about rape, they universally condemned it and thought it should be punished swiftly and severely. However, further observations of police responses to actual cases indicated much more ambivalence. In effect, the officers were unanimously opposed to rape and agreed that it was a serious offense, but in actual practice they rarely encountered cases that fit their specific definitions of rape.

Similar results have been observed for homicide, the crime that usually receives the harshest punishments a society has to apply. For example, anthropologist Henry Lundsgaarde (1977) studied all homicides known to Houston police in 1969. He found (p. 145) that although nearly 90 percent of the reported homicides resulted in the apprehension of the alleged killer, fewer than 50 percent of the suspects received any type of punishment. The explanation for this remarkable fact was not the differential behavior of offenders but rather the social context in which the crimes occurred. The most important factor in the differential response was the victim–offender relationship. Lundsgaarde reports (p. 16) that 61 percent of the killers of relatives, 53 percent of the killers of friends or associates, and 36 percent of the killers of strangers escaped *any* form of legal penalty.

Another problem with the conclusion that there is a great deal of consensus in most societies about serious crime is that it is usually based on asking respondents to react to descriptions of crimes. While in a written or verbal description it can easily be assumed that the criminal is already guilty and all that remains to be decided is a proper punishment, in actual criminal cases people must frequently operate with incomplete evidence, lies, half-truths, and conflicting testimony. People may agree that murder, rape, and robbery are serious crimes worthy of harsh punishment, but the difficult task in real cases is establishing whether these crimes have actually occurred, whether the correct suspect has been identified, and whether there are any aggravating or mitigating circumstances that should be considered. It is in identifying these social processes of discovery and interpretation that the labeling-theory argument that crime is socially constructed is most useful. And, indeed, while available research (e.g., K. Williams, 1976; Myers and LaFree, 1982; Galvin and Polk, 1983; Caringella-MacDonald, 1985; LaFree, Reskin, and Visher, 1985; Lizotte, 1985) has not shown rape processing to be entirely different from the processing of other violent personal offenses, certain characteristics of rape tend to make the criminal-selection process especially ambiguous.

For one thing, because rape cases rarely include eyewitnesses (National Institute of Law Enforcement and Criminal Justice, 1977; LaFree, 1980a; LaFree, Reskin, and Visher, 1985), processing is often reduced to a direct confrontation between accuser and accused. As Peter Berger and Thomas Luckmann point out (1967, p. 29), the observations of an eyewitness to an event take precedence over other, less direct interpretations of reality and as such are "massive and compelling." By contrast, a two-party confrontation in which each party insists on a different reconstruction of an event is likely to be highly ambiguous. Without eyewitnesses processing decisions may depend less on an assessment of whether a rape has occurred than on a perception of whether the victim and the assailant are the *kind of people* who could have been involved (Garfinkel, 1956; Sudnow, 1965; Emerson and Messinger, 1977).

The ambiguity of rape as a legal category is further increased by the fact that it involves both sex and force. The legal definition of rape in most jurisdictions specifies that the accused must have had carnal knowledge of a woman, forcibly and against her will. Officials and the victim herself must distinguish, or at least appear to distinguish, between forcible (and therefore criminal) and consensual (and therefore noncriminal) sexual acts. The difficulty of this distinction is suggested by research linking force and sex in courtship (Kanin, 1967) and marriage (D. Russell, 1982; Frieze, 1983; Finkelhor and Yllo, 1982), by widespread patterns of male aggression and female passivity (Geis, 1977, pp. 29–30; Check and Malamuth, 1983), as well as by a popular culture that often blurs the distinctions among persuasion, seduction, and coercion.

Officials must make decisions about how cases should be processed and how scarce resources should be divided among cases. Labeling theory asserts that these decisions are based less on actual behavior than on definitions constructed through social interaction. These definitions are called *typifications* by the philosopher Alfred Schutz. Schutz (1970) argues that people process new information by comparing it to previously processed information and uncovering similarities between the two. In Schutz's words, "What is newly experienced is already known in the sense that it recalls similar or equal things formerly perceived" (p. 116). Thus, when people encounter a familiar living entity, they also anticipate certain behavior on the part of the entity.

Schutz (1970, p. 116) illustrates this process by describing a hypothetical meeting between a human being and a dog. When an individual sees a dog, he or she immediately assumes that it has "a typical (not individual) way of eating, of running, of playing, of jumping, and so on." Schutz notes that even though we may not see the teeth of the particular dog that is standing in front of us, we can nonetheless draw conclusions based on our prior experience of dogs and their teeth. Such experience may obviously be invaluable to joggers, people who deliver mail or check gas meters, and anyone else who has frequent contact with dogs.

This ability to typify is arguably the most important aspect of human development. It means that we can learn from our experiences and those of others. This frees us most of the time from the burden of constant decision making. It makes it unnecessary for us to develop new definitions for every situation we encounter. It renders our world more predictable, understandable, and manageable. And it sometimes leads us to be dead wrong.

Because typifications are based not on individual cases, but on generalizations, they are obviously subject to error. *Stereotypes*, the term commonly applied to typifications about classes of people, have been especially troublesome to social scientists. For example, Walter Lippmann, in his classic work *Public Opinion* (1922), describes stereotypes as incorrect, illogical in origin, and rigidly resistant to new information. A good example of the potentially negative effects of stereotyping is found in the early research of Richard LaPiere (1936), who compared stereotypes of Armenian laborers in Fresno, California, with data from public records. While local stereotypes characterized Armenians as dishonest troublemakers, LaPiere found that their credit rating was as good as that of other groups and that they appeared less often in court than other groups. Hence, the stereotype was wrong. More recently, researchers have examined the negative effects of stereotypes for members of ethnic and racial groups and for women (Broverman et al., 1972; Hamilton, 1979; McCauly, Stitt, and Segal, 1980). Thus, typifications occupy an ambiguous position in human experience: we clearly cannot do without them, yet they sometimes lead us to simplistic, illogical, or incorrect conclusions.

For legal agents, who frequently must deal with unusual, novel, or dangerous situations, typifications would seem to be especially important (Swigert and Farrell, 1977; Emerson and Messinger, 1977; Hostika, 1979; Tierney, 1982; Loseke and

Cahill, 1984). If we assume that legal agents are subject to the same types of social processes that affect others, then criminal stereotypes, like other typifications, are based in large part on the previous experiences of those doing the typing. In sociologist David Sudnow's (1965, p. 259) study of criminal typifications (which he calls "normal crimes"), he describes some of the stereotypes developed by public defenders:

> In the course of routinely encountering persons charged with (various crimes) . . . , the P.D. (public defender) gains knowledge of the typical manner in which offenses of given classes are committed, the social characteristics of the persons who regularly commit them, the features of the settings in which they occur, the types of victims often involved and the like.

Applying these concepts to rape processing suggests that the more similar the characteristics of victims, offenders, and offenses are to the typifications of rape held by processing agents, the more likely an incident is to result in the conviction of an accused offender. The obvious next question becomes, "What are the typifications of rape held by processing agents?" Previous research provides some clues about the variables that affect reactions to rape cases and, presumably, constitute rape typifications.

Rape Typifications

Much of the recent research on rape has been concerned with how the victim's characteristics affect reactions to her case. For example, research shows that acquittals or less serious penalties are more likely for men accused of raping women who have "bad" reputations or who are reputedly promiscuous (e.g., Holmstrom and Burgess, 1978; LaFree, 1980a; LaFree, Reskin, and Visher, 1985), women with unconventional living arrangements (Clark and Lewis, 1977; Holmstrom and Burgess, 1978), and women identified as chronic alcohol users or as having been drinking when the offense occurred (K. Williams, 1976; LaFree, Reskin, and Visher, 1985). In addition, research suggests less serious reactions to men accused of raping black women (LaFree, 1980b), older women (D. Russell, 1975; but see K. Williams, 1981), and women who failed to report the incident promptly (Holmstrom and Burgess, 1978).

Not surprisingly, research indicates that the type of case also has an important effect on how officials react to it. Given the importance of consent as an issue in rape cases, case characteristics that officials associate with an indication that the victim consented may be especially important. According to Kurt Weis and Sandra Borges (1973), many people think of rape as a sudden, violent attack by a stranger in a deserted public place. To the extent that case characteristics differ from this stereotype, officials may be more skeptical of the case or simply devote less time and energy to processing it. In support of this reasoning, research has shown that defendants receive less serious sanctions when they are accused of raping women who were outside their own homes (Sebba and Cahan, 1975; Clark and Lewis, 1977). Likewise, research (e.g., Borgida and White, 1978; L'Armand and Pepitone, 1982; L. Williams, 1984) shows that convictions are less likely when the victim and offender were previously acquainted.

Of course, lack of consent can also be demonstrated by evidence of force and violence. Research (e.g., Reskin and Visher, 1986) generally confirms that indications of force, such as evidence of a weapon, victim injury, and victim resistance, increase the likelihood of convictions in rape cases. Similarly, because consensual sexual relations do not typically involve more than one partner, assaults by multiple offenders may be more easily interpreted as forcible (LaFree, 1980a). Note that some of these indications (e.g., victim injury) are relatively straightforward and objective, while others are less objective because they are not directly visible (e.g., victim resistance) or are subject to several interpretations (e.g., multiple offenders).

Berger and Luckmann (1967, pp. 34–35) illustrate how subjective meanings in social situations can be made objective by physical evidence, such as a weapon. They relate a story about a man who has an altercation with another man and that night awakens to find a knife embedded in the headboard of his bed. The weapon becomes an expression of an adversary's anger, a subjective emotion physically represented. This scenario permits several related conclusions. First, the meaning of the knife depends on its context, both in time and in space. That is, if the knife had been lying on the nightstand instead of stuck in the headboard, it would have had a different meaning. It would also have had a different meaning

if it had been found lodged in the headboard before the altercation. Second, the meaning of the knife can be shared with
others. That is, other people, including legal agents like police, can inspect the position of the knife in the headboard and
reach similar conclusions. Third, the interpretations of the
meaning of the knife given by the sleeping man and by others, even if seemingly accurate, may nonetheless be incorrect.
For example, it could be that the knife was left by a total
stranger who was trying to burglarize the man's house.

Although recent rape research has devoted less attention
to the effects on case outcomes of defendant characteristics
than of victim characteristics, prior research suggests that at
least two defendant characteristics are of special concern
in rape cases in the United States: the defendant's race and
prior criminal record. Given the long history of black–white
sexual segregation in the United States, researchers have
been especially concerned with assessing differential processing by race in sexual-assault cases. The issue of discrimination against blacks in rape cases is a staple of conflict-theory
research on rape, and I consider it in more detail in the next
chapter. Research (e.g., Farrell and Swigert, 1978; Drass and
Spencer, 1987) suggests that officials are also more likely to
type men with more serious records as guilty, confirming sociologist Harold Garfinkel's earlier (1956) claim that a criminal record indicates to officials that a suspect is "the kind of
person" who could have committed the act with which he is
charged.

APPLYING LABELING THEORY TO THE
PROCESSING OF RAPE CASES

Compared to criminology theories such as differential association or anomie, labeling theory does not lend itself to the
listing of a single set of testable propositions. This is no doubt
due in large part to the fact that compared to most etiological
theories, labeling theory is less closely linked to one theorist.
Instead of a single set of propositions, labeling theory has contributed what sociologist Herbert Blumer (1969, pp. 147–151)
calls a set of "sensitizing concepts," such as Tannenbaum's
discussion of "the dramatization of evil" and Lemert's distinction between "primary" and "secondary" deviance.

Moreover, 25 years after the publication of Howard Becker's *Outsiders*, it is clear that some of the claims made by labeling theorists were exaggerated and others were simply wrong. However, the basic vision of crime and societal reactions to it provided by labeling theory remains essential to criminology. In the chapters that follow, I consider in particular the fundamental labeling-theory proposition that official reactions to crime depend more on socially constructed typifications than on the actual behavior of offenders.

In this chapter I have briefly traced the development of labeling theory and explored some of its implications for the official processing of rape cases. These ideas are applied to the decision making of legal agents in rape cases in Chapters 4 and 5. However, before considering results, I first want to explore in greater detail a perspective whose influence on criminology in the United States has been closely associated with that of labeling theory. Accordingly, the next chapter takes up conflict theory and its implications for the study of official reactions to rape.

CHAPTER 3

The Conflict Perspective and the Legal Processing of Rape Cases

It is certain . . . that rape, an act so rare and so very difficult to prove, wrongs one's neighbor less than theft, since the latter is destructive of property, the former merely damaging to it.

The Marquis de Sade, *The Complete Justine.*

A man's highest job in life is to break his enemies, to drive them before him, to take from them all the things that have been theirs, to hear the weeping of those who cherished them, to take their horses between his knees, and to press in his arms the most desirable of their women.

Genghis Khan, in Lasswell, *Power and Personality.*

Any oppressed group, when obtaining power, tends to acquire the females of the group that has been the oppressor.

Calvin C. Hernton, *Sex and Racism in America.*

The challenges to mainstream criminology that began in the United States in the 1960s with labeling theory gradually gave way in the 1970s to more direct challenges variously called "new," "radical," "critical," "Marxist," or "conflict" criminology. The different strands of these theories, which I collectively refer to here as conflict theory, have continued to evolve up to the present. In this chapter I outline some of the major assumptions of conflict theory and consider how conflict theory can be applied to the study of the legal processing of rape cases.

THE RESURGENCE OF CONFLICT THEORY

The conflict-theoretical tradition is a venerable one in the social sciences. It can be traced from the cynical realism of Niccolo Machiavelli (1469–1527) and Thomas Hobbes (1588–1679), through the historical materialism of Karl Marx (1818–1883) and the complexities added to the Marxian framework by Max Weber (1864–1920), and finally to contemporary theoretical concerns with the state and the legal order (e.g., Vold, 1958; Dahrendorf, 1958; Turk, 1969, 1976; Quinney, 1970, 1973; Chambliss and Seidman, 1971; Collins, 1975; Michalowski and Bohlander, 1976; Beirne, 1979; Kairys, 1982; Hinch, 1983; Messerschmidt, 1986). For criminology, the most fundamental characteristic of conflict theory is perhaps its insistence that individuals or groups with greater social power are better able to create and enforce the criminal law for their own benefit. Social power has itself been the topic of many complex analyses (e.g., B. Russell, 1949; Weber, 1946; Lasswell and Kaplan, 1950; Bierstedt, 1974); however, the most generally accepted definition is probably the one developed by Max Weber (1946), who conceptualized *power* as "the probability of being able to secure one's own ends in a relationship, even against opposition."

Although the central tenets of conflict criminology can be traced back to earlier European and English theorists, its emergence in the United States in the 1970s was due to the convergence of several factors that were unique. The civil rights and antiwar movements, and the legal and illegal efforts of the government to repress the protest and dissent that followed, served to radicalize college students. Moreover, the emergence of the "New Left" as a political force in the 1960s provided a focus for frustration over the protracted war in Vietnam, for opposition to racism, and for discontent over evidence of widespread official corruption.* In short, the status

---

* The term *New Left* was used to indicate that there had been an ideological and stylistic break with the *Old Left*. According to David Greenberg (1981, pp. 499–500), the New Left in the United States is characterized by an emphasis on "participatory democracy, personal liberation, and opposition to racism, militarism, and bureaucratic organizational forms."

quo was being challenged on many fronts in this period, including criminology.

Since the publication in 1958 of German sociologist Ralf Dahrendorf's influential essay on social conflict, it has been common for researchers to contrast conflict perspectives with so-called *consensus perspectives* (e.g., McDonald, 1976; Bernard, 1983). This contrast is perhaps clearest in the work of William Chambliss (1975, pp. 168–169), who constructed a list of eight points of opposition between consensus and conflict paradigms. As is true with most complex questions, such ideal types can be misleading. And yet, a brief consideration of several nonconflict views of law can help demonstrate the originality and persuasiveness of the conflict perspective.

Consensus Perspectives

In general, consensus theorists conceptualize society as a functionally integrated, relatively stable system held together by a basic consensus of values. By "functionally integrated," they mean that the social systems that compose a society, such as legal systems and economic systems, are affected by, and affect, one another. By "relatively stable," they mean that social changes take place slowly and in an orderly manner. Consensus theorists assume that criminal law evolves from culture and is typically consistent with it. Thus, Emile Durkheim, often cited as especially central to consensus views of the law, wrote in the late 1800s that "normally, custom is not opposed to law, but is, on the contrary, its basis" (1933, p. 65). This view of law assumes that members of a society are united by a shared culture and by general agreement on fundamental norms and values. Scholars working in this tradition have tried to develop explanations of how culture becomes formalized into law.

One of the most influential of these explanations was developed by H. L. A. Hart (1961, p. 89), who calls customs "the primary rules of obligation":

> If a society is to live by such primary rules alone, there are certain conditions which, granted a few of the most obvious truisms about human nature and the world we live in, must be clearly satisfied. The first of these conditions is that rules must

contain in some form restrictions on the free use of violence, theft, and deception to which human beings are tempted but which they must, in general, repress if they are to coexist in close proximity to each other.

Thus, Hart maintains that primary rules underlie criminal law, with the result that citizens feel internally motivated to conform.

A similar view is apparent in the turn-of-the-century writings of William Graham Sumner (1906), who argues that laws evolve through social interaction; as social values change they are eventually formalized into law. More recently, Paul Bohannan (1967, p. 47) has argued that "law may be regarded as a custom that has been restated in order to make it amenable to the activities of the legal institutions." As human beings interact, some of their interactions become institutionalized into customs, of which a part are then "reinstitutionalized" into law. Thus, from this perspective, only rules that are upheld through norms that have undergone this "double institutionalization" become law.

When consensus perspectives do mention conflict, it tends to be of a *pluralistic* type. For example, the influential legal scholar Roscoe Pound (1943) conceptualizes society as composed of diverse groups whose interests often conflict. However, these conflicts are minor disputes that take place within a general social context of harmony and shared values. It is the role of law to mediate between the conflicting interests in order to provide social compromises that are in the interests of all members of society, with the least possible damage done to the interests of society as a whole. Thus, Pound views the law as "an attempt to satisfy, to reconcile, to harmonize, to adjust these overlapping and often conflicting claims and demands" (p. 39).

Conflict Perspectives

In contrast to these views of society and the law, the conflict perspective attributes less influence to shared customs and mutual agreement in the maintenance of social order. Instead, conflict theory assumes that people generally pursue their own self-interests, defined in large part by their subgroup memberships (especially, economic class, race, ethnicity, sex, age). Because resources are scarce and their distribution unequal, the self-interests of various groups will necessarily conflict. Dominant groups use power and violence in these conflicts to maintain their superior positions. Law is simply one of the mechanisms used by the powerful to promote their own interests.

In the 1970s conflict ideas were applied to both the creation of law and its enforcement. It is obvious that criminal defendants and convicts in the United States are disproportionately drawn from specific groups: young men, racial and ethnic minorities, the unemployed, and the poorly educated. Positivist criminology theories attempted to explain why these individuals committed crime. Conflict theorists argue instead that powerless individuals are overrepresented in the legal system because laws are written and enforced to protect the interests of the powerful. According to this view, law is neither a reflection of the basic customs of citizens, as Durkheim would have it, nor a series of compromises between diverse but more or less equally matched interests, as Pound would argue. Rather, law is used by the powerful to maintain their own best interests.

Beyond general observations, summarizing contemporary conflict theories of crime is difficult. Much of the difficulty lies in the nature of the work left behind by the best known conflict theorist of all, German scholar Karl Marx. Because criminology was only a peripheral concern for Marx, his writings do not contain a fully developed theory of crime. This has led some students of Marx to state flatly that a Marxist criminology is impossible (see Hirst, 1975; Spitzer, 1980). Regardless of such arguments, it is nonetheless possible to interpret crime, crime policy, and criminology from a "Marxist" perspective. Still, the fact that crime issues are not central to Marx's writings probably makes specific applications of his theories to crime more difficult to defend and easier to challenge. Moreover, Marxian theory is based on the work of a man who was a prolific and complex thinker. The complexity of Marxism naturally encourages disagreement among both Marxists and their critics.

A comprehensive review of the various strands of conflict theory is well beyond the scope of this book. Nonetheless, two related types of conflict theory can be more or less reliably identified, based on the strength of their connections to Marxism: *interest-group* and *Marxist* versions (I. Taylor, Walton, and Young, 1973, pp. 237–267; Akers, 1977, pp. 13–20; Vold and Bernard, 1986, Chs. 15, 16). The major distinguishing feature of interest-group theories is the assumption that the creation and enforcement of criminal law are due to relatively diffuse, pluralistic interests, largely dependent on group memberships by race, class, religion, ethnicity, age, and gender. On the basis of these memberships, groups command varying amounts of power, which in turn affects their ability to enact and enforce criminal law. In contrast, Marxist criminologists emphasize the political and economic structure of society more directly. This follows from Marx's argument that in capitalist societies, the organized state represents the economic interests of those who own the means of economic production.

Interest-Group Theories. One of the earliest examples of an interest-group approach to the study of crime is sociologist Thorsten Sellin's 1938 work, *Culture, Conflict, and Crime.* Sellin claims that during periods of rapid immigration and social change—such as occurred in Chicago in the early part of the twentieth century—groups with different sets of norms and values often border one another. When this happens, the behavior of one group may appear deviant to the other group because of basic disagreements about what constitutes acceptable behavior. For example, imagine a Chicago neighborhood composed of individuals whose families have lived there for several generations bordering another neighborhood predominantly composed of recent immigrants from other countries or black migrants from the rural South. To the extent that the established residents and the newer residents do not share the same beliefs about the proper ways to behave in a variety of situations, a *culture conflict* may exist. Sellin argues that in situations like these the group with the greatest social power will probably succeed in having its ways of behaving defined as normal and the other group's behavior as deviant or criminal.

From the late 1950s through the early 1970s, several other researchers developed conflict theories based on interest-group arguments. For example, the point of departure for criminologist George Vold's (1958) *group-conflict theory* is the observation that a good deal of social interaction is a product of group association. Because resources are always limited, effectively organized groups generally have the power to secure a greater share of scarce resources for their members. A major avenue for securing greater resources is through the control of law. Vold argues that more powerful groups are able to use the assets of the organized state to support themselves in conflicts with other groups. This includes conflicts over determining legal definitions of crime and how these definitions are to be applied.

Similar themes may be found in the work of contemporary criminologists like Austin Turk (1969), Richard Quinney (1970), and William Chambliss and Robert Seidman (1971). For example, Turk's *theory of criminalization* specifies (1969, p. 53) the conditions under which cultural and social differences between legal authorities and their subjects result in conflict, the conditions under which authorities will use the law and criminal definitions against their subjects, and the conditions under which the punishments and deprivations associated with becoming a criminal will be greater or lesser. Similarly, Quinney's work on *the social reality of crime* includes a set of propositions that define how criminal laws are formulated and applied. Quinney argues (1970, pp. 15–23) that "criminal definitions describe behaviors that conflict with the interests of the segments of society that have the power to shape public policy" and that they in turn are applied "by the segments of society that have the power to shape the enforcement and administration of criminal law." Likewise, in Chambliss and Seidman's comprehensive analysis of the criminal-justice system, they maintain (1971, pp. 473–474) that "the higher a group's political and economic position, the greater is the probability that its views will be reflected in the laws."

Marxian Conflict Theories.   Although Marx's writings do not contain a fully developed theory of crime, several generations of scholars since Marx have attempted to generate theories of crime and the law that are consistent with Marxian principles. One of the first to do so, in the early 1900s, was the Dutch scholar Willem Bonger (1916). The central theme of Bonger's conflict theory is that crime is the product of a capitalist economic system, which encourages all people to be greedy and selfish and to pursue their own interests without regard for others. Lower-class people commit a disproportionate amount of crime because the criminal-justice system passes laws that make the greed of the poor illegal (e.g., laws against street crimes) while simultaneously protecting the rights of the rich to pursue their own forms of greed (e.g., by allowing corporations and wealthy individuals to engage openly in behavior that should be considered criminal).

After the 1920s, criminological interest in Marxist conflict theories virtually disappeared in the United States for 50 years. However, a major resurgence of interest began in the early 1970s with the works of Quinney (1973; Quinney and Wildeman, 1977).* Quinney argues that the key factor in understanding crime in the United States is the realization that the social structure is based on an advanced capitalist economy. This economy has gradually placed control of economic life in the hands of fewer and fewer people—people who usually do not even manage or work in the industrial enterprises from which they nonetheless extract huge profits. Quinney claims that the capitalist state is organized to serve the interests of this tiny economic elite. The criminal law is simply one instrument available to the powerful for maintaining the existing economic and social exploitation.

As the 1970s proceeded, a great deal of interest arose among criminologists in developing and refining Marxian crime perspectives. David Greenberg (1981, pp. 6–10) claims that "By the mid-1970s, a specifically Marxian criminology began to take shape." Interest in Marxian conflict theories continued into the 1980s, in an ongoing process whereby theories are proposed, critics challenge them, and more rigorous theories are devised in response to the criticisms. One of the

* Similar developments began in Great Britain at about the same time (see I. Taylor, Walton, and Young, 1973).

most important distinctions to arise out of recent Marxist criminology research is a distinction between the instrumentalist and the structuralist perspectives.

The Instrumentalist Perspective.   In general, the *instrumentalist perspective* conceptualizes the ruling class as a unified and monolithic elite that uses the state directly as an instrument for the domination of society (Miliband, 1969; Gold, Lo, and Wright, 1975). This reasoning may be traced back to a statement by Karl Marx and Friedrich Engels (1973, p. 110) that "the executive of the modern state is but a committee for managing the common affairs of the whole bourgeoisie." This elite creates and enforces laws for their own benefit. Thus, most criminal behavior is only a political response to conditions of oppression and exploitation by this system.

In response to such views of society, sociologists like C. Wright Mills (1956) sought to identify a cohesive, socially connected group of individuals in American society who regularly communicate with one another and have a major impact on the government and its laws. However, as conflict theory continued to develop in the 1970s, many criminologists came to see such explanations as simplistic and inadequate. It was almost as if instrumentalists were assuming that somewhere in the United States, perhaps in a highly fortified bunker underneath the Rocky Mountains, a cigar-puffing band of capitalist members of the ruling class (composed entirely of white Anglo-Saxon males) regularly meets to determine the fate of the rest of society, actively conspiring to keep the poor poor and the rich rich.

Critics argued that instrumentalist perspectives did not adequately explain many of the decisions made by capitalist governments. For example, a study by John Mollenkopf (1975) shows that much of the New Deal legislation passed in the United States in the 1930s to help the nation's economy recover from the Great Depression was strenuously opposed by the majority of rich and powerful capitalists. Similarly, G. William Domhoff (1978) and Claus Offe (1974) show that, contrary to instrumentalist claims, capitalists are not a monolithic group whose interests mesh perfectly, but instead are a group characterized by important disagreements and divisions. Others have pointed out that instrumentalist theory fails to explain how the enforcement of criminal laws can be seen as a benefit only to the rich when it is the poor who are most frequently the victims of street crime (e.g., Greenberg, 1976). One of the consequences of dissatisfaction with the ability of instrumentalist perspectives to adequately explain crime and the legal system has been the development of the structuralist conflict perspective.

The Structuralist Perspective. The *structuralist perspective* assumes that there is an underlying, built-in ("structural") relationship between the political state and the economic system of capitalism which guarantees that the state will operate in the long-term interests of the capitalist class, even without the direct, coordinated participation of individual capitalists (Whitt, 1979; Chambliss, 1979). In this view, the capitalist system and the ruling elite are perceived as less rigid and unified than is suggested by the instrumentalist perspective. In short, for capitalism to survive, it must show some flexibility. Chambliss and Seidman (1982, p. 308) argue that, to be successful, the capitalist state and the legal system must "appear to function as value neutral organs fairly and impartially representing the interests of everyone." Nevertheless, the ruling elite continues to benefit the most from the operation of the organized state, has far more political power than other groups, and retains a disproportionate ability to get the state to serve its own best interests.

RAPE, LAW, AND SOCIAL POWER

This brief review demonstrates that a central theme in conflict theory is the claim that the criminal law is written and applied so as to maintain the power of dominant groups. This theme distinguishes the role of law as a set of rules and norms that define criminal behavior from its role as a bureaucratic system that applies these rules. Starting in 1935 with Jerome Hall's classic study of the development of laws against theft, the argument that criminal law is defined by a ruling group that uses it to maintain its own superior position has been applied to a wide variety of deviant and criminal behavior, including alcohol use (Sinclair, 1964; Gusfield, 1967), vagrancy (Chambliss, 1964), prostitution (Roby, 1969), juvenile status offenses (Platt, 1969), and drug use (Lindesmith, 1965;

Graham, 1972). All of these applications share at least three characteristics. First, they are based mostly on field work rather than on multivariate analysis of secondary data. Second, they tend to assume instrumentalist rather than structuralist conflict perspectives; that is, they emphasize the creation of law by a more or less monolithic ruling elite. And third, they all claim support for the assertion that law is written so as to maintain the interests of a ruling elite.

By contrast, more recent research, using multivariate statistical analysis, has often reached somewhat different conclusions. For example, a study of California state drug laws from 1955 to 1971 by Richard Berk, Harold Brackman, and Selma Lesser (1977) concludes that the creation of law is more in keeping with a pluralistic model of competing organized interests. Likewise, John Hagan and Jeffrey Leon (1977), in a study of criminal codes regulating Canadian juveniles, reject the instrumentalist view of a monolithic elite creating laws in favor of a more pluralistic model emphasizing the tendency of bureaucracies to operate at times out of good intentions and at other times out of a desire to protect their own interests. In general, as tests of conflict models of the law have become more methodologically sophisticated, assertions about the mechanisms by which elites create and impose law have become more complex. Thus, earlier instrumentalist interpretations of law are gradually giving way to structuralist views.

Conflict Theories of Rape

In the 1960s, feminists applied the conflict proposition that laws are written to maintain the position of the powerful by substituting "men" for the "dominant group" and "women" for the "subordinate group" of earlier conflict formulations. This substitution makes good sense. Although neither Marx nor Engels included rape in their theory of class oppression, the link between gender and power is clear in their writings. For example, in his book *The Origins of the Family, Private Property, and the State* (1972, p. 41), Engels wrote:

> The subjugation of the female sex was based on the transformation of their socially necessary labor into a private service

through the separation of the family from the clan. It was in this context that women's domestic and other work came to be performed under conditions of virtual slavery.

As rape became a central focus for feminist theories in the 1970s, a more fully developed conflict theory of the creation of rape law also began to emerge. At the microsocial level, the behavior of individuals in institutionalized relationships like marriages and families is governed by social rules that specify mutual rights and responsibilities. Historically, and in some societies today, some of these relationships were viewed literally as *property* relationships and were governed by principles borrowed from those that dealt with real property. In general, the concept of property implies a set of socially granted rights about access to and disposition of the goods in question. These rights derive from social norms or statutory or common law and are usually protected by the state. The existence of rights implies the possibility of violation (damage or destruction, theft, and trespass). And, importantly, when violations occur, property holders may seek redress under the law.

While slavery is the most obvious example of property rights applied to relationships between human beings, traditionally children have been viewed as the property of their fathers and women as the property of their husbands. Historically, marriage has involved a special type of property relationship, that of *sexual property*, which is defined by sociologist Randall Collins (1975, p. 236) as a relatively permanent claim to exclusive sexual rights over another person. Sexual-property rules are the basic structure of kinship systems; they determine who can mate with whom and under what circumstances. The definition of sexual property is parallel to that of economic property: property is not lands or buildings themselves, but the social relationships that guarantee access to them. While the concept of sexual-property rights does not necessarily rule out female rights over males, Western values, traditions, and laws have typically interpreted sexual-property rights as husbands' rights to exclusive sexual access to their wives and as fathers' rights to protect the sexual-property value of their daughters before marriage.

This reasoning places the origin and meaning of laws

against rape in a social context that is completely different from the one proposed by theorists like Durkheim and Pound. If women were legally the property of men, then rape laws may have developed not primarily to protect women who were raped, but to protect the property rights of their husbands or fathers. This view conceptualizes rape law as developing along with marriage law as a mechanism to protect fathers' sexual property from usurpation by rapists, who could otherwise have claimed their victims as wives. Furthermore, men's characteristic rage at sexual attacks on their wives or daughters is reinterpreted as a socially supported response to the violation of men's sexual-property rights.

Consistent with conflict theory, then, much of the feminist writing on rape claims that the law exists mostly to protect the interests of men. However, few would argue that women in the United States today have the same social status that they did a century or two ago. In the 1970s and 1980s virtually every state in the country enacted new laws at least nominally aimed at protecting rape victims during the adjudication process (Feild and Bienen, 1980, p. 153; Loh, 1980, 1981; Borgida, 1981, p. 212). Hence, earlier critiques of blatant sexism embodied in rape statutes (e.g., LeGrand, 1973; Wood, 1973) have gradually given way to arguments (e.g., Marsh, Geist, and Caplan, 1982; Polk, 1985) that emphasize that even though rape statutes have changed, the application of rape laws may nonetheless still serve the interests of men. For example, in an examination of Michigan's reforms of its rape legislation, sociologist Susan Caringella-MacDonald (1985) concludes that although changes in the law did bring about important reforms, its implementation still results in rape victims being treated differently from victims of other types of crimes.*

The Application of Law in Rape Cases

Conflict-theory predictions about the application of law have generated a great deal of research in recent years. Most often, researchers have examined the variables that predict

---

* The fact that most states have passed major reforms of their rape laws in recent years may yet be in keeping with simple instrumentalist versions of

criminal-justice decisions like arrest, verdict, and sentence in order to determine whether defendants' characteristics (especially race and economic status) are more important than measures of evidence and seriousness of the offense. Apart from the fact that this issue is fundamental to concepts of justice and equality, it has probably attracted research interest because, unlike many other conflict and labeling propositions, it is relatively accessible to empirical test by research methods that have become standard in the social sciences.

For example, using multivariate analyses, many researchers have now examined the proposition that black or poor defendants receive harsher sanctions than others in criminal cases. In general, researchers have variously concluded that there is no evidence of discrimination (e.g., Chiricos and Waldo, 1975; Bernstein, Kelly, and Doyle, 1977; Hindelang, 1978; Wilbanks, 1987); that variables like race and economic class have indirect effects on outcomes through their relationship to other variables like defendant's prior record (Zatz, 1984; LaFree, 1985a); or that discrimination is limited to specific circumstances, including the year in which the case was processed (Thomson and Zingraff, 1981), the racial composition of the victim–defendant dyad (Farrell and Swigert, 1978; LaFree, 1980b; Walsh, 1987), the type of offense (Unnever, 1982; Peterson and Hagan, 1984), or the region of the country where the case was adjudicated (Hagan, 1974; Kleck, 1981).

Some criminologists (e.g., Chiricos and Waldo, 1975; Hindelang, 1978; Kleck, 1981; Wilbanks, 1987) have concluded from this research that criminology should move away from research on labeling and conflict explanations of official reactions to crime and return instead to etiological concerns about the causes of criminal behavior. I think this is a premature

---

conflict theory, although in a way not usually suggested by conflict theorists. If women possess greater power in society today than they previously did, conflict theory would lead us to expect concomitant change in the nature of rape law. Baldly stated, the laws should favor men less and women more. This would lead us to expect an expansion of the social situations in which women could legally charge rape, a contraction in the legal defenses available to men accused, and less emphasis in rape law on the culpability of women. Evidence from states like Michigan suggest that rape laws have indeed generally changed along these dimensions (see Marsh, Geist, and Caplan, 1982; Horney and Spohn, 1987).

conclusion. The problem with most of the recent empirical research on discrimination in the application of the law is that it tends to ignore the social relationship between the offender and the victim (contrary to labeling theory) and the wider social system in which criminal acts take place (contrary to conflict theory). The first of these problems is illustrated by Becker's claim that "the degree to which an act will be treated as deviant depends . . . on who commits the act and who feels he has been harmed by it" (1963, p. 12). Most of the research on differential application of the law has examined only "who committed the act" and not "who feels he has been harmed by it." Thus, labeling and conflict arguments are not necessarily disproved if research demonstrates that sanctions are not particularly harsh when relatively powerless persons in society murder and rape each other.

A second problem is that most of the empirical tests of discrimination in the application of law have not closely examined the social-structural context in which they occur. For example, finding that a society harshly punishes men accused of rape does not necessarily indicate that women are socially powerful in that society. Before we can draw such a conclusion, we must know more about the structure of the society, the relationships between men and women in the society, and the relationship between crime and punishment over time in the society. It could be, for instance, that punishment for rape has more to do with the social position of men than women in a given society.

Thus, while most recent research on discrimination in the application of law has been concerned with whether less powerful members of society are treated differently, my concern here is with also considering the social context of the offense: who is the victim, who is the offender, what is the victim–offender relationship, what groups are threatened by the crime? A brief explanation of the concept of *sexual stratification* should make this strategy clearer.

Race, Gender, and Sexual Stratification

Since the original works of Marx and Engels, conflict theorists have emphasized the differential access of groups to economic rewards. But the conflict argument can easily be applied to other resources that are both valued and scarce. Several decades ago, sociologist Kingsley Davis (1949) argued that sexual access is such a resource. Like other scarce resources, the distribution of sexual access is determined by power relationships within a highly stratified sexual market. Rules of sexual access, like class relationships, are not immutable. They are subject to constant challenge and must be maintained through bargaining, threats, alliances, force, and violence. If rape represents a violation of male sexual-property rights in which the "trespasser" can "despoil" the value of the victim, the notion of sexual stratification suggests that the status of the "trespasser" may affect the perceived seriousness of the violation. In general, the more powerful the group from which the victim is selected as compared to the offender's group, the more serious the violation. Randall Collins (1975, p. 282) expresses this relationship as a proposition: "The greater the power of dominant individuals to appropriate others as sexual property, the stronger the taboo and the greater the outrage at violations of these property rights." This reasoning seems especially useful for analyzing the treatment of blacks and gender-role-nontraditional women in rape cases.

Official Reactions to Interracial Rape. In its extreme form during the period of slavery in the United States, the sexual-stratification system placed few constraints on sexual access to black women by white men. Sexual access to white women by black men, however, was carefully constrained, and sanctions for the violation of these constraints were harsh. Although few would contend that interracial relationships of the antebellum South remain in effect today, it could be plausibly argued that blacks and whites in the United States remain more highly stratified in sexual terms than in economic terms even today. Although there have been increases in recent years, rates of interracial marriage in the United States remain extremely low. Census figures (United States Bureau of the Census, 1987, p. 39) show that of more than 51 million married couples in the United States, only 164,000 are black–white interracial (less than one-half of 1 percent). Moreover, while there is evidence that white Americans have become more supportive of racial integration in the last two decades, surveys and opinion polls continue to show tremendous resistance to the concept of sexual integration of the races (Taylor, Sheatsley, and Greely, 1978; Condran, 1979). In one national survey, 65 percent of white Americans said that they disapproved of marriage between blacks and whites. In a separate study (see Erskine, 1973, p. 283), 83 percent of white Americans polled claimed that they would be "concerned" if they found that their teenage child was dating a black person.

Most studies that have looked for evidence of racial discrimination in the processing of rape cases have considered only the defendant's race and not the racial composition of the victim–defendant dyad. But if official reactions to rape are in part an effort by the white male power structure to protect white women from attack by black men, we might expect reactions to rape to depend more on the racial composition of the victim–defendant dyad than on the offender's race alone. To the extent that relationships between men and women in the United States are still defined by race-specific rules of sexual access, an implicit ordering of official reactions to sexual assault by race is suggested: the assault of white women by black men should result in the most serious sanctions, followed by the assault of white women by white men, black women by black men, and, finally, black women by white men.

Reactions to Nontraditional Rape Victims. The idea that rape laws can serve a social-control function has also surfaced in the feminist literature on rape. In this case the argument is that rape laws are applied so as to control the behavior of women who violate traditional gender-role expectations. Gender-role differentiation requires certain behavior of each sex and accords each sex certain privileges. To maintain gender-role conformity, society invokes both positive and negative sanctions for women and men. Sanctions include both the imposition of punishments and the loss of privileges generally available to others of the same sex. For example, men who fail to support their families may forfeit conjugal rights, or women who compete with men at work may lose social support and be excluded from important informal work groups. Similarly, feminists have argued that women who violate traditional gender roles may forfeit access to justice in the event that they are raped. Importantly, the treatment of nontraditional women by the legal system serves as a warning to both more traditional and less traditional women. Thus, the criminal-justice system can be seen as an institutional arrangement that functions to maintain the gender-role conformity of all women.

Two types of gender-role deviation seem particularly important. First, victims' behavior at the time they are raped may violate traditional gender roles. Hitchhiking provides a clear example. Traditional gender roles assign women to the home. When they must leave, they are often warned to do so in the safety of their own cars or under the protection of reliable male guardians (husbands, fathers, brothers, or sons). Other pre-rape behavior that deviates from traditional gender roles includes permitting oneself to be "picked up" by a man, going to a man's apartment, and walking "unprotected" (i.e., without a responsible man) late at night, in a bad neighborhood, or in a strange or isolated place.

Second, victims' life-style or living arrangements may violate gender-role norms. Thus, women may be seen as deviants if they are sexually active outside marriage; fail to dress "modestly"; are divorced or live with men to whom they are not married; embrace counterculture life-styles; work in "disreputable" occupations (for example cocktail waitress); or pursue traditionally male recreational activities such as riding motorcycles or frequenting bars.

APPLYING CONFLICT THEORY TO THE PROCESSING OF RAPE CASES

Like labeling theorists, conflict theorists often disagree about the precise nature of their theory. Moreover, both proponents and critics often obscure differences between earlier interest-group conflict approaches and subsequent Marxist approaches in their writings. Similarly, differences between instrumentalist and structuralist versions of conflict theory are often blurred. In large part this confusion is a consequence of the fact that conflict theories are still evolving, so that individual theorists frequently change their own positions over time.

There is also some confusion between conflict and label-ing arguments. The two perspectives are often combined by researchers (e.g., Schrag, 1971, pp. 89–91; Bernstein, Kelly, and Doyle, 1977; Nettler, 1984, pp. 186–203), and labeling theorists (e.g., Kitsuse, 1962, 1975; Becker, 1963; Erikson, 1964; Sudnow, 1965; Schur, 1971, 1975) typically emphasize the greater ability of the powerful to resist labels, a funda-mental conflict-theory concern. In fact, the basis for conflict theorist Richard Quinney's (1970) "criminal stereotypes" and labeling theorist David Sudnow's (1965) "normal crime" ap-pears to be similar: less powerful individuals are denied equal justice by the official labeling process.

Confusion between labeling and conflict views is further increased by the fact that as labeling theory evolved in the late 1960s and 1970s, it began to emphasize social-structural interpretations of crime commonly associated with conflict theory and to depart somewhat from its roots in symbolic interactionism. Thus, sociologist Walter Gove (1980, pp. 9–32) argues that labeling theory's early emphasis on the dy-namics of social interaction began to give way to a primary concern with the organization of society and the impact of this organization on the construction of social rules and laws. In short, later labeling-theory formulations began to converge with conflict perspectives.

To avoid some of these ambiguities, this book concen-trates on a single conflict proposition, which I believe is among the most important and enduring contributions of conflict theory to the understanding of crime—namely, that laws are applied to control the behavior of individuals who threaten the power of dominant social groups.

This completes my review of labeling and conflict theories and their implications for the processing of rape cases. Now it is time to turn to the data. In the next two chapters I explore the labeling-theory idea that the official processing of rape cases is based largely on stereotypes of women, men, and the proper behavior of each. Chapter 4 deals with the decision making of rape victims and police, and Chapter 5 examines court outcomes.

CHAPTER 4

Constructing Rape:
The Victim and the Police

People use rules as rhetorical devices in arguing about and constructing accounts of their behavior, but having lists of rules is not going to throw much if any light on what people do.

Albert Cohen, in Laub, *Criminology in the Making.*

In this chapter I examine the official processing decisions made in a set of forcible-sex offenses reported to Indianapolis police for three years in the early 1970s. All these cases were potential felonies.* I exclude male victims—there were very few of them—and nonforcible, statutory offenses. The main purpose of this chapter is to explore the extent to which rape victims and police are influenced by rape stereotypes in deciding how to react to the crime. The results generally show that both the victim and the police are influenced by extralegal characteristics of the incident. Furthermore, while there appear to be many similarities among the decisions made by the victim, the police, and other legal agents, each decision point is also somewhat unique. That is, variables that influence decisions in rape cases do not have the same importance for outcomes at each stage of the criminal-justice process. The results also suggest that rape stereotypes are fairly resistant

---

* The charges involved were rape, armed rape, sodomy, armed sodomy, assault and battery with intent to rape, and assault and battery with intent to gratify. Attempted crimes in all these categories are also included. To control for differences between completed and attempted crimes, I include in the analysis a measure distinguishing them.

to change, even when there are major changes in the organization of the criminal-justice bureaucracies in charge of processing rape cases. However, before we consider the processing of rape cases specifically, it is necessary to describe the general characteristics of the criminal-justice bureaucracy responsible for felony processing.

CRIMINAL SELECTION IN INDIANAPOLIS

Criminal-justice systems in large urban areas of the United States have become organizational labyrinths comprising several functionally dependent and yet largely autonomous subsystems. In general, criminal-justice bureaucracies operate like great sieves, beginning with a large number of cases reported to police but filtering out the vast majority before they reach the criminal courts. The process also resembles a production line, in which suspects are sorted into different categories: some are arrested, others dismissed, some are convicted, others imprisoned. Because the major connection among all the disparate agencies that take an interest in law enforcement is the suspect, I refer to the procedures by which "the guilty" are separated from "the innocent" as the *criminal-selection process*. The research reported here is based on criminal-selection processes in Indianapolis, Indiana.

Indianapolis was reorganized as a "consolidated city" in 1969, which substantially merged its functions with Marion County, in which it is located. Following consolidation, Indianapolis became the twelfth largest city in the United States, with a 1980 population of 1,166,575. For a large midwestern city, the proportion of blacks in Indianapolis is low—about 13.5 percent of the population.

Stages in the Processing of Felonies

Although no two systems in the United States process criminal cases in an identical way, the general outlines are fairly similar in most jurisdictions. The major stages in the processing of felonies in Indianapolis are summarized in Figure 4.1, which conveys some of the complexity of the bureaucracy that is responsible for selecting criminal defendants. My interviews with the legal agents who worked in the crim-

FIGURE 4.1 The Processing of Felonies in Indianapolis

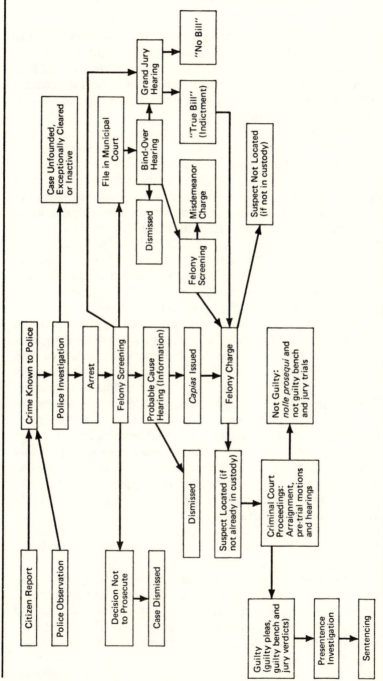

inal-justice system demonstrated that most of them had only a vague understanding of the operation of the parts of the system outside their particular office or department. Thus, it is hardly surprising that most citizens who come into contact with the criminal-justice system find its operation confusing, if not incomprehensible.

Crimes may become known to police through either citizen reports or police observations. However, the vast majority of crimes, including rapes, are brought to the attention of police by citizens. When a police department is notified about a crime, a uniformed police officer is usually dispatched to the scene and is required to file a report. In Indianapolis, as in most other jurisdictions, the uniformed officer can declare a case *unfounded* in this report. Officially, to unfound a case the officer must conclude that the charge is baseless, erroneous, invalid, or frivolous. During the period of my observations, I never witnessed any police officer being questioned by a superior about the decision to unfound a case.

Unless the case is declared unfounded by the uniformed officer, a detective is next assigned to do further investigation. After the investigation, Indianapolis detectives can arrest a suspect, declare the case *inactive* or *exceptionally cleared*, or simply file the case without a final designation. The length of the investigation depends on many factors, including the perceived seriousness of the offense, public interest in the case, and the type of case. Technically, the police are expected to make an arrest only when they have probable cause to believe that a crime occurred and that a particular suspect perpetrated it. *Probable cause* is generally defined as "the existence of circumstances that would lead a reasonably prudent person to believe that the accused person committed the crime charged" (Statsky, 1985, p. 604). In actual practice, police have a great deal of discretion in defining probable cause and making an arrest.

In Indianapolis rape cases, an "inactive" designation generally means that the police accept the complaint as genuine, but have been unable to identify and apprehend a suspect and are no longer actively investigating the case. The "exceptionally cleared" category is used for cases which the police consider to be solved but which they feel do not warrant arrest and prosecution. For example, police frequently designate cases as exceptionally cleared when the victim has identified a suspect but refuses to cooperate in the investigation and prosecution.

Arrests for potentially serious offenses in Indianapolis are next reviewed by a "felony screener" in the prosecutor's office. These screeners are lawyers who examine the statutory requirements for each felony and the preliminary information on the case provided by the police. Common concerns in screening rape cases include whether the necessary elements of proof are present (e.g., the law requires sexual penetration for a rape charge to be filed); the seriousness of the case within specific crime categories (based, e.g., on whether or not the perpetrator was armed and the age of the victim); and the existence of major prosecution difficulties (e.g., victim uncertain about testifying in court). Before making the charging decision, screeners often consult the investigating officer and, occasionally, the victim and other witnesses.

Indianapolis screeners have four major filing options in rape cases. First, they can dismiss all charges—a decision usually made if the prosecutor feels there is insufficient evidence. Second, they can file cases in municipal court, either by reducing the police charge to a misdemeanor (an option frequently used in cases in which the screener feels that the penalty imposed for conviction would be too harsh) or by scheduling a municipal court hearing. The latter option is sometimes used if the prosecutor believes that the victim may later decline to testify. Prosecutors often use the hearing as a "dress rehearsal" for later courtroom appearances: if the victim's testimony goes well at the hearing, prosecutors assume that it has a greater chance of going well in a trial. Third, they can present the case to the grand jury. This option is routinely used in rape cases, especially if they are controversial or have what the prosecutor considers to be evidence problems. Finally, felony screeners can file cases directly in criminal court by ordering a probable-cause hearing by a court commissioner. In these cases they can preserve the original charges, increase them, or reduce them.

In general, *grand juries* are juries of inquiry, which can receive complaints and accusations in criminal cases, hear evidence presented by the prosecutor, and issue *indictments* in those cases in which the jury is satisfied that a trial should be held. In Indianapolis grand juries are composed of six citizens chosen randomly from voter registration records. Unlike *petit juries*, the type with which most of us are more familiar, grand juries do not return verdicts of guilty or not guilty. Instead, they either *"no bill"* a case, which means prosecution ends, or *"true bill"* a case, which means an indictment is issued and the case may be processed as a felony. The Fifth Amendment to the United States Constitution requires grand jury indictments in federal cases. However, the Supreme Court has held that states are not required to use grand juries for indictments. In general, the use of grand juries for indictments has been declining in the United States. However, grand juries were still common in Indianapolis in the 1970s.

If felony screeners send the case to a probable-cause hearing, the commissioner can either dismiss the case or issue a warrant for the arrest of the defendant (called a *capias*).* To summarize, felony charges can originate from a probable-cause hearing, from a municipal court hearing, from a grand jury hearing, or from some combination of these. As recently as 1975, most rape cases in Indianapolis went first through municipal court hearings, then through grand jury hearings; if the grand jury found probable cause, they were then prosecuted in criminal court as felonies. Given the complexity of these proceedings, it was not uncommon for rape cases to require more than a year to come to trial.

Because felony screening sometimes occurs before an arrest has been made, the next processing step depends on whether a suspect is in custody. For suspects already in jail, pre-arraignment motions and hearings on bond reductions are held next. These tend to be short and routine. At this stage, police attempt to locate and arrest those suspects who are not already in jail.

Cases that are not dismissed by the prosecutor or court proceed to the *arraignment*, at which the charges are read, the defendant pleads guilty or not guilty, a public defender is appointed if needed, and, if the case is to be tried, a trial date is set.

---

* *Capias* is a Latin word meaning "that you take." A *capias* warrant is so called because it requires a police officer to take the defendant bodily into custody.

Pretrial motions and hearings, such as the type used to determine whether the defendant is competent to stand trial, are held next. The prosecutor can dismiss (called *nolle prosequi*) a case at any point, although this rarely happened in Indianapolis rape cases once trial procedures had begun. Likewise, although the prosecution had the option of refiling dismissed cases, this happened infrequently in actual practice. If the case is not dismissed, three options remain: (1) guilty plea by the defendant, (2) bench trial, or (3) jury trial. Once a guilty plea is accepted or a guilty verdict returned, the court orders a *presentence investigation* (PSI) of the defendant and sets a sentencing date. The PSI includes detailed background information on the defendant, which may be used by the judge in sentencing.

This complex system of organizations and agents was responsible for applying criminal law to rape cases in Indianapolis. In doing so, it defined rape.

Processing Rape Cases

As we saw in Chapter 2, a central debate between labeling theorists and their critics centers on the meaning of the decisions made by criminal-justice officials. Labeling theorists argue that people are defined as criminal not so much because of their actual behavior as because of their characteristics or the characteristics of the agents and agencies that process them. Critics of labeling theory counter that some behavior is intrinsically criminal, that people show widespread agreement about the seriousness of such behavior, and that the criminal-justice system, although imperfect, generally ferrets out the guilty parties. In this section I explore these two views, using data on the processing of rape cases in Indianapolis.

Figure 4.2 summarizes the major processing decisions made in all forcible-sexual-assault cases reported to Indianapolis police in 1970, 1973, and 1975. I collected these data while I was employed as a researcher by the Marion County Prosecutor's Office. Using police, prosecution, and court records, I was able to trace the cases through the criminal-justice system to the stage at which they were finally dismissed or adjudicated. The figure shows that of 881 cases reported to police, 328 (37.2 percent) resulted in arrest, 153 (17.4 percent)

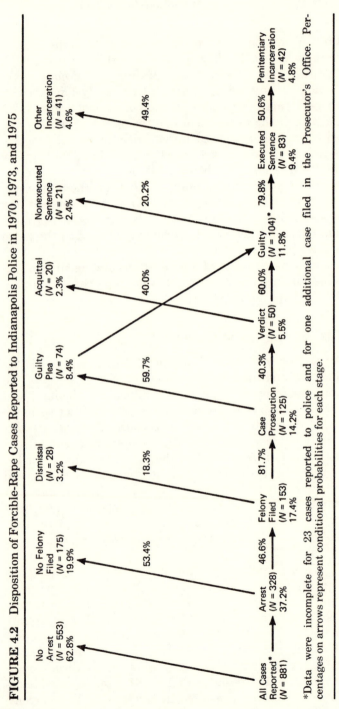

FIGURE 4.2 Disposition of Forcible-Rape Cases Reported to Indianapolis Police in 1970, 1973, and 1975

*Data were incomplete for 23 cases reported to police and for one additional case filed in the Prosecutor's Office. Percentages on arrows represent conditional probabilities for each stage.

source: LaFree, 1980b, p. 845.

were filed as criminal felonies, 104 (11.8 percent) resulted in guilty pleas and verdicts, and 42 (4.8 percent) resulted in a convicted offender being sent to prison. Of the 42 men sent to the penitentiary, 23 (54.8 percent) were still serving time in 1986, while this book was being prepared. According to Indiana prison officials, probable release dates for these 23 men range from late 1986 through 2012. Six of them are scheduled for release before 1990, 13 before 2000, and the remaining four during or before 2012.

Although Figure 4.2 is limited to rape cases in one jurisdiction, it has some interesting implications for the claim that criminal labels are based on factors other than the actual criminal act committed. Most fundamentally, it raises questions about the meaning of the assertion commonly made by critics of labeling theory that decisions in *mala in se* crimes like rape are based on widely shared interpretations of actual behavior. If labels are based on actual criminal behavior, then the label "rape" should distinguish those who committed rape from those who did not. But in this example it clearly does not. To begin with the obvious, these data exclude all rape cases not reported to the police. But the assertion is even problematic if we ignore this obvious problem. If rape labels are based on actual criminal behavior, how many rapes are actually represented by these data? The 881 reported to police? The 328 in which a suspect was arrested? The 104 in which a suspect was convicted? Or the 42 that resulted in prison terms? We could probably build a reasonable defense for each of these possibilities. However, regardless of the argument made, these data seem to confirm Howard Becker's observation that we cannot "assume that the category of those labeled deviant will contain all those who actually have broken a rule" (1963, p. 9).

Nevertheless, it is equally obvious that rape does exist and that these statistics on rape tell us something about its existence. It would be ludicrous to contend that we would find as many examples of the behavior legally defined as rape in a randomly sampled group of Indianapolis men as we would find in the group represented by these 881 cases. But critics of labeling theory overlook two important differences between the kind of actual criminal-justice processing represented here and reactions to crime in the abstract. First, real cases, unlike abstractions, cover an entire range of human behavior and are often difficult to classify. Recall the complexities of the four cases summarized at the beginning of Chapter 1. If we polled citizens of Indianapolis or the officials who processed these 881 cases, we would no doubt find—as other studies of this type have found—that people regard rape as a heinous offense worthy of the most serious punishment (Rossi et al., 1974; United States Department of Justice, 1983). However, we would find more disagreement if we moved from the abstraction of rape to the complexity of real cases. Chances are that fewer people would judge an incident to be rape if it involved a victim and offender who knew each other previously or were in some way socializing before the reported incident (Feild and Bienen, 1980; Burt and Albin, 1981; Shotland and Goodstein, 1983). Fewer still would consider an assault by a husband or ex-husband to be rape (Finkelhor and Yllo, 1982; D. Russell, 1982; Frieze, 1983).

The second difference is that labeling critics usually take an "Olympian view" of actual processing. If we had a good seat among the gods on Mount Olympus, we could determine precisely the real behavior of the individuals involved in these cases. However, nothing could be further from the actual situation in most criminal cases. Rather, legal agents are faced with incomplete, contradictory, and incorrect information, and must operate within rules of evidence that sometimes prevent them from obtaining specific types of information. The agents themselves are by no means universally diligent in obtaining correct information, and in many jurisdictions their caseloads in any event prohibit a full investigation of every case reported.

While these observations will strike few people involved in the study or practice of criminal justice as particularly profound, they have important implications for the way we view crime and the role of criminology. Figure 4.2 may lead us to conclude that evidence of widespread agreement about the kinds of acts condemned as criminal may not necessarily contradict the assertion that deviance and crime are not objective properties of behavior, but rather definitions constructed through social interaction. Obviously, this does not mean that all men in Indianapolis committed rape in the 1970s, or that it makes no sense to distinguish rapists from nonrapists (as some of the later labeling literature suggests). Nonetheless, it seems equally clear that the men actually convicted and punished for rape in this jurisdiction bear only a faint resemblance to all those who—with Olympian eyesight—we could identify as rapists. I turn next to a consideration of how the legal agents in these cases actually went about ascribing or not ascribing criminal labels to the men they processed.

THE RAPE VICTIM

In several respects, the victim herself is the first social-control agent in the complex set of decisions that are necessary to conclude officially that a rape has occurred. Only 2.2 percent of the cases in my Indianapolis study reviewed here became known to the police through their own patrol observations. The vast majority of cases came to police attention through citizen reports. Thus, without the cooperation of victims and other witnesses in rape cases there would be virtually no arrests. Moreover, because the victim is the state's chief witness in a rape case, her active cooperation is a minimum practical requirement for prosecution and conviction.

The Social Nature of Rape Reporting

If we conceptualize the rape victim as the first in a long sequence of processing agents, we can apply to the victim the labeling argument that criminal labels are based not on objective properties of actual behavior, but on socially constructed definitions. On the face of it, it would appear that the rape victim should be less susceptible than other legal agents to the interpretive influences of social constructions of the incident. After all, she was at the scene of the offense and thus has more complete information than anyone who will subsequently make processing decisions in her case. And yet her definition of an act as rape is in several ways as much a social construction as the decision making of the other legal agents who work on the case.

Most obviously, rapes become social events early on because of the participation of family, friends, and witnesses in their aftermath. Recall that in the four cases summarized in Chapter 1, only one of the victims, Jennie Thorsten, called the police herself. Martha Jones was picked up by a passing motorist, who called the police; Cathy Marsh's boyfriend called the police; and Sheila and Rachel Davis's mother took them to the police. Similar patterns have been confirmed in other rape research. For example, researchers Lynda Holmstrom and Ann Burgess (1978, p. 31) interviewed 94 women, age 17 or older, who had been admitted to a city hospital as rape victims. They found that only 22 (23 percent) of these women decided to call the police on their own initiative. In 28 percent of the cases, the victim's family or friends notified the police, in 23 percent a stranger called the police, and in 10 percent the victim was persuaded to call the police by relatives or friends. When the victim was less than 17 years old, the role of others in introducing the case to the legal system was even greater. Of 23 rape victims interviewed, only two called the police on their own initiative. Thus, for a substantial majority of the rape cases in the Holmstrom and Burgess study, the incident was immediately opened to social interpretation through the participation—often against the wishes of the victim—of relatives, friends, and witnesses.

Apart from the social nature of the direct participation of "third parties"* in defining a particular incident and taking action, rapes are social in the sense that the victim herself is a member of a society that holds particular stereotypes about rape. Before the victim can convince others that she has been raped, she must convince herself. This decision is often more complex than we might at first suspect. For example, researchers Cheryl Oros, Kenneth Leonard, and Mary Koss (1980) found that the degree of force in a rape was the most important factor for victims in classifying encounters with men as rape. Women who had been subjected to high levels of violence were more likely to see themselves as rape victims. In contrast, women who were acquainted with the offender prior to the incident were less likely to consider themselves to be rape victims.

The victim's interpretation of the rape is also social in

---

* The role of "third parties" in defining deviance and crime has been explored in detail by sociologists and criminologists (e.g., Garfinkel, 1956; Goffman, 1959; Emerson and Messinger, 1977).

the sense that, like other processing agents, the victim commonly projects her case forward to consider how it will be interpreted by others. Thus, even when a woman is convinced that she is a rape victim, she may fear that others will not believe that she was raped. Recently, Shirley Feldman-Summers and Clark Ashworth (1981) asked 400 women about their willingness to report a hypothetical rape to police and others. The researchers found that women's decisions to report rape were most closely associated with whether they perceived the existence of social support for doing so.

Some of these ideas about the rape victim's willingness to report the assault were directly tested in recent research by Linda Williams (1984). Williams studied 246 female rape victims who went to a rape crisis center for help, 146 who had reported the rape to police and 100 who had not. Her results suggest that some of the same stereotypes are at work in victims' interpretations of rape that are more commonly attributed to police and judges. For example, victims whose homes were broken into or who were attacked in their cars were most likely to report, followed by those assaulted in public or abducted from a public place. Women who were raped in a social situation (e.g., on a date or while studying with their attackers) were least likely to report the incident to police. Furthermore, women who were raped by strangers were more likely to report than those raped by relatives or friends. Similarly, women who were threatened with a weapon or were subjected to a high degree of violence were more likely to report.

Changes in Rape Stereotypes

If crime categories like rape are the result not only of criminal behavior but also of widely held stereotypes about the characteristics of rape, there is the possibility that these stereotypes change over time. Indeed, labeling theorists (e.g., Becker, 1963, p. 12; Gusfield, 1967) argue that the enforcement of laws and rules depends in part on social movements and periodic campaigns against various types of crime and deviance. A major focus of the modern feminist movement has been to change rape stereotypes (see, e.g., Rose, 1977; Burt and Albin, 1981). An indication that these stereotypes have indeed changed is indirect support for the argument that criminal labels are applied because of social definitions rather than actual behavior. A study by sociologists James Orcutt and Rebecca Faison (1988) provides a partial test of this idea.

Orcutt and Faison hypothesized that declining support for traditional female sex roles in the 1970s and 1980s should have been accompanied by an increase in the rates at which women reported rape to the police. Because the view of the rapist as a stranger is a prominent stereotype, they further predicted that rates of rape reporting involving nonstrangers should increase as attitudes toward women's roles changed. To test these hypotheses, the authors examined U.S. data on sex-role attitudes and criminal victimization for the 1970s and 1980s. Consistent with their hypotheses, they found that women in the United States became more likely to report rape throughout the 1970s and 1980s and that this increase was the greatest for rapes in which the victim and offender were previously acquainted. At the same time, they did not find similar increases in a control analysis based on robbery victims.

Thus, the research on the rape victim's decision to report generally supports the claim that criminal labels depend on definitions constructed through social interaction. Obviously, each victim's decision is a complex one, and there are many reasons that a woman may decide not to report even when she defines the incident as rape. However, research suggests that part of her decision is based on her own stereotypes about rape and her perceptions of others' stereotypes.

POLICE REACTIONS TO RAPE

In several ways police are the most important official processing agents in sexual-assault cases. The police officer is typically the victim's first contact with the criminal-justice system, and police are the only officials who participate in cases from initial report to final disposition. Also, the police provide the pool of arrestees from which the prosecution selects defendants. More cases are screened from the system by police than by any other agents in the system. Recall that of the 881 cases reported to Indianapolis police in this study, only 328 (37.2 percent) resulted in arrest. Major decisions made mostly by the police in criminal cases include the decision to unfound and to arrest and the severity of the initial charge. In addition, police play an important role in determining whether criminal cases should be filed as felonies. Police are also important as witnesses in those cases which are tried.

Police and Rape Cases in Indianapolis

Several changes were made in the social organization of the Indianapolis Police Department from 1970 to 1975 that had implications for the processing of sexual-assault cases. Before 1973, all sexual-assault cases were investigated by a Homicide and Robbery (HR) Unit. Because Indianapolis detectives generally considered homicide the highest-status detective work and robbery the next highest, sexual assaults were likely to receive less attention and resources than homicides and robberies. All detectives in the HR Unit were male; most were long-term veterans of the Police Department. Before 1973, nearly all rape cases were investigated by one male officer, a police veteran who had joined the department in 1951. In a single year, he was officially responsible for investigating 357 rape cases. To get some indication of the relative importance of rape and homicide investigation, it is interesting to note that at the same time one detective was assigned 357 rape cases in one year, six detectives were responsible for investigating approximately 50 homicides each year.

Public concern about rape and its treatment by the police in Indianapolis began to increase dramatically in the early 1970s. In addition to the growing national attention being focused on rape, two local women's groups campaigned diligently for reform of the criminal-justice system's treatment of rape victims. Women United Against Rape (WUAR), the larger and more influential of the two groups, began in 1972 as a joint enterprise of the already existing Women's Anti-Crime Crusade (founded in 1962) and the Mayor's Task Force on Women. WUAR was managed by a loosely organized board of directors, elected by those in attendance at annual meetings. The organization worked to improve police treatment of rape victims, encouraged more effective prosecution of rape cases, and lobbied for the reform of Indiana rape laws. The

Victim Advocate Program (VAP) began in March 1975, when a WUAR member became dissatisfied with what she perceived as the conservativism of WUAR and formed her own group. The major ongoing project of the VAP was to provide volunteers who offered emotional support to victims of violent crimes while their cases were being processed by the criminal-justice system.

The growing attention paid to rape victims in Indianapolis in the early 1970s had tangible effects on the way police treated rape cases. After 1973, a specially delegated Sex Offense (SO) Unit was created in the Police Department and given responsibility for processing all sexual-assault complaints. Four of the six staff detectives originally assigned to the unit were women, including its director. The Police Department also created a victim assistance program to serve as a liaison between the police and victims of violent crime, including rape. Victim assistance personnel provided transportation to and from court, offered counseling and support, and made referrals to other counseling and medical agencies.

In order to determine how police processed rape cases and whether their practices had changed as a result of the reforms, I examined police records on rape cases for 1970, 1973, and 1975. I chose 1970 because it was the earliest year for which reasonably complete records were available. Because cases take up to two years to be adjudicated, 1975 was the latest year I could include in the study (these data were collected in 1977). This procedure resulted in a data set of 904 cases; 30.3 percent had been reported to police in 1970, 33.3 percent in 1973, and 36.4 percent in 1975.*

Seventeen detectives each investigated 10 or more of the cases included in the analysis. I interviewed 15 of these detectives (one refused to be interviewed and I could not locate the other, who had retired from police work). The detectives I interviewed were responsible for processing 73.6 percent of the 904 cases in the analysis. I questioned detectives about their attitudes toward rape, their strategies for processing rape

---

* The difference between the 904 cases reported here and the 881 cases discussed in Figure 4.2 is explained by missing data. I was unable to match prosecution and court records with 23 of the cases available in the police data.

cases, their opinions about rape victims and suspects, and their perceptions of how the processing of rape cases in Indianapolis had changed in recent years.

Description of the Police Data

Characteristics of the police data are summarized in Table 4.1. The first four variables in the table are measures of how the police processed the cases. Indianapolis police offered three official reasons for unfounding cases: (1) problems with the complainant's moral character or conduct (70.9 percent), (2) lack of cooperation from the victim (20 percent), and (3) technical reasons (9.1 percent).

Cases unfounded because of problems with the complainant's moral character or conduct most often involved complainants who were drinking or using drugs when the incident was reported or investigated, complainants who were "runaway" juveniles and were believed by police to have fabricated the rape accusation, or complainants who were hitchhiking at the time of the offense. The following excerpt is typical of police reports in cases unfounded because of the complainant's moral character or conduct:

> I received the above assignment to investigate a rape . . . and have been to the alleged victim's apartment on two occasions and couldn't get anyone to answer the door. I talked to other tenants in the building and they stated that [complainant] makes it a practice to take different men into her apartment at all times of day or night, drinks heavily and they do not believe that anyone would have to rape her.

Cases were unfounded for technical reasons when they occurred outside the Indianapolis Police Department's jurisdiction. Reported rapes occurring out of jurisdiction were first unfounded and then turned over to the appropriate police agency.

For all rape cases reported to Indianapolis police during the three years of the study, I determined whether an arrest was made. I was able to collect complete information on 324 men who were arrested.* I created charge-seriousness scores

---

* Police charges were missing for four of the men who were arrested, so these cases had to be dropped from this part of the analysis.

TABLE 4.1 Police Processing of Rape Cases in Indianapolis[a]

		Distribution	
Variable	Coding	N	%
Outcomes			
Unfounded	0 No	844	93.4
	1 Yes	60	6.6
Arrest	0 No arrest	580	64.2
	1 Arrest	324	35.8
Charge	Interval scale (1–22)	Median =	15.07
Felony screening	0 Dismissed, misdemeanor	176	54.3
	1 Felony	148	45.7
Characteristics of Victim and Suspect			
Race composition[b]	Black defendants and victims(BB)	383	44.1
	Black defendants and white victims(BW)	199	22.9
	White defendants and victims(WW)	287	33.0
Victim age	0 18 or older	594	65.6
	1 17 or younger	224	27.0
Suspect age	0 21 or older	606	73.0
	1 20 or younger	224	27.0
Victim Behavior			
Alleged nonconformity	0 No	874	96.6
	1 Yes	31	3.4
Victim resistance	0 None	695	77.6
	1 Physical resistance	206	22.3
Promptness of report to police	0 Less than 1 hour	513	59.4
	1 1-24 hours	290	33.6
	2 More than 24 hours	60	7.0
Interpersonal Context			
Victim–suspect relationship	0 Strangers	435	49.7
	1 Acquaintances	440	50.3
Location of incident	0 Outside home	556	69.6
	1 In home	243	30.4
Number of offenders	0 One	676	74.8
	1 More than one	228	25.2
Evidence			
Physical injury	1 None	268	29.7
	2 Minor, self-treated	596	66.1
	3 Hospitalized	37	4.1
Eyewitness	0 No	714	79.2
	1 Yes	188	20.8
Weapon	0 None	599	68.4
	1 Firearm, knife, other	276	31.6

TABLE 4.1   (*continued*)

Variable	Coding	Distribution N	%
Outcomes (continued)			
Offense type	0 Attempted sexual assault	138	15.3
	1 Sexual assault	766	84.7
Victim willing to prosecute	0 No	188	20.8
	1 Yes	714	79.2
Suspect identification	0 No	378	41.8
	1 Yes	527	58.2
System Characteristics			
Detective unit	0 Pre-SO Unit	553	62.2
	1 SO Unit	336	37.8

[a] Variation in total number of cases is due to missing data.
[b] Less than 1 percent of all suspects and victims were nonwhite other than black. Because I expected the same effects for other nonwhite racial groups, I combined black and other nonwhite in the analysis. This produced no changes in the interpretation of results.

for each of the suspects who were arrested by assigning the mean prison term imposed by statute for conviction (e.g., for a 10- to 20-year sentence, charge seriousness equals 15, or 30/2). Because sentences were almost always *concurrent* (i.e., served at the same time rather than consecutively) in this jurisdiction, I used only the most serious charge for each case. Charge-seriousness scores ranged from 1 (assault and battery, disorderly conduct) to 22 (rape of a victim under 12 years of age, kidnapping). Seriousness scores from 71 percent of the cases were between 10 and 15 points (63 percent of the charges were 15 points); 6.2 percent were less than 10 points; and 22.9 percent were greater than 15 points.

Table 4.1 shows that of the 324 suspects arrested, 148 (45.7 percent) were eventually charged with felonies. Nominally, the prosecutor's office is responsible for this decision; however, my observations indicated that the screening decision was strongly influenced by detectives. Deputy prosecutors and judges generally agreed that detectives were usually in the best position to know the evidential strength of cases at the early stages of processing. As one Marion County judge put it, "The police are out there a lot and they're pretty good judges of character." Although prosecutors occasionally dismissed cases that detectives believed should be filed, it was very unusual for a prosecutor to file felony charges when the detective opposed prosecution.

The labeling argument that official processing decisions in criminal cases are based less on the actual behavior of the accused than on the interpersonal context of the incident generally suggests that outcomes should be affected more by extralegal than legal variables. However, in actual practice, distinctions between legal and extralegal factors are complex. For example, the victim's willingness to testify is legally required, but as suggested in our discussion of the victim's decision to report a rape, her willingness may in turn be conditioned by official reactions to her complaint. Other variables, such as whether the assault involved a weapon and whether sexual penetration occurred, are legal considerations for the seriousness of the charge but not for the decision to arrest or file the case as a felony. And for variables like seriousness of the offense, which clearly is a legal concern, the law does not specify how much weight officials should assign. Thus, distinctions between legal and extralegal variables must be interpreted as relative rather than absolute.

The analysis included measures of (1) victims' and suspects' characteristics (race, age), (2) victims' behavior (allegations of nonconformity, victim resistance), and (3) the interpersonal context of the incident (e.g., victim–suspect relationship, number of offenders). Only 11 (1.2 percent) of the cases involved white defendants and black victims. The small number of such cases made meaningful statistical analysis impossible, so they were excluded. For the remaining cases, I distinguished between black offender–white victim cases and black and white intraracial cases.*

To provide a partial test of the argument that nonconformist women are less likely to have their cases defined as rapes, I examined police records for any allegations that the victim had engaged in some type of nonconformist behavior,

---

* The race-composition variable was dummy-coded in the analysis as two vectors, with white intraracial assaults being the excluded category.

either at the time of the offense or in general. Such allegations included: (1) hitchhiking, (2) drinking at the time of the offense, (3) being at a tavern or bar without a male escort, (4) allegedly engaging in sex outside of marriage, and (5) willingly entering the suspect's car, house, or apartment. Note that none of these behaviors constituted criminal offenses for adults; however, several of the victims coded for alleged nonconformity were arrested for juvenile status offenses, either as runaways or curfew violators. In the analysis, I coded the victim-nonconformity variable as positive if police records indicated that the victim had engaged in any of these types of behavior.

In keeping with labeling arguments, I also included measures identified in the rape literature (e.g., Holmstrom and Burgess, 1978; Sanders, 1980; Stanko, 1981–1982; Schwendinger and Schwendinger, 1983; L. Williams, 1984) as related to stereotypes about the authenticity of reported sexual assaults. Generally, this literature shows that assaults (1) by prior acquaintances, (2) occurring outside the victim's home, (3) perpetrated by only one offender, (4) in which the victim did not physically resist, and (5) that were not reported promptly by the victim are less likely to be interpreted as genuine.

To control for evidential differences between cases, the analysis included six measures of evidence. Indiana law provided more serious penalties for assaults involving a weapon, sexual penetration, or both. In addition, I included the following as measures of evidence: physical injury, the presence of an eyewitness, the victim's ability to identify a suspect, and her willingness to testify. Although corroboration of the assault by a witness was not legally required in this jurisdiction, I expected the effect of witnesses to be important for police decision making.

In order to determine whether changes in the organization of the Police Department affected the processing of rape cases, I included a variable that distinguished cases processed by the newly formed Sex Offense Unit from those processed by the Homicide and Robbery Unit.

To examine which factors had the greatest influence on police decision making in these rape cases, I treated the four outcome variables listed at the top of Table 4.1—unfounded, arrest, charge, and felony screening—as dependent variables. However, the extreme skew in the "unfounded" outcome (only 6.6 percent of the cases were unfounded) made the validity of multivariate statistical analysis questionable in this case, so it was excluded. In an analysis of the remaining three police decisions, I treated the other variables in Table 4.1 as independent variables. I performed two types of multivariate statistical analysis, depending on the way in which the dependent variable was measured. For charge seriousness, an interval-level variable, I used ordinary least-squares multiple regression procedures (see Hanushek and Jackson, 1977; Lewis-Beck, 1980). Because arrest and felony filing are dichotomous (yes–no) outcomes, I used a weighted least-squares analysis for these variables. Table 4.2 is a summary of the statistically significant results.* (For the full results, see Appendix 4.1 at the end of this chapter.)

DETERMINANTS OF POLICE DECISIONS IN RAPE CASES

To allow a less technical presentation of the major findings, Table 4.2 shows the best predictors of each of the three police decisions, rank ordered by the size of their standardized regression coefficients, or beta weights. *Beta weights* are standardized coefficients that show the amount of change in a dependent variable for a change in an independent variable of one standard deviation. Because beta coefficients are standardized, we can compare them within each equation. Thus, the beta coefficient for victim nonconformity in Table 4.2 tells us that police were less likely to make an arrest when there were allegations of victim nonconformity. It also tells us that victim nonconformity was more important than the victim–suspect relationship but less important than the victim's decision to prosecute as a predictor of arrest.

---

* Exceptions to the above are: (1) I included suspect identification only in the analysis of Arrest—after arrest, all suspects have obviously been identified; and (2) I included charge seriousness only in the analysis of Felony Screening. I included the type of detective unit (i.e., SO or HR) in all three equations to allow interpretation of the product terms.

TABLE 4.2 Best Predictors of Arrest, Charge, and Felony Screening in Indianapolis Sexual-Assault Cases, 1970–1975

Arrest (N = 769)		Charge (N = 324)		Felony Filed (N = 324)	
Variable	Beta	Variable	Beta	Variable	Beta
1. Suspect identification	.541	1. Offense type	.378	1. Charge seriousness	.206
2. Victim will testify	.137	2. Weapon	.255	2. Number of offenders	−.167
3. Victim nonconformity	−.056	3. Victim age	.213	3. Victim age	−.164
4. Report promptness	−.025	4. Report promptness	−.185	4. Victim will testify	.093
5. Victim–suspect relation	.024	5. Black suspect–white victim	.134		
6. Weapon	.023	6. Victim will testify	.081		

Note: All variables significant at $p < .05$ except number 6 for Charge and number 3 for Felony Filed, which were significant at $p < .10$.

The Arrest Decision

Consistent with feminist arguments, Table 4.2 shows that the victim-nonconformity measure was a significant predictor of arrest—this despite the fact that victim nonconformity was cited in relatively few cases. In fact, none of the 31 cases in which victim nonconformity was alleged resulted in arrest. Hence there was no variation in this variable for the analysis of charge severity and felony filing, and it had to be dropped. My interviews with police who processed rape cases showed that they often associated the victim's nonconformity with her carelessness before the incident or her outright complicity in the incident. But at the same time, police clearly did not record all possible instances of victim nonconformity in the records. For example, even though none of the cases in which police alleged victim nonconformity were included among those adjudicated as felonies, prosecution and court personnel alleged that an additional 22 percent of the cases subsequently filed as felonies involved victim nonconformity, despite the fact that I measured nonconformity the same way in the analysis of court outcomes as in the police analysis.

The reason that police do not include all possible instances of victim nonconformity in their official reports probably has more to do with the nature of criminal-justice processing than with definitions of nonconformity held by police and other legal agents. Police reports are available to defense attorneys and are routinely used by both prosecution and defense representatives. Detectives know that their allegations of victim nonconformity effectively eliminate cases. They make decisions about genuine rape complaints on the basis of many considerations, including the victim's apparent moral character and her willingness to cooperate with the investigation. These decisions are then *justified* by reporting those features of the incident that support the conclusions already reached (e.g., unfounding, arrest). These processes are illustrated by comparing police justifications for unfounding with those for arrest. These two excerpts are from unfounded case reports:

1. The report is questionable as to the facts that happened and the way they happened. I think it is fabricated. . . . However, trying to pin the girl down is hard. Her foster parents

have a lot of trouble with her for lying and she ran away from home. . . .

2. I interrogated the above alleged victim. . . . She stated that she ran away from home . . . and she met a girlfriend. I learned from her mother that the girl has run away from home five times. One time she slept and had intercourse with a Mexican about three months ago and had intercourse freely. . . . Girl seems to have mental problems and evidently likes to have sex.

In neither report do police provide a specific, legally justifiable reason for unfounding. Instead, both reports assume that no crime occurred ("the report is questionable," "the alleged victim") and then support this assumption with negative assessments of the complainant's moral character (e.g., "her foster parents have a lot of trouble with her for lying," "(she) evidently likes to have sex").

These two excerpts are strikingly different from the next two, which both resulted in arrest:

1. Victim stated that she was raped by an acquaintance. Mother was at the above location on my arrival and accompanied victim to General Hospital where she was checked. Both stated that they would prosecute. Car number 65 was on the scene at the hospital and has the name of the suspect.

2. Victim stated that the subject drug her to the residence . . . and raped her. Victim stated she screamed and hit the subject several times. Witnesses downstairs heard the victim screaming at approximately 0700 hours. When the police arrived, the victim pointed out the house where the rape occurred and the subject was arrested. Victim was taken to General Hospital. . . .

In these two reports the complainant is referred to as the "victim." Both reports assume that a rape occurred and that it will be handled as a crime. Key elements necessary for prosecuting the case (e.g., "both said they would prosecute," "witnesses downstairs heard the victim screaming") are included. In the two unfounded reports, the police maintain a separation between the complainant's version of what happened and what they personally think happened. By contrast, the two reports resulting in arrest are written as if the officers are merely reporting objective facts; there appears to be no disparity in the complainant's statement, the officer's statement, and what really happened.

Arrest was also less likely when the victim did not promptly report the incident. One detective stated simply, "A woman who has actually been raped would call the police immediately." Arrest was more likely when the incident involved a weapon.

Table 4.2 shows that arrest was *more* likely for prior acquaintances than strangers. This finding seems to contradict research (e.g., Holmstrom and Burgess, 1978; Shotland and Goodstein, 1983) showing that a prior relationship between victim and offender results in higher rates of dismissal and acquittal. Indeed, my interviews with detectives included many references to the belief that rape complaints involving acquaintances are less likely to be valid. This statement by one detective is typical:

> The victim–offender relationship makes a big difference. I'm leery of those cases [i.e., cases in which victim and offender are acquainted]. I have in the back of my mind, "Did this guy really do this, or didn't he?"

The contradictory findings for prior victim–suspect relationship here are explained by noting differences between arrest and subsequent processing decisions. A prior relationship makes arrest easier by increasing the chances of locating and identifying a suspect. But as we shall see in later chapters, a prior relationship often hurts the prosecutor's case by making a consent defense possible. Interviews also suggested the police sometimes used arrest to temporarily protect the victim from further attack and that this function was particularly important in cases of assault by relatives or prior acquaintances.

Charge Seriousness and Felony Filing

As Table 4.2 indicates, charges were more serious when the offense included sexual penetration and when a weapon was present. Charges were also more serious when the victim was white and the suspect black, when the victim made clear her intention to prosecute, and when the victim was less than 18 years old. Charges were less serious for incidents that were not promptly reported.

The best predictors of the decision to file a case as a felony were charge seriousness, number of offenders, and the victim's age. Not surprisingly, more serious offenses were more likely to be filed as felonies. Offenses involving more than one offender were less likely to be filed as felonies. Interviews indicated that detectives were suspicious of sexual assaults involving more than one offender—particularly when these cases also involved more than one victim, when victims and offenders were acquainted prior to the incident, or when victims and offenders were all young. Several detectives referred to cases with these characteristics as "party rapes" and suggested that such incidents deserved less serious attention than other complaints.

Compared to other men, those accused of assaulting women under 18 years of age were less likely to be charged with a felony. However, my interviews with police suggested that the victim's age affects cases in different ways, depending on other case characteristics. Consistent with the analysis of charge seriousness, police considered sexual assaults of young victims as particularly serious offenses. At the same time, however, many of the incidents involving women under 18 years old had other characteristics that made them seem less serious to the police. For example, incidents involving women under 18 years were more likely to involve young suspects (correlation = .19, $p < .001$) who were acquainted with the victim (correlation = .13, $p < .001$). Detectives whom I interviewed argued that some rapes reported by young women, especially cases in which the suspect was also young and known to the victim prior to the incident, were "date rapes" and did not warrant felony prosecution.

As with arrest and charge decisions, the probability that men would be charged with felonies was greater for cases in which the victim made clear her intention to testify. Given the importance of the victim's testimony for subsequent prosecution, her willingness to testify is essential for filing cases as felonies.

Police Decisions Before and After Formation of the Sex Offense Unit

Note that the measure of whether a case was processed by the old Homicide and Robbery Division or the newly formed Sex Offense Unit does not show up as statistically significant in the three police decisions reported in Table 4.2. This finding surprised me, because my interviews with detectives who had investigated rape cases before and after the creation of the SO Unit led me to expect major differences in the way cases were treated by police during the two periods. These expected differences can be illustrated by comparing the comments of two detectives, whom I refer to as Officers McKenna and Drake.

McKenna is a 60-year-old white male with a high school education. He has worked for the Police Department for 26 years. He investigated rape cases and other violent crimes for 20 years before the formation of the SO Unit. Officer Drake is a 35-year-old white male. At the time of the interview he was writing his master's thesis in psychology at an Indianapolis university. He has been with the Police Department less than 10 years and originally joined the police force as an investigator in the crime laboratory. He was transferred to the SO Unit shortly after its formation. Both McKenna and Drake have investigated hundreds of rape cases during their police careers.

The views of these two men toward women, rape, and the role of the detective in investigating rape cases were strikingly different. Officer McKenna's comments during my interviews with him were filled with the kinds of rape stereotypes that so enrage citizens concerned about rape victims. For example, he claimed that the rape shield law in Indianapolis is a bad law because many women

> play up to a guy. [They] let him take them out and buy drinks for them and lead the guy on. These women are prick teasers. Your dick doesn't have much of a conscience. Some guys just can't control it.

He believed that feminists have had a dangerous effect by counseling women to physically resist rape, noting that "sexual intercourse never killed anybody." He asserted that increases in black offender–white victim rape are due to integration in the schools. Black boys now have to go to school with the whites. White girls see these blacks every day and begin to think they're not as bad as their mothers told them they were.

In contrast, Officer Drake's description of rape and rape investigation was much more in tune with contemporary feminist thought:

> You're talking about a crime of violence, but with an intimate factor. The rapist takes something from the rape victim—it is much more intimate and demeaning. This creates more awareness of the crime than you get with something like robbery. The approach to handling the crime should be entirely different. The victim of a sexual crime has lost so much more. It weighs psychologically on the victim. There is a certain degree of psychological trauma that can't be removed.

McKenna, who had been investigating rape cases 10 times longer than Drake, took a much more callous approach to rape investigations. When I asked him about the first thing he did in a rape investigation, he said:

> First I talk to the victim. If the story doesn't seem too good, I give her a lie detector test. You must first determine if she is telling the truth.

In contrast, Drake claimed a much more sympathetic involvement with cases:

> With these cases you have to get emotionally involved. You suffer sometimes when you do, but the price is worth it.

When I asked McKenna how the handling of rape cases could be improved, he said he didn't think there was any need to change the procedure. In fact, he saw the recent changes in the handling of rape cases as unnecessary at best and detrimental at worst. In contrast, Drake applauded the changes that have been made and suggested that much more could be done:

> We need to take rape squads and insure adequate staffing on the basis of training and education. College degrees contribute to capability, verbal skills. College doesn't necessarily make good cops, but these skills are important. Make college education a requirement for the squad. Also extensive training in crisis intervention and specific training in sexual deviance

literature. . . . I would recommend continued in-service training. New techniques, new approaches. Continual training. Also
should have periodic meetings with the squad for any innova-
tive ideas they have. . . . I would also make the squad an independent group. Give it control over its own investigations.
Take away the paramilitary organization.

Given the differences between the HR and SO units suggested by interviews like these, how can we explain the fact
that the new detective unit had no significant impact on arrest, charge seriousness, or felony filing? The answer becomes
clearer if we examine Table 4.3, which compares final police
dispositions of rape cases processed before and after the creation of the SO Unit. As we might expect, Table 4.3 shows
that police were less likely to unfound and to exceptionally
clear cases after the creation of the SO Unit. In fact, police
unfounded about five times more reported rapes before the SO
Unit than after. However, the results also show that SO detectives were more likely to leave cases inactive and that
there was no difference in the likelihood of arrest before and
after the creation of the SO Unit.

In general, the results suggest that changes in the pro-

TABLE 4.3   Police Disposition and Filing Decision
by Detective Unit[a]

Disposition	Homicide and Robbery Unit	Sex Offense Unit
Unfounded	9.6 (53)	2.1 (7)*
Cleared by arrest	36.0 (199)	36.0 (121)
Exceptionally cleared	19.6 (108)	11.0 (37)*
Inactive	34.8 (192)	50.9 (171)*
Total	100.0 (552)	100.0 (336)
Arrests: Dismissed, Misdemeanors	57.8 (115)	49.6 (60)
Arrests: Felonies	42.4 (84)	50.4 (61)

[a] Cases processed by both units were excluded from the analysis.
* Chi-square significant at $p < .001$.

SOURCE: LaFree, 1981, p. 587. © 1981 by the Society for the Study of Social
Problems, Inc. Original version appeared in *Social Problems* 28 (1981). Used
by permission.

cessing of rape cases after the creation of the SO Unit occurred at points of least resistance. Unfounding is probably the most controversial police decision in rape cases: it directly challenges the authenticity of the complainant's claims, cases are typically unfounded before a thorough investigation has been launched and usually on the authority of only one police officer, and once a case is unfounded there is little chance that it will reenter the criminal-justice system at a later time. (In fact, none of the 60 unfounded cases in this study received any further investigation.) But to change the criteria for unfounding is a relatively simple matter, requiring only changes in the categorization of reported offenses. Likewise, the rates at which cases are exceptionally cleared can be changed simply by changing record-keeping practices.

In contrast, arrest and felony filing require tangible elements (e.g., a suspect, evidence) and set into motion a protracted legal process that demands police participation from start to finish. Arrest rates remained unchanged before and after the SO Unit, and although the SO Unit increased the percentage of cases filed as felonies, the increase was not statistically significant. Overall, the main processing differences after the creation of the SO Unit were simply that police classified more cases as inactive and fewer as unfounded or exceptionally cleared.

Comparing the HR and SO Units

Although the analysis so far does not show that outcomes were significantly different for the HR Unit and the SO Unit, it is still possible that the effects of the other independent variables on police decisions were different for the two units. For example, perhaps measures of victim nonconformity had a greater effect on the decision to arrest for detectives in the HR unit than for detectives in the SO unit. To test for this possibility, I did the multivariate analysis a second time, including variables called "product terms." These variables are so named because they are the product of multiplying one variable by another. I created one product term for each of the independent variables by multiplying it times whether the case was processed by the HR Unit (coded 0) or the SO Unit (coded 1). Significant effects for these product terms tell us that the independent variable has different effects depending on which unit, HR or SO, is processing the case.

The results are summarized in Table 4.4 (for the full analysis, see the bottom half of Appendix 4.1), which compares the standardized effects of significant independent variables for the HR and SO Units.* Table 4.4 shows that at least one variable had different effects for the HR and SO Units for each of the three police decisions. However, the results do not uniformly support the idea that police from the SO Unit were more likely than HR Unit police to rely on legal considerations in making decisions. For arrest, the effect of the victim's willingness to prosecute declined after the creation of the SO Unit. However, the effect of black intraracial cases, the promptness of the victim's report, and the victim's identification of a suspect increased. The SO unit was less likely than the HR unit to arrest when both the victim and offender were black or when the victim reported the rape less promptly. The SO unit was more likely than the HR unit to arrest when the victim was able to identify a suspect clearly. For both charge seriousness and felony filing, the effect of the victim's age was reduced, and, for charge seriousness only, the effect of report promptness was also reduced. In general, most of the important variables for predicting these outcomes—victim nonconformity, black offender–white victim cases, victim–suspect relationship, number of offenders, presence or absence of weapon, offense type—had the same effects for the HR and SO Units.

CONCLUSIONS ABOUT POLICE REACTIONS TO RAPE

We may now ask ourselves, What are the implications of these findings for the claim that official labels are based less on actual behavior than on the social context of the incident? The answer is complex. Three of the important variables—

---

* Coefficients for the HR Unit in Table 4.4 are simple unstandardized regression coefficients from an analysis including detective unit by independent variable product terms (see Appendix 4.1). Coefficients for the SO unit are obtained by adding unstandardized coefficients from the product terms to unstandardized coefficients for the main effects. For example, the SO Unit effect for Race (BB) is .010 + (−.061) = −.051 (see LaFree, 1981; LaFree, Reskin, and Visher, 1985; Fiala and LaFree, 1988).

TABLE 4.4 Unstandardized Effects of Independent Variables on Police Decisions in Homicide and Robbery Unit and Sex Offense Unit

Variable	Arrest (N = 769)		Charge (N = 324)		Felony Filed (N = 324)	
	HR Unit	SO Unit	HR Unit	SO Unit	HR Unit	SO Unit
Victim age			1.61	-1.05	-1.71	.086
Race (BB)	|.010|	-.051				
Report promptness	-.020	-.060	-1.09	.82		
Willingness to prosecute	.165	.113				
Suspect identification	.538	.633				

Note: |Statistically insignificant|

85

type of offense, presence of weapon, and statutory seriousness —are probably the clearest measures of the actual criminal behavior that occurred. The fact that these variables have major effects on police decisions would seem to be contrary to the labeling argument.

In contrast, the strongest support for the labeling argument are the findings for victim nonconformity, race composition, and number of offenders. It seems probable that these variables relate more closely to stereotypes about the kinds of victims, offenders, and cases that are likely to constitute bona fide rape cases than to determinations of defendants' actual behavior.

Other important variables, especially whether a suspect was identified and whether the victim was willing to testify, are more difficult to classify. On the one hand, neither *necessarily* represents discriminatory action on the part of legal agents; on the other hand, both depend to an unknown extent on the ways in which police react to cases. For example, the reasons for not apprehending a suspect may range from the victim's inability to identify him to the failure of police to allocate sufficient resources to ensure his identification and apprehension. Likewise, the victim's willingness to testify may be solely dependent on or totally independent of her prior experiences with the legal system. Thus, different outcomes may still depend on case stereotypes even when they can be traced back to arguably legitimate variables.

One of the important mechanisms for these underlying relationships is simply the allocation of scarce resources. In a study of how victim characteristics affect felony screening decisions in the New York County District Attorney's Office, sociologist Elizabeth Stanko (1981–1982, p. 237) concludes that felony screeners indirectly take into account victims' social class, sex, race, and life-style:

> But the implicit . . . use of such attributes in the charging process is not—or at least not only—a measure of outright prosecutorial bias. More often it emerges as the pragmatism of a prosecutor intent on maximizing convictions and using organizational resources efficiently.

I observed similar processes in my interviews with detectives:

> You don't have time to work on every case fully—you have to pick the most important ones. The ones I like to work on are the ones where a woman is raped in her own house. If a woman can't be safe in her own house, where can she be safe? In a tavern, they can at least try to avoid the situation. I always work harder on cases where they couldn't help it than on cases like an ex-boyfriend.

While the detective quoted here does not claim that women raped outside of their homes are fabricating charges or that they deserve whatever happens to them, she does acknowledge that such cases are likely to get less of her attention than other cases. These allocation decisions in turn affect such so-called legal variables as whether a suspect is identified and apprehended and whether the victim decides to prosecute.

Taken together, the results suggest that the behavior of the police in these cases fell somewhere between the popular television image of the unbiased champion of the crime victim and the image of the sexist, racist brute offered by some critics. Although victim nonconformity was alleged in only 31 cases, none of these cases resulted in arrest. Likewise, assaults by black men on white women resulted in more serious charges; black men accused of assaulting black women were less likely to be arrested by members of the SO Unit; men accused of assaulting women aged 18 or older received less serious charges; and women who did not report promptly were less likely to see a suspect arrested. But contrary to the labeling thesis, there was ample evidence that police decisions also depended on more or less standard legal issues, including the type of offense, the seriousness of the charge, and the presence or absence of a weapon.

A related issue is whether the system reform, most notably the creation of a special SO Unit, was responsible for increasing the percentage of cases defined as rape and reducing the effect of legally irrelevant variables on processing decisions. Generally, the results do not support this interpretation. The SO Unit did reduce the percentage of unfounded and exceptionally cleared cases; but arrest and felony filing rates, more important in terms of subsequent processing, remained unchanged. Similarly, although the determinants of these processing decisions did change after the formation of the SO

Unit, the changes did not consistently result in less reliance on extralegal variables.

An important question, given the differences I observed in interviews with members of the HR and SO Units, is, Why didn't the reorganization of the Police Department result in more basic changes? First, some factors are difficult to change no matter how enlightened or motivated the public official. Arrest and felony screening require elements, such as a reasonable suspect and a victim willing to testify, that are often beyond the police officer's ability to influence. The data suggest that detectives in the SO Unit changed those things easiest to change (and most politically expedient), including the rates at which they unfounded and exceptionally cleared cases and the frequency with which they recorded victim nonconformity in the official records.

Second, measuring the determinants of arrest, charge, and felony screening is only one way of assessing change in the system. For example, according to my observations and interviews, it seems very likely that sexual-assault victims received more humane treatment from the SO Unit than they did earlier from the HR Unit. Nonetheless, if this was so, it was not translated into markedly different processing outcomes. In fact, members of the SO Unit were less likely than their predecessors to arrest when the victim and suspect were both black or when the victim did not promptly report the incident.

Thus, the results of comparing the processing decisions of rape cases before and after the creation of the Sex Offense Unit seem to confirm sociologist Amitai Etzioni's conclusion that "human beings are not very easy to change after all" (1972, p. 45). Despite widespread grass-roots support for changes in the processing of rape cases, backed by national and local media pressure for reform, the major effect on police appears to have been more considerate treatment of rape victims rather than changes in the percentage of offenders arrested and charged. And even the fate of this reform is in question. While I was finishing the research reported in this book, Officer Drake, the energetic young detective I quoted above, was transferred out of the Sex Offense Unit. Insiders in the Police Department told me that he was considered to be a troublemaker who was "rocking the boat." He subsequently quit the Police Department and became a manufacturer's representative for a local pharmaceutical company. I asked him what he thought would happen to the Sex Offense Unit in the future, if public interest in rape once again declined. While he was obviously not a disinterested party, his response was pessimistic:

> When the pressure fades, the program will lapse back into a lackadaisical, inefficient system. It is one of the lousy parts of our society.

In the next chapter, I follow the rape cases that were filed as felonies in criminal court as they move through the next stages of legal processing. Again, I am especially interested in the claim, most often associated with the labeling perspective, that official definitions of crime are based not on objective properties of behavior, but on definitions constructed through social interaction.

APPENDIX 4.1 Regression Coefficients and Standard Errors of Predictors of Arrest, Charge, and Felony Screening

Variables	Arrest		Charge		Felony Screening	
	b	B	b	B	b	B
Victim age	-.145 (.020)	-.056**	1.61 (.600)	.213**	-.171 (.091)	-.164*
Victim nonconformity			1.11 (.391)	.134*		
Race composition (BW)	|-.010 (.011)	-.010|				
(BB)	.023 (.013)	.024*				
Victim–suspect relationship			-1.09 (.516)	-.185**	-.186 (.076)	-.167**
Number of offenders	-.020 (.008)	-.025**	2.01 (.381)	.255**		
Report promptness	.012 (.007)	.023**	1.98 (1.13)	.081*		
Weapon	.165 (.018)	.137**	3.82 (.482)	.378**		
Willingness to prosecute					.728 (.231)	.093**
Offense type	.538 (.022)	.541**				
Suspect identification	|-.043 (.036)	-.042|	|.273 (.258)	.062|	|.122 (.254)	.118|
Detective unit						
Charge seriousness					.024 (.006)	.206**
Product Terms (Independent Variable by Detective Unit)						
Victim age	-.061 (.024)	-.044**	-2.66 (.726)	-.309**	.257 (.143)	.180*
Race (BB)	-.040 (.015)	-.034**	1.91 (.565)	.301**		
Report promptness	-.052 (.027)	-.050*				
Willingness to prosecute	.095 (.022)	.081**				
Suspect identification						
R² with product terms/ without product terms	.675/.641		.371/.261		.147/.102	
Number of cases	769		324		324	
R² increment for product terms	.034 (p < .05)		.056 (p < .05)		.045 (p < .05)	

Note: |Statistically insignificant| * .10 < p < .05. ** p < .05. Attrition in sample size is due to missing data. Standard errors are given in parentheses.

SOURCE: LaFree, 1981, p. 588. © 1981 by the Society for the Study of Social Problems, Inc. Original version appeared in *Social Problems* 28 (1981). Used by permission.

CHAPTER 5

Constructing Rape: The Courts

What matters is the character of stereotypes, and the gullibility with which we employ them.

Walter Lippmann, *Public Opinion.*

Once a case is filed in criminal court, the major question of interest to both prosecution and defense, as well as to the parties they represent, is whether the defendant is to be officially labeled guilty. In this chapter I examine the 152 forcible sex offenses adjudicated by Indianapolis courts in 1970, 1973, and 1975. As before, the sample does not include male victims or nonforcible, statutory offenses. I collected information on the defendants' and victims' characteristics from police, prosecution, and court records. I recorded measures of evidence from prosecution files, defendants' criminal histories from police records, and final dispositions from court records. During the 12 months of data collection, I also did field observations in the prosecutor's office and criminal courts and interviewed most of the judges, prosecutors, defense attorneys, and other court personnel who processed these rape cases.

On the face of it, tracing cases from the police through the prosecutor's office and into the courts would seem to be a relatively straightforward task. In practice, however, it is often extremely difficult because of the largely autonomous organization of the individual components of criminal-justice bureaucracies. This can make even basic comparisons difficult. For example, in Indianapolis, the police and the courts assigned different identification numbers to the same cases.

As a result, the only way to match police records with court records was to compare the actual contents of individual cases. In many cases, this required a relatively simple matching of defendants' names in the police and court records. However, with common names, it was also necessary to compare other case characteristics to guarantee an accurate match.

Even after police and court records were matched, other analysis problems remained. Most importantly, the amount of information available on criminal cases increases as they move further into the system. Thus, the researcher is able to include more variables in the analysis of cases that remain in the system through more processing stages. The least information is usually available for cases in which a suspect is never identified; the most information is available from cases in which an offender is convicted. To understand the potential importance of this, recall that for 42 percent of the sexual assaults reported to police in this study, no suspect was ever identified (see Table 4.1, p. 70). For these cases, the only information on the defendant that was generally available were his basic characteristics (e.g., a white male more than 30 years old). Thus, potentially important variables like the defendant's criminal record were simply unavailable at this stage of processing.*

By contrast, after cases are filed as felonies, there is usually a great deal of information about them in official records, including the background and characteristics of a definite suspect and detailed information about the victim and the incident. However, while the amount of information available on criminal cases steadily increases as they move through the system, the number of cases remaining steadily declines.

---

* The fact that the amount of information on each case increases as it is processed is closely associated with the organization of legal decision making. In general, the official criteria for later decisions tend to be more specific and clear than the criteria for earlier decisions. For example, the decision to unfound is typically made by one officer with few guidelines. The decision to arrest is somewhat more structured, but still based on the extremely flexible notion of *probable cause*. In contrast, the official criterion for conviction in a court trial is *guilt beyond a reasonable doubt*. Thus, as the case moves through the system, the criteria for making decisions generally become more precise.

Thus, although my original sample included 881 cases of reported rape, only 50 cases reached the trial stage—a relatively small sample for multivariate analysis. Hence, researchers who want to trace the same cases from initial report to final disposition must choose either analyses of many cases and few variables or few cases and many variables. For these reasons, the analysis of court decisions presented in this chapter is somewhat different from the analysis of police decisions presented in the last chapter—even though I am still following the same cases with which I began.

CHANGES IN THE PROCESSING OF INDIANAPOLIS RAPE CASES

Major processing outcomes at the court stage are guilty pleas, jury or bench trials, and dismissals. Table 5.1 summarizes the methods by which the sexual-assault cases in the study were adjudicated. The table suggests several basic changes over the five-year period of the study. First, more than twice as many rape cases were adjudicated by guilty plea, jury, or bench trial in Indianapolis in 1973 (54) and 1975 (46) than in 1970 (24). Second, the percentage of cases pled guilty in 1970 was nearly twice as great as the percentage pled guilty in 1975. Third, the number of jury trials increased dramatically from 1970 to 1975. It is worth empha-

TABLE 5.1   Court Adjudication Type by Year of Offense for Indianapolis Sexual-Assault Cases

Outcome	1970 %	1973 %	1975 %	Total %
Pled guilty	60.0 (18)	56.2 (36)	34.5 (20)	48.6 (74)
Jury trials	3.3 (1)	18.8 (12)	41.4 (24)	24.4 (37)
Bench trials	16.7 (5)	9.4 (6)	3.4 (2)	8.6 (13)
Dismissals	20.0 (6)	15.6 (10)	20.7 (12)	18.4 (28)
Total	100.0 (30)	100.0 (64)	100.0 (58)	100.0 (152)
Convictions: Guilty pleas, verdicts	73.3 (22)	76.6 (49)	56.9 (33)	68.5 (104)

sizing that Indianapolis, a city with more than 1 million inhabitants, had only one jury trial for a forcible-sex offense in 1970—despite the fact that there were nearly as many arrests in 1970 as 1973 and 1975 (see Table 4.3, p. 82). Fourth, the number of bench trials declined steadily from 1970 to 1975. And finally, the total number of cases filed as felonies doubled from 1970 to 1973.

My field work in Indianapolis convinced me that these changes were closely related to changing social conceptions of rape. In 1970 rape was just beginning to receive national attention, primarily from a small group of activists. With little public pressure to treat rape cases seriously, the legal system favored easier, less costly types of adjudication. Thus, in all but one case, rapes adjudicated in 1970 were either plea-bargained, dismissed, or tried by judges.

By 1973 the situation had changed dramatically. Rape had been elevated to a national issue by the feminist movement, articles about rape were appearing with frequency in the national and local press, and in Indianapolis, Women United Against Rape had been formed and was actively campaigning for changes in the treatment of rape cases. Moreover, interest in rape was by no means limited to radical elements of the feminist movement. In fact, in Indianapolis, many of the members of WUAR were housewives who did not regularly participate in other movement activities. In 1973 the prosecutor—an elected official—responded to growing public pressure by more than doubling the number of rape cases filed in criminal court. Even with a doubled caseload, the prosecutor's office accepted fewer guilty pleas and scheduled fewer bench trials and more jury trials. Also, on the assumption that women might be more effective than men in rape prosecution, the prosecutor assembled a group of female attorneys to prosecute and screen all sexual-assault cases.

In 1975 a liberal, Democratic prosecutor was elected, swept into office partly in reaction to the Republican Watergate scandal. By now, rape was perceived as a full-fledged social problem at both the local and the national levels. In the early part of the year, Indiana became one of the first states in the nation to pass a "rape shield law," which made evidence of the victim's past sexual history inadmissible in court. The new prosecutor worked to increase the proportion of rape cases tried by taking a harder line on plea bargaining. Somewhat ironically, these reforms had the effect of *reducing* the overall conviction rate, which declined from a high of 77 percent in 1973 to 60 percent in 1975. The main reason for this decline was the new policy on plea bargaining fewer cases and trying more: because guilty pleas are automatic convictions while trial outcomes are uncertain, one effect of reducing plea bargaining was to lower overall conviction rates.

DESCRIPTION OF THE COURT DATA

The attitudes toward rape held by Indianapolis prosecutors and judges reflected the same kind of diversity that we observed among police in Chapter 4. Some viewed rape victims as having unique problems in the criminal-justice system, others saw rape as no different from other crimes, and still others saw rape victims as often contributing to their own victimization. One veteran judge I interviewed had just finished reading feminist Susan Brownmiller's book, *Against Our Will* (1975). He noted that after reading the book,

> I became more aware of the problem. I know how severely violent it can be. I share their frustrations. I don't know if I would recommend to someone to report it or not. Someone has to do something about these bastards.

He went on to say that from his experience, rape cases are different:

> It has torn my heart to see some victims who have stayed around to see the verdict and then the jury says "not guilty". . . . [This] is very damaging to the psyche. I used to think that it required physical injury, but even those cases are sometimes a problem—it is just a different standard.

Other judges were much less sympathetic to rape victims. One man who presided over several of the rape trials in my study told me:

> The typical rape case involves a tremendous amount of asking for it. The average rape is a girl, well-endowed . . . went to a tavern, drank all night, expected a sexual encounter and got raped—he used more force than she expected.

The same judge continued:

> I believe biologically it is wrong to entice a man knowing the situation you're creating and then saying "no." There is a button a man has that cannot be turned off and on like a light switch. And a man can go to prison for a very long time because of it.

In order to test the labeling-theory proposition that official processing decisions in these cases depend more on rape stereotypes than on actual behavior of offenders, I used procedures similar to those outlined for police decision making in Chapter 4. As before, I reviewed the rape literature for variables expected to affect court outcomes. The variables are summarized in Table 5.2. The main difference between this analysis and the earlier police analysis is that at the court stage more variables were available for analysis.

The first three variables listed in Table 5.2 are all court outcomes: whether the case is tried or pled guilty; if tried, the verdict; and, regardless of adjudication method, whether guilty.* Plea bargaining and trials usually involve more participants than either prior or subsequent processing decisions, including deputy prosecutors, defendants and their counsel, judges, detectives assigned to cases, and victims. Guilty pleas are complex decisions, in terms of both the number of parties involved and the meaning of the results. Defendants who plead guilty generally receive less serious sentences than those found guilty by trial, but the trial option offers the defendant the possibility of complete exoneration. For the most part, it is in the prosecutor's interest to plea bargain cases that are unlikely to result in guilty verdicts.†

I analyzed verdicts for all 50 defendants tried by a judge or jury in these cases. If the societal reaction to rape is conditioned by characteristics of the victim, the defendant, and the incident, then the courtroom is a strategic arena in which to

---

* I have chosen not to present data on sentencing outcomes here because the results were substantially similar to those for the analysis of court decisions. The interested reader should see LaFree (1979, Ch. 10).

† For a more general discussion of the dynamics of plea bargaining in felony cases, see Heumann (1978), Mather (1979), Brereton and Casper (1981–1982), Maynard (1982), LaFree (1985b).

TABLE 5.2 Court Processing of Rape Cases in Indianapolis ($N = 124$)

Variable	Coding	Distribution %
Outcomes		
Guilty plea	Tried by judge or jury (0)	40.3
	Pled (1)	
Verdict	Not guilty (0)	56.0
	Guilty (1)	44.0
Conviction	Not guilty (0)	22.6
	Guilty by trial or plea (1)	77.4
Characteristics of Victim and Suspect		
Race composition[a]	Black defendants and victims (BB)	40.3
	White defendants and victims (WW)	31.5
	Black defendants and white victims (BW)	28.2
Victim age	Interval scale (7–78)	$\overline{X} = 23.43$
Defendant age	Interval scale (16–53)	$\overline{X} = 24.82$
Criminal record (excluding sex offenses)	No arrests (0)	24.2
	Arrests, no convictions (1)	12.9
	Convictions, no time imposed (2)	17.7
	Convictions, time imposed (3)	45.2
Criminal record for forcible-sex offenses	No arrests (0)	62.9
	Arrests, no convictions (1)	19.4
	Convictions (2)	17.7
Victim Behavior		
Alleged victim misconduct/ nonconformity	No (0)	78.2
	Yes (1)	21.8
Victim living arrangements	Both parents or husband (1)	30.1
	Other (0)	69.9
Alleged victim carelessness	No (0)	63.7
	Yes (1)	36.3
Promptness of report to police	Less than 1 hour (0)	61.2
	1–24 hours (1)	33.1
	More than 24 hours (2)	5.8
Interpersonal Context		
Victim–defendant relationship	(dummy coded)	
	(1) Strangers (1, 0)	51.7
	(2) Relatives (1, 0)	4.2
	(3) Prior acquaintances (0, 1)	44.1

TABLE 5.2 *(continued)*

Variable	Coding	Distribution %
Location of offense	Victim's residence (1)	28.4
	Other (0)	71.6
Number of offenders	One (0)	78.2
	More than one (1)	21.8
Evidence		
Physical injury[b]	None reported (0)	29.3
	Minor (1)	65.0
	Hospitalized (2)	5.7
Number of witnesses	Interval (0–3)	$\overline{X}$ = .30
Prosecution evidence	Interval (1–8)	$\overline{X}$ = 2.32
Defense evidence	Interval (1–8)	$\overline{X}$ = .30

[a] Only two of the victims and one of the defendants in the sample were nonwhite other than black. These cases are included with black victims and defendants in the analysis. Only one case involved a white defendant and a black victim. This case was added to the black defendant–black victim category in the analysis.
[b] No physical injury (other than the rape itself) was assumed unless it was explicitly mentioned in the records.

observe these effects. The adversarial nature of court trials guarantees a direct confrontation between the accuser and the accused. And the courtroom provides an important opportunity for the defense to challenge the credibility of the complainant through references to her prior sexual behavior, bad moral character, and deviant or nonconformist conduct.

I also examined the likelihood of conviction for all cases either pled or tried. Because the central question for the defendant as well as the victim in criminal cases is whether the accused is judged guilty, this variable provides an estimate of the relative effect of the independent variables on convictions, controlling for the type of adjudication.

To apply the labeling-theory argument about typifications in rape cases, I examined variables related to the victim's moral character and conduct (alleged victim nonconformity and carelessness, type of living arrangements), the victim's and the defendant's social attributes (race composition of the victim–offender dyad, age), the characteristics of the incident (scene of the offense, number of accomplices), the victim–defendant relationship, the defendant's prior criminal record, and evidence.

Nonconformity is a measure of the victim's activities prior to the reported assault; carelessness measures her activities at the time of the assault. Nonconformity was coded positively on the basis of either sexual (e.g., the victim had illegitimate children, the victim was sleeping with her boyfriend) or nonsexual (e.g., the victim was allegedly a drug dealer or a runaway) evidence. The most common examples of victim carelessness included victims who were out alone late at night or early in the morning, were alone at a tavern or bar, or were hitchhiking.

Compared to the cases that dropped out before being filed as felonies, these cases included much more detailed information about evidence. I created evidence scales based on eight evidence types identified in the official records: (1) recovered weapon, (2) defendant or accomplice confession, (3) expert testimony, (4) defendant identification, (5) identification of car, scene, or property, (6) physical evidence, (7) circumstantial evidence, and (8) photographs of a car or scene. Some evidence favored the prosecution and some the defense. For example, a polygraph examination indicating that the defendant lied was coded as expert testimony for the prosecution, while a polygraph examination indicating that the defendant answered truthfully was coded as expert testimony for the defense.

GUILTY PLEAS AND VERDICTS
IN RAPE CASES

I again use multiple regression analysis to determine which variables predict guilty pleas, verdicts, and convictions. The statistically significant results are summarized in Table 5.3. (Full results are presented in Appendix 5.1 at the end of this chapter.) As before, I list the variables in terms of the relative size of their standardized regression coefficients —that is, their *beta weights*.

Victim Nonconformity

As with the analysis of police decisions, when the victim allegedly engaged in nonconformity, an acquittal was more likely.* One prosecutor told me:

> It's tough [to try the case] if the victim comes across as being loose, or if the victim has frequented bars. Also important is where she was when she was picked up and what time of night it occurred.

Defense attorneys were equally aware of the importance of the victim's moral character. An Indianapolis defense attorney who had a local reputation for his ability to win especially difficult cases told me:

> It's kind of a pitiful thing. The girl most likely to be raped is a girl who he can probably get away with it on. If he plans carefully he can beat the case—that's not right, but it is a fact of life. . . . I've known people who have made a good living robbing drug dealers, homosexuals, and houses of prostitution. These are all carefully cased. The same thing is true of a carefully cased rape.

These findings are especially important when we consider that in cases that reached court, the victim's moral character had already been screened repeatedly. Recall from the analysis of the police in Chapter 4 that cases in which the victim's moral character was evaluated negatively were often unfounded and that one of the best predictors of the decision to arrest was victim nonconformity.

Case Characteristics

Offenses that took place in the victim's residence were less likely to be pled guilty and to result in convictions. In general, legal agents considered assaults in the victim's home to be strong cases—unless the victim had invited the offender

---

* I experimented in the analysis with treating sexual and nonsexual nonconformity separately. However, although examining them independently yielded weaker effects, both sets of effects were in the same direction. I report here results for the two measures combined.

TABLE 5.3 Best Predictors of Guilty Pleas, Verdicts, and Convictions in Indianapolis Sexual Assault Cases, 1970–1975

Guilty Pleas (N = 124)		Verdicts (N = 50)		Convictions (N = 124)	
Variable	Beta	Variable	Beta	Variable	Beta
1. Defense evidence	–.341	1. Criminal record (sex offenses)	.642	1. Black intraracial	–.257
2. Offense at victim's residence	–.315	2. Report promptness	–.314	2. Offense at victim's residence	–.250
3. Number of witnesses	.240	3. Multiple offenders	.286	3. Victim's nonconformity	–.225
4. Black defendant	–.230	4. Prosecution evidence	.272	4. Defense evidence	–.186
5. Victim age	.212	5. Defense evidence	–.220	5. Criminal record (nonsex offenses)	.162
		6. Victim nonconformity	–.218		
		7. Black intraracial	–.212		

Note: All variables significant at *p* < .10.

into her home. The fact that officials considered assaults occurring in the victim's own home to be stronger cases may explain why they were less willing to plea bargain in these cases. Paradoxically, this same fact probably explains why assaults occurring in the victim's home were *less* likely to result in conviction: because guilty pleas guarantee conviction, while court trials do not.

As the time that elapsed before the victim reported the assault increased, the chances of a guilty verdict declined. A veteran deputy prosecutor stated simply, "A rape case must be reported immediately to have value." Processing agents' assumptions that rapes are more likely to be valid if reported promptly is probably reinforced by other characteristics of rape. As we saw in the discussion of the victim's decision to report a sexual assault to the police, women who feel that their rape accusations may not be taken seriously are more likely to delay reporting. If the victim's own assessments are accurate, these cases may indeed be legally weaker.

In fact, the promptness-of-report variable is a good example of how complex the distinction between legal and extralegal criteria really is. Clearly, the promptness of the victim's report is not necessarily a measure of what actually happened and is therefore legally irrelevant. Yet a common typification of rape is that if a woman does not report it at the earliest possible moment, she is going through a set of mental processes that may indicate that it was not a bona fide rape, that she has ulterior motives for defining the act as rape. Yet promptness of report has direct legal and evidential implications for the processing of the case above and beyond rape stereotypes, because the quality of several types of evidence in rape cases diminishes over time. For example, as time between the incident and the report increases, medical examinations are of decreasing value in establishing the nature of the incident, and witnesses and police officers are less likely to be able to testify in support of the violent nature of the incident or the traumatized condition of the victim following the incident.

Jurors were more likely to define cases as rape when more than one man was charged. In the earlier analysis of police decision making I observed the opposite effect. Two different processes appear to be at work here. In the early stages of processing, cases involving multiple offenders are considered suspect by officials because these attacks often involve younger victims with some previous relationship with offenders and often occur in public places. However, after extensive early screening, the multiple-offender cases that are left are often perceived as more serious cases. Prosecutors and judges whom I interviewed claimed that sexual assaults by more than one man involved greater suffering and humiliation for the victim. Also, assaults by multiple offenders may directly affect reconstructions of the case by allowing prosecutors to compare the defendants' accounts for discrepancies. And in some cases an accomplice is persuaded to cooperate with the prosecution against other defendants in exchange for a more favorable plea agreement.

As the number of witnesses increased, so did the likelihood of a guilty plea. Witnesses strengthen the prosecution's case by providing independent verification of the incident. They undoubtedly serve as a powerful incentive to the defense to work out a guilty plea. The witnesses variable is probably not even more important in predicting these outcomes because of the type of witnesses coded here. Genuine eyewitnesses were extremely rare. Most of the cases involving witnesses were people who observed the victim shortly after the offense had occurred.

Victim's Age

As the age of the victim increased, so did the likelihood that the defendant would plead guilty. Feminist Diana Russell (1975) and others (e.g., Clark and Lewis, 1977) have suggested that the rape of younger women and virgins is taken more seriously by society. Evidence that assaults of older women were more likely to result in guilty pleas than in court trials could be interpreted as support for this argument. But my observations suggested that, if anything, processing agents in Indianapolis reacted with more concern for older than for younger rape victims. Given the fact that courtroom appearances tend to be especially traumatic for rape victims, I suspect that older women were simply less willing than younger women to cooperate in the full prosecution of cases— which would encourage the prosecution to plea bargain.

Defendant's Characteristics

Defendants with more serious criminal records for sex offenses were more likely to be found guilty in jury trials, and prior nonsex-offense criminal records meant that defendants were more likely to be convicted. The public tends to be ambivalent about using defendants' prior criminal record as an indicator of their current or future criminal behavior. On the one hand, many people believe that defendants should be judged only on the charges against them and not on the basis of their previous behavior. On the other hand, many assume that offenders who have been convicted once are likely to commit new crimes and thus view the defendant's prior record as a good indication of his current and future behavior.

This ambivalence is also reflected in the law. While barring evidence of the defendant's criminal record in general, most states provide several exceptions under which the defendant's criminal history may legally be admitted into evidence. In Indiana the most important exceptions were allowed when the defendant testified and when the defense introduced witnesses who testified about the defendant's moral character.

Regardless of the law and its intent, in actual practice officials know the defendant's criminal record and frequently use it to make decisions. Although jurors generally do not have the same easy access to the defendant's criminal record, they frequently receive cues, formally or informally, that allow them to draw reasonable conclusions. For example, information on the defendant's criminal record in the jury trials my colleagues and I observed was frequently obvious either through the testimony of witnesses or simply through the failure of the defendant to testify. In one trial we observed, the prosecutor identified the defendant as "the one wearing jail clothes." Although the defense attorney naturally objected and the jury was admonished to disregard the statement, the point had obviously been made.

The relative importance of the defendant's prior record for forcible-sex offenses compared to other felonies was different for overall convictions than for court trials. For trials, the defendant's record for sex offenses had the larger effect, while for convictions in general, the defendant's record for all felonies was more important. This probably reflects differences between trials and guilty pleas. Jurors depend on prior record for sex offenses to indicate whether the defendant committed the specific offense charged, but prosecutors are probably more concerned with the defendant's overall criminal history as a guide to how tough they should be in plea bargaining.

Because the white offender–black victim cases were excluded from the analysis, all cases involving black victims necessarily involved black offenders. However, for white victims, offenders could be either white or black. To examine whether black defendants received harsher treatment regardless of the victim's race, I experimented with substituting defendant's race for the race-composition variables in the analyses. For verdicts and convictions in general, black intraracial cases were treated less harshly, while black offender–white victim cases were treated more harshly. In fact, whether cases were black intraracial was the single best predictor of overall convictions. However, the pattern was different for guilty pleas. Here, regardless of the victim's race, black defendants were less likely to plead guilty. I could not determine from my observations whether black defendants were more reluctant than white defendants to plead guilty or whether the prosecution was less willing to plea bargain when the defendant was black (see also Petersilia, 1983; Zatz and Lizotte, 1985). I return to the issue of race and official reactions to rape in the next chapter.

Evidence Measures

At least one of the two evidence measures had a statistically significant effect on each of the three court outcomes. More defense evidence meant that guilty pleas and verdicts were less likely. Defense evidence was the most important determinant of whether the defendant pled guilty. More prosecution evidence meant guilty verdicts were more likely. Although it may seem obvious that the amounts of prosecution and defense evidence are legally relevant concerns, in fact their relationship to cases is complex.

Both officials and nonofficials often think of evidence as a fixed commodity attached to the case. Thus, attorneys routinely speak about "how much evidence" there is in a particular case or suggest that "the evidence shows" something.

In actual practice, evidence is not a fixed commodity but a purposefully constructed set of documents, testimony, and material objects. In no case is only one set of evidence possible. Moreover, evidence does not create itself. Its generation requires human labor and interpretation and, usually, economic resources. Because evidence must be generated, officials create more or less of it depending on their conceptions of cases. Cases that they are less interested in winning, for whatever reasons, generally receive less work and thus generate less evidence. Conversely, more evidence can also be generated. For example, a prosecutor told me:

> You can "ham up" rape cases sometimes. . . . You can add a doctor's determination that sexual intercourse occurred, even though . . . the test only proves that she had sexual intercourse in the last three days.

The relationships among evidence, case outcomes, and the amount of resources devoted to particular cases can be related to case typifications in subtle ways. For example, agents clearly prefer devoting more resources to some types of cases than others. Indeed, any organization operating within a fixed budget is likely to develop mechanisms for weighing the relative costs of obtaining various types of information. Legal agents frequently estimate the resources that various aspects of cases will require and how much will be gained by investing the necessary resources. Their allocation of scarce resources is clearly linked to their case typifications.

The relationship between processing outcomes and the generation of evidence is perhaps best illustrated by the guilty-plea outcome—a decision that requires agreement between the prosecution and the defense. For the defense, there is a clear reciprocal relationship between amount of evidence and a guilty plea: a guilty plea is a more viable option to the defense when it can provide less evidence to support its case. At the same time, defense attorneys may not look for evidence as diligently when they know their clients are going to plead guilty anyway. Like the defense, the prosecution gains nothing by assembling a large amount of evidence for a case that is to be pled guilty. However, to encourage the defense to plead guilty, some prosecution evidence may be necessary. Thus, while the prosecution tends to generate less evidence in cases that are pled than in court-tried cases (compare the effects of prosecution evidence on guilty pleas and verdicts in Table 5.3), cases with little defense evidence are especially likely to result in guilty pleas.

CONCLUSIONS: COURT PROCESSING

By the time a case reaches the courts, the victim's account of the incident has been repeatedly tested and challenged. Deputy prosecutors whom I interviewed typically presumed the defendant's guilt. One prosecutor stated: "By the time they get to us, there is a good likelihood that it's based on fact." Because guilt is usually assumed, the primary decision facing prosecutors at this stage is the likelihood of the defendant's conviction, given various processing strategies. This means that even though prosecutors frequently believe that the defendants they process are technically guilty, they are still likely to be concerned about how case characteristics are going to be interpreted by the jury or judge. Thus, rape typifications held by prosecutors affect not only their willingness to believe that a case is in fact rape but also their willingness to present a case to a jury.

It is important to observe that the decision making of legal agents throughout the criminal-selection process is constantly informed by their hunches about how the case will be treated at subsequent stages in the system. Thus, the victim may believe that she was raped but may not pursue the case because of her perceptions of how the police and court will define the case. Likewise, police decisions are strongly influenced by their beliefs about how court officials and juries will define cases. These processes are of particular sociological interest because they are not based on "what really happened" so much as on perceptions of how what really happened will be interpreted by others.

CRIMINAL BEHAVIOR AND TYPIFICATIONS

The major purpose of the analysis of police decisions in Chapter 4 and court decisions in this chapter has been to evaluate the assertion, often associated with the labeling perspective, that official definitions of crime are based not on objective properties of behavior but rather on definitions constructed through social interaction. This argument is central to a concern with the quality of justice dispensed by our legal system. If suspects are arrested, convicted, and sentenced not because of what they have done but because of the stereotyping of official agents, the system is clearly unjust. If, however, legal processing decisions are based only on the seriousness of the behavior committed and not on the characteristics of the offender or the incident, the system is essentially a just one.

The results provide evidence that both criminal behavior and typifications affected the processing of the rape cases in this study. In support of the view that legal reactions are based mostly on the criminal behavior of defendants, the seriousness of the charges, whether a weapon was present, the type of offense, the victim's willingness to testify, her ability to identify a suspect, and the strength of prosecution and defense evidence all affected police and court outcomes. In general, these variables were the best predictors of the police decisions—both before and after the formation of the Sex Offense Unit—and were also very important in the court decisions reviewed in this chapter.

In contrast, the results also show that decisions in these cases were affected by the stereotypes and social constructions of the legal agents making the decisions. For example, measures of the victim's alleged nonconformity and her age and race affected official decision making. Likewise, defendant attributes, especially his race and criminal record, affected official decisions, as did characteristics of the incident, including the victim–offender relationship, the promptness of the victim's report to the police, the racial composition of the victim–defendant dyad, the scene of the offense, and the number of offenders. However, the effect of these variables on processing decisions was complex. As with the analysis of police decision making in Chapter 4, the use of stereotypical victim and case attributes by prosecutors reflects not only outright bias but also pragmatism in the allocation of scarce organizational resources (see also Stanko, 1981–1982).

At one level, the debate over whether official crime statistics primarily reflect the behavior of criminals or the social definitions of legal agents is a misguided one, because all human definitions are ultimately based on social constructions—whether these constructions are rooted in reality, fantasy, or somewhere in between. It is the essence of the human condition that people actively construct their own perceptual world, and it is this constructed world—not the world as it really is—to which we ultimately respond. Furthermore, because we are meaning-creating organisms, it follows that we always remain one step removed from the world we are constructing. In the case of the criminal-justice system, legal agents are involved in processes of perception and social construction even if they ultimately base their opinions solely on measures that are widely held to be legal considerations—like criminal behavior and crime seriousness.

The results clearly show that all rapes are not treated equally by the legal system. Both my interviews with legal agents and the statistical evidence suggest that legally irrelevant characteristics of cases affect their treatment. At the same time, the proposition that crime is simply a definition constructed through social interaction does not, by itself, adequately characterize these data on Indianapolis sexual-assault cases. Although the distinction between legal and extralegal effects is itself complex, these cases were clearly influenced by measures of the seriousness of the criminal behavior alleged. Applied to these cases, the assertion that criminal labels are only social constructions is an exceedingly cruel one for the hundreds of women whose lives were disrupted, destroyed, and in several instances ended by the sexual assaults included in this study.

In Chapter 1 I suggested that despite the complexity of criminal-justice decision making, the subject matter of criminology is relatively straightforward: legal agents applying law to behavior. For most of this century, North American criminology was dominated by efforts to determine why people committed criminal behavior. This focus, which sociologist David Matza (1969, p. 143) once called the "great task of disconnection" because it separates the study of crime from the study of social reactions to crime, is clearly not adequate for explaining the results presented here. In the 1960s, labeling theorists studied the problems of a criminology that focused exclusively on criminal etiology and challenged criminologists to consider the importance of social reactions in defining crime. However, once labeling theorists came to the conclusion that crime statistics did not accurately represent criminal behavior, many simply began to ignore criminal behavior altogether. This is no doubt one of the reasons for the resurgence of interest in recent years in research on the causes of crime.

Emulating the physical sciences, criminologists have too often assumed that the application of law to behavior must follow only one path: it is based either on legal factors like the defendant's behavior or on extralegal factors like the victim's moral character. Distinctions between trees and nontrees, planets and nonplanets, and nitrogen and non-nitrogen may be relatively clear; however, as I have endeavored to show in the last two chapters, distinctions between legal and extralegal factors are not clear. Thus, there is no reason to believe that relationships between legal decisions and other factors are the same for all types of crime, in all jurisdictions, and for all time periods. Certainly, I would not make this claim for sexual assaults processed in Indianapolis in the 1970s and 1980s. Rather than an ongoing debate about whether criminal outcomes depend exclusively on legal or extralegal factors, criminologists should begin to focus on the precise criteria that distinguish legal from extralegal variables; on the processes by which these criteria emerge, persevere, and change; and on how such considerations vary, depending on the crime, the jurisdiction, and the time period.*

The results presented in this chapter suggest that the common division in North American criminology between an emphasis on either criminal etiology or criminal labeling is misguided. Without the labeling emphasis on the social construction of crime, we ignore the essential insights that all persons construct their own perceptual worlds and that it is our duty to learn more about these processes and how they change over time. And without the etiological emphasis on causes of crime, we ignore the facts that crimes like rape are all too real and that it is the responsibility of criminologists to determine why they occur and what can be done to prevent them.

---

* For some research that moves in this direction, see Nagel and Hagan (1982), Nagel (1983), and Peterson and Hagan (1984).

Although the primary focus of the last two chapters has been on the labeling-theory argument that criminal definitions are not based exclusively on objective properties of criminal acts, the results of my research also have important implications for the conflict perspective's concern with the application of law for the control of social behavior. In terms of the argument that black men accused of raping white women are treated more severely than other victim–offender race combinations, the analysis of the police data has shown that charges were more serious when the suspect was black and the victim white, and the analysis of the court data has shown that acquittals were more likely for black intraracial cases. For the argument that nonconformist women are less likely to have rape charges result in conviction and punishment of the offender, the analysis of the police data has shown that not a single case in which victim nonconformity was alleged resulted in an arrest. Likewise, cases in which prosecutors and defense attorneys alleged victim nonconformity were less likely to result in guilty verdicts and guilty pleas. In the next part of the book, I consider the evidence for the social-control argument more directly. Chapter 6 examines the processing of rape cases in terms of the race of the victim and the offender, and Chapters 7 and 8 consider the processing of rape victims who are alleged to have engaged in nonconformist behavior.

APPENDIX 5.1 Regression Coefficients and Standard Errors of Predictors of Guilty Pleas, Verdicts, and Convictions

Variables[a]	Guilty Pleas (N = 124)		Verdicts (N = 50)		Convictions (N = 124)	
	b	B	b	B	b	B
Victim age	.008(.003)	.212*				
Race composition (BB)			−.212(.114)	−.212*	−.192(.067)	−.257*
Defendant race	−.241(.091)	−.230*				
Victim nonconformity			−.199(.098)	−.218*	−.140(.054)	−.225*
Victim living arrangements			.117(.122)	.107		
Defendant age			−.010(.009)	−.152		
Criminal record (excluding sex offenses)					.048(.029)	.162*
Criminal record for forcible-sex offenses			.378(.073)	.642*	.075(.046)	.158

Location of offense	−.343(.092)	−.315*			−.204(.072)	−.250*
Number of offenders			.332(.133)	.286*		
Victim injury	−.118(.077)	−.131	−.303(.114)	−.314*		
Report promptness	.192(.068)	.240*	−.196(.241)	−.100		
Witnesses						
Relatives						
Prior acquaintances	.151(.084)	.154	.091(.042)	.272*	.109(.070)	.148
Prosecution evidence	−.030(.032)	−.087			.003(.025)	.012
Defense evidence	−.302(.072)	−.341*	−.163(.081)	−.220*	−.124(.058)	−.186*
R^2 With evidence/without evidence[b]	.281/.157		.574/.496		.184/.164	
R^2 Increment for evidence	.124($p < .01$)		.078($p < .01$)		.020($p < .05$)	

Note: Attrition in sample size is due to missing data. Standard errors are given in parentheses.

* Significant at $p < .10$.

[a] See Table 5.2 for variable identifications.

[b] R^2 was adjusted for number of cases.

CHAPTER 6

Rape and the Social Control of Blacks

In 1855 white men sitting in the Kansas legislature, duly elected by other white men, passed a law that sentenced white men convicted of rape of a white woman to up to five years in prison, while the penalty for a black man convicted of the same offense was castration, the costs of the procedure to be rendered by the desexed.

W. Haywood Burns, in Kairys, *The Politics of Law.*

The crossroads of racism and sexism had to be a violent meeting place. There is no use pretending it doesn't exist.

Susan Brownmiller, *Against Our Will.*

In 1987, a police chief in the small, steel-producing town of Homewood, Pennsylvania, ordered fingerprints from all the town's black male residents after a police investigation into five rapes involving a black assailant had stalled (*The New York Times*, 1987). The American Civil Liberties Union strongly protested, arguing that this practice violated the constitutional rights of blacks. As the situation began to draw national media attention, Homewood police arrested a suspect in the rape cases—a black man who had not been included in the fingerprinting program. Nearly 150 years after the Civil War, the connection between race and sexual assault is still a sensitive one in the United States. In this chapter I explore the connection through an examination of the proposition that law is applied to control the behavior of individuals who threaten the power of dominant social groups. More specifically, I consider whether the application of rape laws in our society still reflects a social-control system in which the rape of a white woman by a black man is treated as a more serious crime than a rape involving a different victim–suspect racial combination.

Conflict theorists have long maintained that the economic resources available to individual members of society are distributed according to the relative power of the groups to which they belong. From this perspective the criminal law is interpreted as a mechanism created and enforced by powerful subgroups to maintain their own favorable access to resources and to limit the access of less powerful subgroups to these resources. The concept of sexual stratification, introduced in Chapter 3, suggests that sexual access may be viewed as a resource that is unevenly distributed in most societies. Hollywood images of romantic love notwithstanding, dating and courtship patterns are anything but open. Like economic resources, sexual access is determined by power relationships within a highly stratified sexual marketplace. Rules of sexual access are guidelines for who can date and marry whom. Thus, marriage and courtship possibilities are generally constrained by the same subgroup memberships that constrain access to economic rewards—especially race, social class, ethnicity, and religion. Moreover, conflict theory suggests that for sexual stratification, like economic stratification, the law is used by more powerful groups to maintain their own favorable position.

It is important to keep in mind that sexual-stratification systems are not immutable. Instead, rules of sexual access, like class relationships, are subject to constant challenges and can be maintained only by the resources available to those in power, ranging from bargaining and threats to coercion and violence. If rape is reinterpreted as a violation of this sexual-stratification system, the possibility arises that society's reactions to rape depend in part on the relative social positions of victims and offenders. In general, the more powerful the group to which the victim belongs vis-à-vis the group to which the offender belongs, the greater the seriousness of the violation and hence the more severely the crime is treated by the legal system.

Although few would claim that the social position of

blacks and whites in the United States has remained unchanged in the past century, it remains apparent that white
men still overwhelmingly occupy the elite positions in our society. Moreover, there is clear evidence that the United States
remains a sexually stratified society with regard to race. As
discussed in Chapter 3, rates of interracial dating, courtship,
and marriage remain low, and whites consistently show more
resistance to sexual than economic and educational integration. In this chapter I consider more specifically the possibility that official reactions to rape cases still contain evidence
of longstanding assumptions about the relative harm of sexual violation, depending on the races of the victim and the
offender.

RACE AND PROCESSING
DECISIONS IN RAPE CASES

Although there has been a great deal of research on discrimination against blacks in the application of law, the results have often been contradictory. However, many of the
contradictions can be explained by identifying when the research was done. Virtually all research on the effects of race
on official reactions to rape published before 1970 concludes
that black defendants receive more serious official sanctions
than white defendants (e.g., Johnson, 1957; Bullock, 1961;
Partington, 1965; Koeninger, 1969).

In contrast, most research completed after 1970 concludes
either that there is no evidence of discrimination (e.g., Chiricos and Waldo, 1975; Bernstein et al., 1977; Hindelang,
1978; Wilbanks, 1987) or that discrimination is limited to
specific circumstances, such as the year in which the case was
processed, the type of offense, and the region of the country in
which the case was adjudicated (e.g., Thomson and Zingraff,
1981; Unnever, 1982; Peterson and Hagan, 1984; Zatz, 1984).
Part of the explanation for these changes in conclusions about
discrimination against blacks are undoubtedly due to corresponding changes in official reactions to black defendants
over time. Overtly racist laws such as the one described by W.
Haywood Burns at the beginning of this chapter have been
eliminated. Moreover, it seems likely that there has been
some real movement toward more nearly color-blind process-

ing of criminal cases in the United States in the past few decades.

However, much of the recent research on discrimination against blacks in legal processing is still limited in at least two respects. First, given the history of sexual segregation by race in this country, the race composition of the victim—defendant dyad—and not the individual race of either offender or victim—may be the most important racial consideration in processing decisions. The sexual-stratification argument would lead us to expect cases involving black offenders and white victims to be treated most seriously while cases involving white offenders and black victims and black intraracial cases to be treated least seriously.

Second, most of the recent studies of discrimination against blacks in criminal processing have not examined the entire range of criminal-justice processing. While evidence of discrimination by race in any single outcome may not be overwhelming, the cumulative effect of race may still be considerable. Thus, studies examining only one or two processing outcomes may or may not support a view of discriminatory processing, depending on independent variables included, methods used, and specific outcomes examined.

At the outset we should also realize that complete consensus about the extent of discrimination against blacks by the legal system is probably unlikely because of fundamental differences in assumptions about the legal system and its operation. For example, criminologist William Wilbanks (1987, pp. 40–41) points out that in a recent survey of police use of deadly force completed by the International Association of Chiefs of Police, the researchers conclude that there was no evidence of racial bias. Yet in a review of the same literature sponsored by the National Urban League, researchers conclude that racial discrimination was a major factor in police use of deadly force. In general, concluding whether a cup is half empty or half full may be resolved only by knowing the assumptions of the observer. In fact, we should not try to wish away the complexity of the racial-discrimination issue by immediately assuming that the cup is either empty or full. Instead, we need to try to understand in all its complexity the question of how race relations are reflected in the legal processing of rape cases. To illustrate this complexity and to introduce the issues examined in this chapter, I next review two rape cases involving different racial combinations of victim and offender. In the first case, a black defendant was charged in the rape of a white woman. In the second, two black defendants were charged with raping a black woman. Both cases were tried in the early 1980s.

THE RAPE TRIAL OF CHARLES JACKSON

Carrie Brighton* was a 22-year-old white female. She was slim, with long red hair and large brown eyes. Our courtroom observers described her as "attractive." She worked as a bartender at the Starship, an Indianapolis disco. While returning to her apartment from work at 4:00 one morning, she was approached by a young black man carrying a knife. She ran, he caught her, and he dragged her into his car. He then drove her away, demanding that she give him her money. She gave him the money she had, told him that she had more money at her apartment, and suggested that they go back there. He said, "Don't look at me and don't make any noise." He told her, "If you lied to me about anything, I'll kill you." When they returned to her apartment, she gave him more money. He then told her to take off her clothes. He also took off his clothes and then forced her to have oral and vaginal sex with him.

During her courtroom testimony, Brighton explained that:

> I was so scared. I knew he could hurt me. I knew he had a knife. I thought I could live through a rape, but I wanted to live a lot longer.

Brighton continued talking to the assailant and tried to keep him calm. She told him that she had a roommate coming home. After a while he gave back part of the money he had taken and left. She locked the door and stayed in her apartment alone until 5:00 P.M. that day. Brighton decided not to call the police because she thought it would only be his word

---

*All the names in these accounts are fictitious.

against hers. However, a few days later, she saw the intruder again and decided then to call the police.

A major part of the prosecution's case was that the assailant had also attempted to rape Sheila Davidson and Beth Drury, two other residents of Carrie Brighton's apartment complex. Davidson also worked at the Starship disco. Both were young, attractive, with long hair. Davidson testified that a man followed her home from the disco one night and came to her apartment door. He asked to use her telephone. He had a knife. He backed her into a corner outside of her apartment. When she began screaming, the assailant ran. Davidson called the police about 40 minutes later, but the police were unable to locate the suspect.

Beth Drury testified that one night she met a girlfriend at the Starship after work and left the disco alone at 3:00 A.M. As she was walking from her car to her apartment, a man came up behind her, grabbed her, and spun her around. He was holding a knife. Although she was not married, Drury told the man that her husband would be home any minute. The assailant warned her not to yell or scream for help. He kept saying, "Be quiet! If you scream, you'll get hurt." He said, "You're coming with me." But when she began screaming, he fled.

Drury testified that afterward, "I went into my apartment and was hysterical." She remained there for 30 or 35 minutes and then called her next-door neighbor, who also worked nights. Drury's neighbor advised her to call the police. She said, "I didn't want to. I didn't want to get involved in this." Instead, she moved out of her apartment and spent several days living with her mother and then with a man she had been dating. When she drove back to her apartment complex a week later, she saw the intruder walking toward her apartment. She left immediately and called the police. The police arrived shortly afterward and arrested Charles Jackson, a 25-year-old black male, at the scene. Jackson did not resist. The officers found no knife on him. Carrie Brighton and Sheila Davidson both identified Jackson in a police lineup. He was charged with rape, criminal confinement, and robbery against Brighton.

Charles Jackson was about 6 feet tall, weighing 200 pounds. He had a short, Afro hairstyle and a mustache. There were only two witnesses for the defense: Jackson and his wife. Jackson testified first. He claimed that on the night of the reported rape he was at the apartment complex where Carrie Brighton lived "looking for a friend." He testified that he did not see Brighton that night, but that he had previously met her. He claimed that he had once stopped on a highway and helped her repair her car. He also said that he had been in Brighton's apartment on two occasions. On one of these visits, Jackson claimed, he and his brother had stayed for at least two hours and Brighton had given them a marijuana "joint." He said that Brighton had known who he was, including his name, before the reported rape and before the police lineup. He flatly denied the charge that he raped Carrie Brighton and claimed that he had never before seen Sheila Davidson or Beth Drury.

During cross-examination, the prosecutor pointed out that Charles Jackson had been convicted of theft at age 15 and of carrying an unlicensed firearm at age 18.

Jackson's wife testified that he was a "good husband" and had a regular job at the time of his arrest—which he lost when he went to jail. However, she was unable to say where her husband was from 2:00 to 4:00 A.M. on the night of the incident, noting simply that "on weekends, he went out with friends."

In his closing argument the defense attorney acknowledged that "everything Carrie Brighton said happened to her," but claimed that Charles Jackson "wasn't the man." He suggested that Brighton had made the wrong identification because she was extremely frightened. The defense attorney noted that the police thought the case was so "flimsy" that they did not even examine Jackson's car or Brighton's apartment for fingerprints. He tried to show that Jackson was himself a victim because of his race and his criminal record. He noted that the only description Beth Drury gave of her assailant was that he was "a black man." He pointed out that "it's only people with bad [criminal] records who are chosen to be in police lineups." The defense attorney also implied that the three victims had talked to one another before the trial so that their stories would be consistent in court.

In her closing argument the prosecuting attorney asked the jurors to focus on the "similarities" among the three victims. She asked the jurors to consider why these women would submit themselves to the degrading courtroom experience if they weren't telling the truth. She also asked why Jackson's brother did not testify and why Jackson's wife was unable to say where he was on the night of the incident. She noted that Jackson was a big man and that Brighton had done the reasonable thing by not fighting him. She reminded the jury that Jackson had a criminal record and concluded that "this man belongs in prison."

The jurors agreed, returning a guilty verdict on all counts. A month later Jackson was sentenced to 50 years in the Indiana State Penitentiary.

THE RAPE TRIAL OF JAMES MARTIN AND JEFFREY PHILLIPS

On the evening of September 12, 1978, Sharon Robertson, an attractive, 22-year-old black woman, was accidentally locked out of her Indianapolis home. While she was waiting for her roommate to return, James Martin, a 20-year-old black man, walked by, and Robertson asked him to go to a nearby liquor store with her to buy some whiskey. By the time the two returned from the liquor store, Robertson's roommate had returned, and Robertson fixed all three of them cocktails. At about 7:30 that evening Jeffrey Phillips, a 21-year-old black man, came by Robertson's house, and James Martin invited him in. Phillips was carrying a pistol. In court testimony, Robertson claimed that she asked Phillips to put the pistol away, which he did.

Later that evening, Robertson asked Martin to return with her to the liquor store, saying that she wanted to buy some cigarettes. Phillips said that he was leaving anyway and would drop her off. Robertson, Phillips, and Martin left together in Phillips's car. However, instead of driving Robertson home after taking her to the liquor store, they went for a ride. According to Robertson, Phillips said, "We'll smoke this 'joint' and then we'll take you home." Robertson testified that shortly afterward, Phillips brought the car to a stop and said, "We don't have to worry about police here." She said that Phillips then pulled out the gun, which he had stored under his car seat, and told Martin to get out of the car. According to Robertson, Phillips was "waving the gun in my face." Phillips ordered Robertson to remove her clothing and forced her to have sexual intercourse with him. Later, Martin returned to the car and said, "You gave him some. I want some, too." Martin then forced Robertson to have sexual intercourse with him.

While Martin was in the back seat of the car with Robertson, a sheriff's deputy drove up. The deputy asked Phillips for his driver's license. Martin then drove away, with Robertson and Phillips in the back seat. Robertson claimed that she did not scream out to the deputy because she knew that Martin had a gun. Two blocks away, the car smashed into a bench. Phillips got out of the car and ran. Robertson claimed that James Martin said to her, "Come on, baby, let's run!" Robertson responded, "I ain't going nowhere." Martin left without her. Robertson testified that she picked up the gun, which was in the car near her feet, and threw it into the grass. She said that she was afraid that Phillips or Martin would return to the car and shoot her. The same deputy sheriff who had just questioned Martin drove up shortly afterward. Robertson told the deputy that she had been raped. Martin was arrested at the scene. The police also recovered a .38-caliber revolver after Robertson told them where she had thrown it. The gun was not loaded, but another police officer found bullets in Phillips's pants, which had been left on the roof of the car. Phillips was also arrested after he walked back to the car. Robertson was taken to a hospital.

The defense attorney was a black woman. During her cross-examination of Robertson, she asked her whose marijuana the three of them had smoked. Robertson said that it belonged to James Martin. The defense attorney also asked her how much whiskey she had bought on the day of the incident. Robertson responded, "A half-pint." The defense attorney asked a series of questions about what everyone had had to drink, whether the whiskey had been mixed with anything, whether there had been ice in it. She also asked several general questions about Robertson's behavior on the day of the incident:

Defense attorney:

Miss Robertson, isn't it true that you spent a good deal of time drinking and smoking |on the day of the reported rape|?

Robertson:

It wasn't but one or two hours.

Jeffrey Phillips was the first witness for the defense.

Defense attorney:

We might as well start with the most difficult question first. Did you rape Sharon Robertson?

Phillips:

No, ma'am. I didn't.

Phillips claimed that when he arrived at Robertson's house, he had other plans for the evening, but Robertson asked him to take her to a liquor store. He said that she offered him and Martin marijuana after they left the store. According to Phillips, after smoking the marijuana, Robertson said to him, "Let's get down." He claimed that she was "really hot." The defense attorney asked Phillips if he had had sexual intercourse with Sharon Robertson. Phillips replied that he had not. He said that after they began to have intercourse, it became clear to him that Robertson was not sexually stimulated, so he said to her, "That's the way it is. Why don't you and James get down?" Phillips claimed that he had run from the police because his driver's license had been suspended and he "was afraid."

Defense attorney:

Who had the marijuana?

Phillips:

Sharon Robertson.

Defense attorney:

It was her idea to ride around?

Phillips:

Yes.

Defense attorney:

Did she ever object to having sex with you?

Phillips:

No. In fact, when we were riding around, she was sitting with her leg on mine.

During the prosecutor's cross-examination, he asked Jeffrey Phillips if he always carried a gun when he went out.

Phillips:

> I carry it.

Prosecutor:

> If Sharon Robertson was ready as you say, why didn't you go back to her house? [The liquor store was only two blocks away from Robertson's house.]

Phillips:

> I asked her if she was ready to go back, and she said, "No, let's drive around and smoke a joint."

Prosecutor:

> You never pointed the gun at Robertson?

Phillips:

> No.

Prosecutor:

> Do you consider yourself to be a "ladies' man"?

Phillips:

> I hate to sound conceited, but yes.

Prosecutor:

> They're begging to go to bed with you, is that right?

James Martin was the next witness for the defense. Contrary to Sharon Robertson's testimony, he claimed that he first ran into her outside of her house at 2:00 in the afternoon and that they began smoking marijuana immediately. Martin claimed that he gave Robertson the money for the liquor she bought because he was less than 21 years old and couldn't buy the liquor himself. He claimed that she bought rum, not whiskey, and that she bought a pint, not a half-pint. Martin also claimed that he gave Robertson money for cigarettes.

During his closing argument, the prosecutor focused on the plausibility of the defendants' accounts.

Prosecutor:

> A willing and wanting woman wants to drive out to "no man's land" and do it in the car? Does this make sense to you? People don't have sex with guns.

The prosecutor portrayed Robertson as "a friendly person whose behavior was reasonable" and as "a woman whose body was violated." The prosecutor noted that if Robertson did not appear overly emotional following the incident, that was because "people react to trauma in different ways." Sharon Robertson "has suffered in her own way."

The prosecutor portrayed Phillips as a person who thought only of himself and as "someone who is not as 'cool' as he thinks he is."

> You've seen the degrading experience to be a rape victim in Marion County. Would you go through with this if it didn't really happen?

The defense attorney began her closing arguments by noting that "this is just another case for the state, but it is the most important thing that ever happened to these two men." She described Phillips as "a ladies' man" but pointed out that he was also "a Christian who worked with underprivileged kids." She portrayed Martin as a person who was used by Robertson. Both were described as "just kids"—"two young men, never in trouble before." The defense attorney described Robertson as a "party girl" who took advantage of both defendants to protect herself from being arrested for possession of marijuana. She claimed that Robertson's description of the "alleged incident" sounds like it came "from a grade B movie." She concluded:

> There was a party. There was alcohol, and there were three willing participants. There was marijuana, and there were three willing participants. There was sex, and there were three willing participants in that, too. Sharon Robertson never once uttered those three little words, "Take me home." All she had to do when the policeman came was to yell, in her big outdoor voice, "Rape!" Instead, she says [softly] "Rape." We're not talking about rape. I submit that it is impossible to have sex with anyone, living or dead, with a gun in your hand.
>
> We're talking about a party. We had drinks, we had marijuana, now we'll go have some fun. Robertson was thinking, if you are found with marijuana, you go to jail. But there was another alternative. She figured, it's thee or me, so it's good-by y'all. There is not a rape situation here, and it would be a tragedy to convict the defendants on the basis of the evidence presented. You promised me that you wouldn't convict unless you were convinced beyond a reasonable doubt. You have to return a verdict of not guilty.

Following a brief deliberation, the jury acquitted both defendants on all counts. After the trial, the judge told our courtroom observers that she disagreed with the jury's verdict and that if she had heard the case as a bench trial, she would have convicted. She thought that the defendants' guilt was a close question but that the jurors had let their own negative impressions of Sharon Robertson cloud their judgement.

COMPARING THE JACKSON AND PHILLIPS-MARTIN CASES

Of course, I can make no particular claims about the representativeness of these two cases. Yet they may serve to illustrate how difficult it is to sort out the effects of individual variables like race on processing decisions. The two cases are generally consistent with the sexual-stratification argument that official reactions to rape depend on the racial composition of the victim–defendant dyad. In the first case, a black man charged with raping a white woman was found guilty and sentenced to 50 years in prison. In the second, two black men charged with raping a black woman were acquitted of all charges. But how can we tell that jurors in these cases were reacting to the race of the participants and not to other characteristics of the cases? In general, we want to know if the victims' and defendants' races have an effect on verdicts even when other aspects of the cases are similar.

Similarities

In fact, we can note some similarities between the two cases summarized above. In both, the victim was 22 years old and unmarried. Courtroom observers and jurors rated both women as attractive. Neither was living with a spouse or parents. Both were portrayed in the courtroom as individuals who frequently drank and stayed out late at night. One white male juror said of Carrie Brighton:

> It would be less than one would hope for one's daughter. She's a bartender and works to 3:30 A.M. I had a feeling that she was

a party girl, and I guess that sexual intercourse was not new for her.

In the same trial, a white female juror concluded that Brighton's morals were not "exceptionally high." "She was not a virgin." Similarly, a white female juror described Sharon Robertson's background as:

> Not a very good one. I think a young girl shouldn't be out on [her] own. You just don't drink, smoke pot, and be out late if you're brought up good.

There were also some similarities between the defendants in the two cases. In both cases, the defendants were in their early 20s, all three were presented as individuals who drank and used drugs. All three were from lower-class to lower-middle-class backgrounds. All three testified in court. Courtroom observers and jurors perceived all three defendants as presenting a positive courtroom appearance. In the trial of Charles Jackson, a white male juror admitted that he felt some identification with the defendant. He thought the defendant seemed to have physical qualities that would have allowed him to "pick a good girl." In the same case, a white female juror noted, "He didn't look like a rapist or a bad guy. If I saw him on the street, I never would have guessed him to be a rapist." Similarly, a black female juror described Jeffrey Phillips as not looking "like the type of guy who would want a girl who didn't want him." In the same trial, a white female said that Phillips "seemed like he wouldn't rape anyone. Like a kid; didn't seem he would force anyone to do anything."

In terms of evidence, too, there were similarities. Both cases were characterized by relatively little evidence apart from the testimony of victims and defendants. In neither case did the victim sustain serious physical injury. In both cases, the state introduced only one exhibit. In the trial of Charles Jackson, the state introduced a license plate taken from Jackson's car that read, "I love everybody and you're next." The state argued that this license plate indicated Jackson's frame of mind. In the Phillips-Martin trial, the only exhibit was the recovered gun. The defense in both cases introduced only one witness apart from the defendants: the defendant's wife in the trial of Charles Jackson and Phillips's mother in the Phillips-Martin trial. In neither case did the defense introduce any exhibits.

Differences

Yet there were also obvious differences between the cases. In the Jackson trial, the defendant claimed that he had previously known Carrie Brighton, but Brighton denied this and neither Brighton nor Jackson claimed that there had been any legitimate socializing between them prior to the rape. In contrast, Sharon Robertson, Jeffrey Phillips, and James Martin all agreed that Robertson had spent time socializing with Phillips and Martin prior to the alleged rape.

The cases also differed in terms of allegations about drug use. Charles Jackson claimed that he had previously smoked marijuana with Carrie Brighton; however, Brighton never admitted this. In contrast, Sharon Robertson admitted smoking marijuana with Phillips and Martin. This admission probably hurt the prosecution in the Robertson case in several ways. First, it no doubt reduced Robertson's credibility. Second, it supported the defense interpretation of the incident as consensual. Finally, it allowed the defense to argue that Robertson's motive for claiming that she had been raped was her fear of being arrested for possession of marijuana.

Although there was little physical evidence in either trial, in the Jackson case three separate rape victims testified against the defendant, while in the Phillips-Martin trial two defendants testified against a single victim. Although a gun was recovered in the Phillips-Martin case, the defense attorney managed to portray carrying a gun as normal behavior for inner-city blacks and to convince jurors that Sharon Robertson had never been frightened by it.

In order to determine whether the race composition of the victim—offender dyad has an impact on how legal agents process cases, it would be ideal if we could eliminate all differences between the cases except for race. Obviously, we cannot do this when we study actual cases. However, we can statistically control for some of the important legal and evidential differences between the cases and see whether race has an effect net of such differences. I turn to this task in the next section.

THE EFFECT OF RACE COMPOSITION ON LEGAL DECISION MAKING

To examine the possibility that the punishment received by black men charged with rape depends more on the race of the victim than on evidence, I return to the data on suspects charged with sexual assault in Indianapolis introduced in Chapters 4 and 5. As before, police, prosecution, and court records provided data on defendants' and victims' social characteristics. For each case, I recorded measures of evidence from the prosecution files, defendants' criminal histories from police records, and final dispositions and sentences from court records. I again used field observations and interviews with legal agents to help interpret the official data.

Of 881 forcible-sex offenses reported to Indianapolis police in 1970, 1973, and 1975, 44.1 percent involved black defendants and black victims (BB), 31.9 percent involved white defendants and white victims (WW), 22.7 percent involved black defendants and white victims (BW), and 1.2 percent involved white defendants and black victims (WB).* There were only 11 cases involving white offenders and black victims—too few to include in the multivariate analysis.† To analyze

---

*The proportion of cases in each victim–offender racial combination varies somewhat from the proportions reported in earlier chapters because of missing data.

†Two (18.2 percent) of the 11 white suspects accused of sexually assaulting black women were arrested and had their cases filed as felonies. One man pled guilty; the prosecution dismissed the second case. The man who pled guilty received a two-year executed sentence in a minimum-security institution. Prior research (e.g., Curtis, 1975; Stember, 1976; LaFree, 1982; Wilbanks, 1985) has offered a variety of explanations for observed differences in rates of interracial and intraracial crime. It is important to note here that at least part of the difference in rates of BW and WB rape can be explained purely on the basis of demographic relationships between blacks and whites. Sociologist Peter Blau (1977, pp. 22–23) expresses this phenomenon as a general principle: "All minority groups, singly or in combination, are more

the other three racial combinations, I recoded the race-composition variable to form two separate measures. BW cases were coded 1 if they involved a black defendant and a white victim and 0 otherwise; BB cases were coded 1 if both victim and defendant were black and 0 otherwise.

My main strategy was first to identify the major processing decisions made by legal agents from the time a case was reported until it was either disposed of or dismissed and then to determine whether the victim's and offender's race affected these processing decisions, controlling for evidence and case characteristics. Altogether, I examined the impact of race composition on nine decisions. I examined the *arrest* decision for 870 of the reported assaults. For 339 suspects who were formally charged with an offense, I examined *charge seriousness*.* For 326 arrestees, I examined the *felony screening* decision to file felony charges.† Only 151 cases (47 percent) in which a suspect was arrested were ultimately filed as felonies in the criminal courts. For the 151 felony cases, I examined the decision either to continue *case prosecution* or to dismiss charges (*nolle prosequi*). None of the 28 cases dismissed by the prosecutor's office at this stage were later refiled. The remaining 123 cases were adjudicated through *trial* or plea agreements. For 50 cases adjudicated by trial, *verdict* measured the outcome.

---

involved in intergroup relations with a group constituting a majority than the majority group is with them." To understand this, consider the fact that blacks constitute 11 percent of the population, so if black offenders pick victims on a purely random basis, then about 89 percent of all victims raped by blacks will be white. Conversely, if white offenders randomly pick victims, only 11 percent of all victims raped by whites will be black. This reasoning has been applied specifically to rape and other personal crimes by sociologist Robert O'Brien (1987), who shows that the rate of BW rape in the United States can be entirely explained by the fact that rates of violent crimes by blacks—against both black and white victims—are much higher than rates of violent crime by whites.

*As in previous chapters, charge-seriousness scores were assigned to each offense according to the mean prison term imposed by statute. Thus, an indeterminate sentence of 10 to 20 years received a charge-seriousness score of 15.

†Thirteen men who were charged with an offense were never arrested, either because the charge was dismissed before they were apprehended or because the police were unable to locate them.

The judge had primary responsibility for sentencing convicted offenders in the cases examined. I included three sentencing measures. For the 103 men who were convicted, *sentence type* measured whether the sentence included incarceration in prison. The alternatives to prison incarceration were probation, suspended sentences, fines, or some combination of these. Twenty percent of the men convicted of rape received a nonprison sentence. For the 82 men who were incarcerated, *place of incarceration* distinguished between sentences to the maximum-security state penitentiary and incarceration in a local jail or minimum-security institution. Both offenders and officials frequently expressed the opinion that confinement in jail or a minimum-security institution (most often, the state farm) was "easy time"—a less serious sanction than incarceration in the state penitentiary. Only 51 percent of the men who received prison time of any type were sent to the state penitentiary. Finally, for the 82 men who received prison sentences, *sentence length* measured the average length of the sentence imposed.*

Proportion of Cases by Race Composition

The nine processing decisions just identified form a funnel in which fewer cases remain at each subsequent stage and both official punishment (e.g., prison, probation) and unofficial punishment (e.g., pretrial detention, time required

---

*A forcible-rape conviction in this jurisdiction carried an indeterminate penalty of from 2 to 21 years, or life imprisonment if the victim was under the age of 12. Armed rape and armed sodomy carried sentences of from 10 to 30 years. Men convicted of forcible sodomy faced sentences of from 2 to 14 years. Assault and battery with intent to rape carried a penalty of from 1 to 10 years. Punishment for assault and battery with intent to "gratify sexual desires" depended on the age of the victim. For victims between 12 and 17, the penalty was from 1 to 5 years. If the victim was under 12 years old, the penalty was from 2 to 21 years. Kidnapping was sometimes included with charges for forcible-sex offenses. The penalty for kidnapping in Indiana was life imprisonment. I estimated indeterminate sentences by taking the mean of the high and low sentence (e.g., $2-21 = 11.5$ years). Life sentences were rare, but when encountered, I assigned them 40 years, based on earlier sentencing research (e.g., Chiricos and Waldo, 1975). For concurrent sentences, I included only the most serious charge in the estimates.

FIGURE 6.1 Percentages of Black Suspect–White Victim (BW), Black Intraracial (BB), and White Intraracial Incidents for Eight Processing Stages

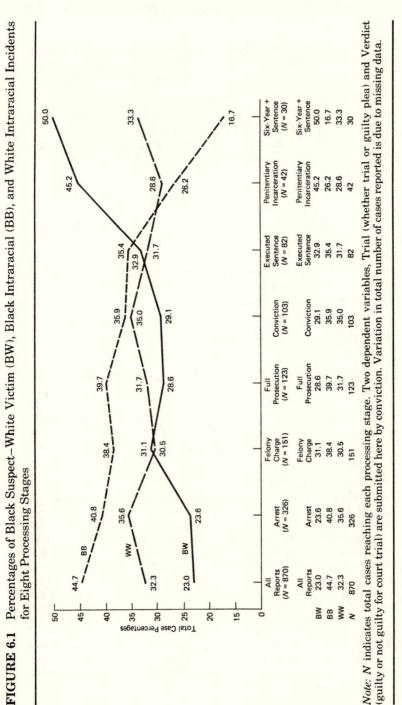

	All Reports (N = 870)	Arrest (N = 326)	Felony Charge (N = 151)	Full Prosecution (N = 123)	Conviction (N = 103)	Executed Sentence (N = 82)	Penitentiary Incarceration (N = 42)	Six-Year + Sentence (N = 30)
BW	23.0	23.6	31.1	28.6	29.1	32.9	45.2	50.0
BB	44.7	40.8	38.4	39.7	35.9	35.4	26.2	16.7
WW	32.3	35.6	30.5	31.7	35.0	31.7	28.6	33.3
N	870	326	151	123	103	82	42	30

Note: N indicates total cases reaching each processing stage. Two dependent variables, Trial (whether trial or guilty plea) and Verdict (guilty or not guilty for court trial) are submitted here by conviction. Variation in total number of cases reported is due to missing data.

SOURCE: LaFree, 1980b, p. 848.

for defense) increase for cases that remain in the system through later stages. The conflict argument would lead us to expect a higher proportion of black offender–white victim cases and a lower percentage of black intraracial cases as we move from earlier to later stages of processing. Figure 6.1, which compares percentages of black suspect–white victim, black intraracial, and white intraracial cases during official processing provides striking support for this prediction. Figure 6.1 shows that from case report to final sentencing, the percentage of cases involving black suspects and white victims steadily increased, the percentage of black intraracial assaults steadily declined, and the percentage of white intraracial assaults remained relatively constant.

The cumulative effect of these shifts was substantial. Black men accused of assaulting black women accounted for 45 percent of all reported rapes, but for only 26 percent of all men sentenced to the state penitentiary and for only 17 percent of all men who received sentences of six or more years. By contrast, black men accused of assaulting white women accounted for 23 percent of all reported rapes, but for 45 percent of all men sent to the state penitentiary and for 50 percent of all men who received sentences of six or more years. Percentages of cases involving white victims and defendants fluctuated between a high of 35.6 percent (arrest) and a low of 28.6 percent (penitentiary incarceration). The percentage of white intraracial assaults resulting in prison sentences of more than six years (33.3 percent) was almost identical to the percentage of white intraracial assaults among all reported cases (32.3 percent).

In addition to demonstrating the overrepresentation of black suspect–white victim cases and the underrepresentation of black intraracial cases, Figure 6.1 shows substantial variation in the size of percentage differences in race composition between processing stages. In fact, the proportion of black suspect–white victim cases actually declined for the decision to prosecute fully. Also, the percentage change between report and arrest and between full prosecution and conviction for black suspect–white victim cases was small: .6 percent and .5 percent, respectively. However, although race composition appeared to be differentially important across processing outcomes, the results strongly supported the argument that official reactions to black men charged with rape depend on the race of the victim.

Effect of Race Composition on Individual Outcomes

To provide more complete information on the nature of the relationship between race composition and outcome, I next estimated simple correlations between each of the nine criminal-justice outcomes and race composition. Table 6.1 shows correlations (Pearsonian r), the proportion of variance (r-square) in one variable that is explained by the other, and the sample size for each outcome.

These results also generally supported the conflict argument. Eight of nine outcomes indicated that black–white interracial assaults are likely to result in more serious sanctions for offenders; five of these relationships were statistically significant. Seven of nine outcomes indicated that black intraracial assaults were likely to result in less serious

TABLE 6.1   Correlations Between Racial Composition and Nine Official Processing Decisions in Forcible Sexual-Assault Cases

	Black–White Interracial		Black Intraracial		
	r	r^2	r	r^2	N
Arrest	.01	.00	−.04	.00	870
Charge seriousness	.17[c]	.27	−.06	.00	339
Felony screening	.17[c]	.03	−.04	.01	326
Case prosecution	−.11	.01	.06	.00	151
Trial	.08	.00	.06	.00	123
Verdict	.12	.01	−.26[a]	.07	50
Sentence type	.16[a]	.03	−.03	.00	103
Place of incarceration	.27[b]	.07	−.17	.03	82
Sentence length	.30[b]	.09	−.13	.02	82

[a] $p < .05$.   [b] $p < .01$.   [c] $p < .001$.
Note: Variation in total number of cases is due to missing data.

SOURCE: LaFree, 1980b, p. 849.

sanctions; one of these outcomes was statistically significant. Of the three outcomes that contradicted the conflict argument, none was statistically significant. Sexual assaults involving black offenders and white victims accounted for 27 percent of the variation in police charge seriousness, 9 percent of sentence length, 7 percent of the measure of place of incarceration, and 3 percent of the felony-screening and sentence-type decisions. Black intraracial assaults accounted for 7 percent of the variation in verdict and 3 percent of the variation in the place of incarceration. In contrast, the most important of the contradictory findings (case prosecution for black–white interracial offenses) accounted for only 1 percent of the variation in that outcome.

Multivariate Analyses

While these results were generally supportive of the proposition that the law is applied most harshly to black men charged with raping white women and least harshly to black men accused of raping black women, other interpretations are clearly possible. For example, as critics of conflict theory have noted (e.g., Chiricos and Waldo, 1975; Hindelang, 1978; Kleck, 1981; Wilbanks, 1987), it may be that there are legal differences between BW and other cases that explain the results. In an effort to control for the possibility that legal differences between the cases are what explain their different treatment, I next reexamined the nine decisions including measures of evidence as control variables.

In this part of the analysis I included four measures of offense seriousness and evidence: (1) victim willingness to prosecute, (2) witnesses, (3) weapon, and (4) type of offense. Research (Skolnick and Woodworth, 1967; Black, 1971; Myers, 1979; Myers and LaFree, 1982) suggests that more serious sanctions are likely when victims make clear their willingness to prosecute suspects. I found that women who reported their sexual assault to police declined prosecution in 20.9 percent of the cases. Although corroboration was not formally required in this jurisdiction, eyewitness identification by other witnesses obviously clarifies issues of consent and identification. Whether the assault involved a weapon relates both to the seriousness of the case and to the issue of consent. More than 31 percent of the cases reported to police involved a fire-arm or knife. The type of offense—whether rape or attempted rape—also reflects the offense's seriousness. About 15 per-cent of the cases reported to police were classified as at-tempted sexual assaults.

As we have seen in previous chapters, the legal system has traditionally been ambivalent about how a defendant's prior criminal record should be interpreted. While criminal law and legal procedure provide various mechanisms for ex-cluding the effect of the defendant's criminal record on official outcomes, research (e.g., Farrell and Swigert, 1978; Garber, Klepper, and Nagin, 1982; Hagan and Bumiller, 1983) consis-tently shows that criminal record is one of the most important issues considered by officials in making processing decisions. To control for the possibility that the results were due to the differential seriousness of defendants' criminal records, I in-cluded an ordinal measure of criminal history (scaled from 0 to 3). Forty-six percent of the men had previous convictions with prison time imposed; 18 percent had previous convic-tions, but no prison time imposed; 18 percent had previous ar-rests, but no convictions; and 18 percent had no prior felony arrests. I also included a dichotomous measure of each de-fendant's age, which was coded 1 if he was 20 years old or younger and 0 if he was more than 20 years old.

I took advantage of the longitudinal quality of the data in two ways. First, each outcome was based on the results of the preceding outcome. For example, only cases filed as felonies were analyzed for prosecution or dismissal. Second, results of earlier decisions were incorporated as independent variables for later decisions. Thus, for all defendants who were charged with felonies, charge seriousness was included in the analysis of subsequent processing decisions. For all convicted defen-dants, type of conviction—whether guilty plea or verdict—was included in the estimation of sentencing decisions. And for the analysis of verdicts, I included a dichotomous variable —jury or bench trial—to control for the type of trial.

Table 6.2 presents the results of a multivariate analysis with all the independent variables, including the indicators of black suspect–white victim and black intraracial cases, to predict the nine processing outcomes. The columns of num-bers marked R in Table 6.2 are called *multiple correlation co-*

TABLE 6.2 Stepwise Multiple Correlations with Nine Processing Outcomes as Dependent Variables for Forcible Sexual-Assault Cases

	Zero Order		First Order		Second Order		Third Order		Fourth Order		Fifth Order	
	R	R^2	R	R^2	R	R^2	R	R^2	R	R^2	R	R^2
Arrest	.39	.16	.41	.17	.42	.18	.42	.18	.42	.18	.42	.18
(N = 780)	PREF		WEAPON		WITNESS		TYPE		RACE (BW)		RACE (BB)	
Charge seriousness	.41	.16	.49	.24	.51	.27	.52	.27	.52	.27	.52	.27
(N = 341)	TYPE		WEAPON		RACE (BW)		PREF		WITNESS		RACE (BB)	
Felony screening	.18	.03	.23	.05	.25	.06	.25	.06	.26	.06	.26	.07
(N = 324)	CHARGE		WITNESS		RACE (BW)		PREF		WEAPON		RACE (BB)	
Case prosecution	.12	.01	.16	.03	.18	.03	.19	.04	.20	.04	.20	.04
(N = 151)	CHARGE		RACE (BW)		TYPE		WEAPON		WITNESS		D-AGE	
Trial	.15	.02	.18	.03	.19	.04	.22	.05	.24	.06	.24	.06
(N = 125)	CHARGE		WITNESS		RACE (BB)		RACE (BW)		D-AGE		WEAPON	
Verdict	.34	.11	.47	.22	.52	.27	.56	.31	.57	.32	.58	.33
(N = 49)	CRIMREC		D-AGE		WEAPON		WITNESS		TYPE		BENCH	
Sentence type	.34	.11	.39	.15	.41	.17	.43	.19	.43	.19	.44	.19
(N = 103)	CRIMREC		CHARGE		RACE (BW)		TYPE		WITNESS		RACE (BB)	
Place of incarceration	.39	.15	.46	.21	.48	.23	.50	.25	.52	.27	.54	.29
(N = 81)	GILTYPE		RACE (BW)		WEAPON		CRIMREC		CHARGE		TYPE	
Sentence length	.41	.17	.54	.30	.58	.34	.60	.35	.60	.36	.60	.36
(N = 82)	GILTYPE		CHARGE		RACE (BW)		D-AGE		WEAPON		WITNESS	

Note: Race-composition variables are underlined to facilitate comparisons. Item identifications are: RACE (BW) = black defendants and white victims; RACE (BB) = black defendants and victims; D-AGE = defendant age; CRIMREC = defendant criminal record; BENCH = trial by jury or judge; WITNESS = eyewitness; WEAPON = presence of weapon; TYPE = offense type; CHARGE = charge seriousness; GILTYPE = conviction by plea; PREF = victim willingness to testify.

SOURCE: LaFree, 1980b, p. 850.

137

efficients. Very generally, these are measures of how closely associated independent variables are to each outcome (or dependent) variable. When R is squared, it is called *the coefficient of determination*; it expresses the amount of variation in the dependent variable that is explained or accounted for by the independent variable or variables in each equation.* The results in Table 6.2 are arranged so that the best single predictor of each outcome appears first (as a "zero-order" relationship), the second-best predictor appears next ("first-order" relationship), and so on. For example, prosecution preference (PREF) was the variable most highly correlated with the decision to arrest, and it shows up in the zero-order column with an $R = .39$. By the fifth order, variables measuring weapon, eyewitness, type of assault, black–white interracial, and black intraracial have been added, providing an $R = .42$ with six independent variables in the equation.

Table 6.2, then, shows us how early in the analysis race-composition variables entered each equation and, further, how much of an additional contribution specific variables made to explaining each processing outcome. According to Table 6.2, the black–white interracial composition variable entered six of the nine outcomes by the second order. The largest increment in explained variance (R-square) produced by adding race composition was for place of incarceration (R-square increment = .06); followed by sentence length and case prosecution (R-square increment = .04); and sentence type and felony screening (R-square increment = .02). Overall, the inclusion of the race-composition variables does improve prediction of outcomes appreciably, with the greatest increases occurring for later, sentencing outcomes.

In a final part of the analysis, I reestimated equations for each of the processing outcomes including only those independent variables which had significant ($p < .10$) net effects. Beta coefficients for the analysis are shown in Table 6.3. Re-

---

*A more detailed explanation of the multiple correlation coefficient and the coefficient of determination may be found in most intermediate-level statistics textbooks; see, for example, Kerlinger and Pedhazur (1973) and Blalock (1979).

TABLE 6.3   Beta Coefficients for Independent Variables with Processing Outcomes in Forcible Sexual-Assault Cases ($p < .10$)

				R^2
Arrest	.408	−.120	.079	.177
	PREF	WEAPON	WITNESS	
Charge seriousness	−.393	.265	.146	.265
	TYPE	WEAPON	RACE (BW)	
Felony screening	.157	.127	.105	.063
	CHARGE	WITNESS	RACE (BW)	
Verdict	.305	.330	−.243	.275
	CRIMREC	D-AGE	WEAPON	
Sentence type	.349	.173	.140	.170
	CRIMREC	CHARGE	RACE (BW)	
Place of incarceration	.380	.235		.209
	GILTYPE	RACE (BW)		
Sentence length	.352	.342	.210	.340
	GILTYPE	CHARGE	RACE (BW)	

Note: Race-composition variables are underlined to facilitate comparisons. See the note to Table 6.2 for item identifications.

SOURCE: LaFree, 1980b, p. 851.

call from earlier chapters that beta coefficients indicate the amount of net change in the dependent variable for a unit change in each independent variable.

The prediction equations for two outcomes (case prosecution and trial) were not statistically significant ($p < .10$) and results are not presented. Thus, there was no indication that race composition had a net effect on these two outcomes. Race composition had a significant effect on five of the remaining seven outcomes. Black offender–white victim cases were the most important racial consideration in all five of these outcomes. This variable entered the equation at the second order for four of the outcomes and at the first order for one outcome. All the significant results were in the direction predicted by the conflict proposition. Compared to other defendants, blacks who were suspected of assaulting white women received more serious charges, were more likely to have their cases filed as felonies, were more likely to receive prison sentences if convicted, were more likely to be incarcerated in the state penitentiary (as opposed to a jail or minimum-security facility), and received longer sentences on the average.

Reviewing the Evidence for Differential Treatment by Race

The main purpose of this part of the analysis was to explore the proposition that blacks accused of sexual assaults against whites receive more serious treatment than other race combinations from the legal system. Taken together, the results indicate that processing decisions in these sexual-assault cases were affected by the race composition of the victim–defendant dyad, and the cumulative effect of race composition was substantial.

In general, the results confirmed the sexual-stratification perspective on racial discrimination in official reactions to rape. Thus, the effects are clearest when we consider race composition rather than the individual race of defendant or victim. This is because black offenders charged with raping white women are treated more harshly and black offenders charged with raping black women less harshly. When examined in the aggregate, these two effects tend to cancel each other. Moreover, as expected, having data on the entire criminal-justice system is important in terms of examining racial discrimination. While evidence of discrimination by race for any single outcome was not overwhelming, the cumulative effect of race (as illustrated in Figure 6.1) was nonetheless considerable. Hence, studies examining only one or two processing outcomes may or may not support a view of discriminatory processing, depending on independent variables included, methods used, and specific outcomes examined.

But note also that conclusions about discrimination drawn from this analysis are relative. While these cases yielded substantial evidence of differential treatment based on the race of the victim and offender, there were also negative findings. None of the independent variables, including race composition, had significant effects on case prosecution and on whether the case went to trial. Moreover, race composition did not have a significant effect on arrest and verdict. For the other decisions, race composition was often less important than type of offense, weapon, witnesses, and charge seriousness. In general, this raises the question of how much evidence is necessary to show discrimination and at what point racial discrimination is serious enough to warrant our attention.

Most of the recent research on official reactions to crime (including the present study) has tried to provide answers to questions like these through analyses that distinguish legal from extralegal influences on decision making. The characteristic form of this approach is to use multivariate-analysis techniques to determine whether variables like race have any effect on processing decisions when legal variables are controlled. This approach has at least two fundamental limitations that we must keep in mind. First, far from being an objective benchmark, the law itself may simply justify oppressive, unequal, and unjust relationships. Civil rights leader Martin Luther King, Jr., once remarked, "We can never forget that everything Hitler did in Germany was 'legal' and everything the Hungarian freedom fighters did in Hungary was 'illegal.'"

In the United States before the Civil War, laws against rape explicitly treated black and white offenders differently. For example, the penal code of antebellum Georgia required capital punishment for slaves and "free persons of color who were convicted of committing a rape or attempting it on a free white female" (Cobb, 1851, p. 987). In contrast, a white man convicted of raping a black female slave or a free black woman was fined, imprisoned, or both at the court's discretion. From 1930 to 1980, 3,820 people were executed for all crimes in the United States, according to government statistics (United States Department of Justice, Bureau of Prisons, 1981). For the offense of murder, 49.4 percent of all those executed were black (1,630 out of 3,297). Although rape is no longer a capital offense in the United States, after murder it is the crime for which offenders have most often been executed. Government statistics (United States Department of Justice, Bureau of Prisons, 1981) show that of 453 legal executions for rape in the United States since 1930, 405 of those executed (89 percent) were black. The 11 states making up the old southern Confederacy accounted for 87 percent of these rape executions and for 91 percent of all black rape executions (United States Department of Justice, Bureau of Prisons, 1971, p. 11; Murchison, 1978, pp. 519–520). Moreover, government figures do not take into account illegal executions. Criminologist William Bowers (1974, p. 40) concludes that in the last two decades of the nineteenth century, illegal lynchings actually outnumbered state-sponsored executions (by 1,540 to 1,214) and that most lynchings were perpetrated on blacks in the South. Bowers notes that even in the beginning of this century, lynchings still constituted more than one-third of all (legal and illegal) executions. Similarly, Donald Partington (1965) found that every single man executed for rape in the state of Virginia between 1908 and 1963 was black. In short, it is important to remember that the issue of differential treatment by race in rape cases in the United States is always one of whether there is *still* evidence for differential treatment rather than whether there is *any* evidence.

A second limitation of separating legal from extralegal variables is that, as we have seen in previous chapters, it is always a relative rather than an absolute process. Hence, to the extent that conclusions about racial discrimination are in turn based on these distinctions, they too must be relative rather than absolute. An example of this limitation from the present study may be observed by considering how a prior relationship between victim and offender is associated with the race composition of the victim–offender dyad. I did not include the victim–offender relationship as a legal variable in the analysis in this chapter because it was not a required element of sexual-assault cases in Indiana (except that the victim and offender cannot be husband and wife, which never occurred in these data) and because Indiana law did not recognize it as a mitigating factor. We have already seen in the analysis of police and court decisions in Chapters 4 and 5 (see Tables 4.2 and 5.3) that the victim–suspect relationship did not have a statistically significant effect on any of the outcomes except arrest (where prior association with the suspect increased rather than decreased arrest chances). Similarly, including the victim–suspect relationship in a reanalysis of

the data presented in this chapter did not change the results.*
Yet, despite the fact that the impact of race on processing outcomes in these data cannot be explained by whether the victim and offender were acquainted, it seems clear that prior
relationships between victim and offender still influenced the
processing of these interracial and intraracial sexual assaults
in individual cases.

This point may be illustrated by the trials of Charles
Jackson and Phillips-Martin. In the BW case, Carrie Brighton denied any prior relationship with defendant Jackson.
But in his testimony, Jackson claimed that he had known
Brighton prior to the reported assault and that they had once
smoked marijuana together. However, he backed away from
arguing that the alleged rape had been consensual, relying
instead on a misidentification defense in the courtroom. This
seriously hurt his case, because he was asking jurors to believe that, on the one hand, Brighton knew him well but that,
on the other hand, she incorrectly identified him as her assailant. Our interviews with jurors showed that most of them
simply did not believe Jackson. We might ask ourselves, Why
didn't Charles Jackson attempt a consent defense? Brighton
seemed vulnerable to this type of defense: young, unmarried,
frequently out late at night, working at a bar. Although she
claimed that her assailant had threatened her with a knife,
no weapon was ever recovered. I suspect that part of the reason for the identification defense in the Charles Jackson case
was the important but unstated fact that jurors would have
been unlikely to believe that Brighton, a white woman, had
been having an ongoing relationship with Jackson, a black

---

*In three of the nine equations—arrest, charge seriousness, and felony
screening—the victim–offender relationship had significant effects. As in the
analysis in Chapter 4, the results for arrest showed that suspects acquainted
with victims were more likely to be arrested—a likely consequence of the
fact that suspects acquainted with the victim are easier to locate and arrest.
Suspects who had been acquainted with the rape victim also received more
serious charges and were more likely to have their cases filed as felonies.
However, in both of these equations, the effect of victim–offender race composition was still significant and was greater than that of the victim–offender
relationship (for similar results, see Walsh, 1987).

man. My guess is that the defense implicitly recognized the fact that because interracial courtship and marriage are relatively uncommon, jurors would be less likely to accept a consent defense as plausible in this BW case.

But imagine for a moment that Carrie Brighton as well as Charles Jackson had been black. In this situation, Jackson could have more plausibly argued that he had known Brighton for some time, that they had smoked marijuana together, and that she had not been raped, but had consented to sexual intercourse. No weapon was recovered for use as evidence of forcible rape. In fact, recall that in the Phillips-Martin trial, jurors apparently discounted a recovered gun as evidence of forcible rape. These comparisons suggest that race composition can have subtle impacts on the interpretation of rape cases by making certain types of social situations more or less likely in the view of official processing agents.

Of course, the difficulty of separating racial discrimination from legal processing decisions is not limited to the interpretation of the social attributes of the victim and the alleged offender; it also applies to considerations that many researchers would treat as obviously legal. For example, in the above analysis I followed a widespread convention in recent criminological research by including defendant's criminal record, measures of offense seriousness, and weapon as legal variables. However, as sociologists Ronald Farrell and Victoria Swigert (1978) have pointed out, criminal record is an unbiased measure of the defendant's actual behavior only if he has not previously been the victim of differential treatment. Thus, if the system unfairly selects certain types of people as offenders at one time, using a measure of criminal record as a legal variable at a later time merely legitimizes earlier discriminatory decision making.

Similarly, while such measures as offense seriousness and weapon are routinely used by researchers as legal indicators of behavior, they are themselves established through the subjective decision making of legal agents. Thus, in Indianapolis, both charge seriousness and whether the offense was officially classified as involving a weapon changed throughout the processing system as bargaining between prosecutor and defense continued, new evidence was introduced, and old evidence was disproved. As anyone familiar with the court system can confirm, charges are routinely dropped, added, or reduced as cases move through different stages of processing. Clearly, not all of these changes represent corresponding changes in the perceived severity of cases or strength of evidence.

Even in the courtroom, seemingly obvious legal considerations, such as presence of a weapon, can be closely linked to racial stereotypes. Although both Carrie Brighton and Sharon Robertson claimed that their assailants had been armed, interpretations of these claims in the two cases were totally different. In the case of Carrie Brighton, testimony about a weapon was interpreted by jurors as an aggravating factor. Yet in the Sharon Robertson case, the defense attorney successfully argued that carrying guns was so prevalent in inner-city Indianapolis that the mere presence of a gun did not support Robertson's story of rape. Ironically, the defense attorney in the Robertson case at one point actually blamed Robertson for not having made an attempt to use the gun on her attackers: "If somebody had just raped me and there was a gun there wouldn't be two defendants—there would be two bodies."

IMPLICATIONS AND CONCLUSIONS

It is clear from the analysis that black offender–white victim rapes resulted in substantially more serious penalties than other rapes, even controlling for the case characteristics that are most often included in this type of research. Moreover, black intraracial assaults consistently resulted in the least serious punishment for offenders. Most of the recent multivariate statistical attempts to determine whether there is evidence of racial discrimination in the legal system have tried to measure whether the race of the defendant has any effect on processing decisions when legal variables are controlled. Researchers who find no effect of race typically conclude that the system is not discriminatory and hence that research should focus on criminal etiology rather than on the decision making of officials. The most important problem with this conclusion is that it is based on the assumption that we can clearly distinguish legal from extralegal variables in research on discrimination and can therefore control for the effects of the former.

As the results show, the distinction between legal and extralegal variables is relative rather than absolute. Thus, supposedly legal variables, such as offense seriousness and presence of weapon, are in fact determined through the same subjective processes of legal agents that we are studying in the first place. Other variables that are commonly treated as legal indicators, such as the defendant's criminal records, are themselves dependent on earlier processing decisions, which may or may not have been discriminatory. Still other measures of legal differences between cases are ambiguous for other reasons. Some, like the promptness of the victim's report, are probably a mixture of components that are legally relevant (for example, medical evidence erodes over time) and discriminatory (many observers feel that women who do not report rape immediately have something to hide). Others, like prior victim–offender relationship, are generally not legal considerations and yet may tap attitudes about the relative severity of the crime.

In fact, regardless of the conclusions we reach about racial discrimination in a particular jurisdiction at a particular time, we should reject the idea that it is pointless to test for discrimination in other jurisdictions or at other times. Instead, an important task of criminology should be to monitor continually the treatment received by societal subgroups in various situations, parts of the system, and time periods.

At the same time, conflict theorists have sometimes been too quick to interpret data such as those presented in this chapter in terms of what philosopher Jeffrey Reiman (1984, p. 112) calls a *conspiracy theory* of criminal justice. Reiman defines the conspiracy theory as an explanation that assumes that powerful members of society actually conspire to maintain their favorable position. This criticism generally corresponds to the distinction between instrumental and structural versions of conflict theory introduced in Chapter 3. For example, the analysis described in this chapter shows rather conclusively that outcomes in rape cases depend on the race composition of the victim–offender dyad. A conspiracy theory would highlight the racist attitudes and behavior of the legal agents responsible for these processing decisions, perhaps even suggesting that white legal agents actively discuss mechanisms for treating cases more or less harshly depending on the race of the victim and the offender. However, my field observations in this jurisdiction indicated that overt racism was relatively uncommon. Instead, it seems most likely that race relations are embedded in a larger social system, which is often much more complex than a simple conspiracy theory would suggest.

In the next two chapters we move from the argument that the application of rape laws in the United States still contains vestiges of a sexual-stratification system in which the law is used to control the behavior of black men to the argument that rape laws are still used to control the behavior of nontraditional women. In fact, the evolution of law regarding blacks and women in Western cultures is in some respects parallel. Most fundamentally, both share a history of being legally recognized as the personal property of others. In his classic study of race relations in the United States, Gunnar Myrdal concludes that the positions of blacks and women are both rooted in a "paternalistic order of society" (1941, p. 1078). Forty years later, feminist Susan Brownmiller (1975, p. 254) updates the connection between women and blacks and applies it specifically to rape:

> Rape is to women as lynching was to blacks: the ultimate physical threat by which all men keep all women in a state of psychological intimidation.

Chapter 7 reintroduces the feminist-conflict argument that the application of law to nonconformist women in rape cases may serve to control the behavior of all women; the chapter examines how allegations of nontraditional behavior on the part of victims can affect the content and outcome of rape trials. Chapter 8 then directly tests the argument, using the verdicts of jurors in a set of Indianapolis rape trials

CHAPTER 7

Rape and the Social Control of Women

Come on! Girls think they know so much these days. They try to lead a man on and then they get so far he can't stop and the woman hollers rape.

Juror, Wendy Yates case.

You asked me how sure I was the decision I made was right. When we went back to the jury room to get our coats after we gave the verdict, we were really down. I mean we were all really down in the pits. There wasn't much hard evidence, like someone seeing him, and we were really depressed that we might have sent an innocent man away . . . for a long time. . . .

Juror, Russell/Chan case.

If . . . no husband were able to use his own force or that of family members, relatives, neighbors, or the community to press his children toward obedience at any age, to eject from his house a man who is courting his wife, to threaten his wife for welcoming flirtations or going on dates with another, to press her to stay in the domicile he has chosen, to persuade her not to abandon the children when she would like to go off alone, to take care of the home and children . . . it is easy to see that a substantial part of the structural strength of the family would be undermined.

William Goode, "Force and Violence in the Family."

In this chapter I take up the feminist-conflict argument that when there is evidence that a woman has behaved sex-role nontraditionally, her charge of rape is less likely to result in the case being defined as a serious crime. The origins of this idea in criminology are related to more general developments in the social sciences, especially in the study of marriage and the family. Most societies most of the time distinguish between what they expect women and men to do, and they maintain conformity to these gender-role expectations through systems of positive and negative sanctions. However, in the 1960s an increasingly active debate began among social scientists about the nature of the social forces that actually hold marriage and family systems together. The traditional view, which had dominated North American social science for most of the century, assumed that sex-role differences were necessary for the proper functioning of the family and, by extension, the society. Adherents claimed that the different social roles played by men and women were complementary. This view is clear in the influential writings of sociologists Talcott Parsons and Robert Bales (1954), who argue that gender-role differentiation in marriage and the family operates for the mutual benefit of all family members. Thus, the husband engages in work outside the home and other *instrumental* activities that create essential links between the family and the economic arena, while the wife performs work inside the home and other *expressive* activities that maintain family cohesiveness and stability.

Critics of this traditional view of the family have come to consider descriptions of sex roles such as that of Parsons and Bales to be sentimental abstractions with little connection to reality. For example, in the quotation at the beginning of this chapter, sociologist William Goode argues that the family is held together not only by attraction and mutual reward but also by force, violence, and coercion. Similarly, conflict theorist Randall Collins (1975, p. 230) suggests that relationships between men and women are strongly influenced by the brute fact that on the average, men tend to be physically bigger and stronger than women. As the feminist movement gained momentum in the 1970s, feminist writers began to develop the theme that relationships between men and women in marriage and family are based as much on power, violence, and coercion as on mutual trust, understanding, and love. These ideas cleared the way for reinterpretations of other aspects of male–female relationships. Rape was an obvious concern because it combines relations between men and women with issues of power and violence.

RAPE AS SOCIAL CONTROL

One of the most controversial themes in the recent feminist reinterpretation of rape is the argument that rape functions as a social mechanism for controlling women's behavior. This idea is stated bluntly by feminist Susan Brownmiller in her book on rape (1975, p. 15): "It is nothing more or less than a conscious process of intimidation by which *all men* keep *all women* in a state of fear." What Brownmiller is suggesting here is that the threat of rape restricts the movement and behavior of all women, including those who never become rape victims. To the extent that such restrictions keep women in traditional sex roles—roles that are subordinate to those of men—all men may indirectly benefit.

We can take issue with several of the assumptions implicit in Brownmiller's statement. For example, it is debatable to what extent rapists, or men in general, consciously calculate the effect that rape will have on women in general. However, a variety of research has been done that is consistent with the idea that women are very much aware of the possibility of rape and that they change their behavior in response to this awareness. For example, criminologists (Reiss, 1967; Hindelang, Gottfredson, and Garofalo, 1978; Braungart, Braungart, and Hoyer, 1980; Ortega and Myles, 1987) have consistently found that women in the United States report greater fear of violent crime than men, despite the fact that with the single exception of rape, they are much less likely than men to be victims of violent crime. In a study of adult men and women in three large U.S. cities, Stephanie Riger, Margaret Gordon, and Robert LeBailly (1978) found that compared to men, women reported significantly greater fear of being alone at night or in places that they perceived as dangerous. Likewise, sociologist Mark Warr (1985) found that in a sample of 181 women living in urban areas, two-thirds reported being "very fearful" of rape. Warr concludes (p. 242) that "both the prevalence and magnitude of fear of rape are remarkable. . . . It is beyond question that rape is currently a central fear in the lives of a large proportion of women."

Recent research also suggests that women's fear of rape has tangible effects on their behavior. Again, the criminology literature (e.g., Hindelang and Davis, 1977; Hindelang,

Gottfredson, and Garofalo, 1978) consistently shows that with the exception of gun ownership, women take more precautions than men to avoid becoming crime victims.

For Brownmiller and other feminists, the key issue in interpreting rape and society's response to it is the gender-role behavior of the victim. Thus, she claims (p. 254) that

> Women have been raped by men . . . as group punishment for being uppity, for getting out of line, for failing to recognize "one's place," for assuming sexual freedoms, or for behavior no more provocative than walking down the wrong road at night.

The image of male–female relations that emerges from the work of Brownmiller and other feminist writers is one in which women occupy an inferior position in society and men use a variety of mechanisms—including rape and the selective enforcement of rape laws—to keep women in this position. Although this argument was developed by feminists more or less independently of academic criminology, the underlying assumptions about human behavior, society, and law are similar to the conflict theory that developed in criminology during the 1970s.

Like the feminist writers, conflict theorists emphasize the importance of law in maintaining existing power structures. Barbara Reskin and I argue (1981) that legal protection, like other scarce resources, may be withheld from some individuals on the basis of their race, age, economic status, or gender. In addition, some individuals forfeit legal protection because they live outside the legal or moral structure of society. For example, homosexuals, prostitutes, and drug dealers who are robbed, beaten, or blackmailed seldom feel free to appeal to the legal system, and when they do, they are generally less likely to receive the same treatment as others who seek justice. Similarly, if women who violate traditional sex roles and are raped are unable to obtain justice through the legal system, then the law may be interpreted as an institutional arrangement for reinforcing women's gender-role conformity.

Most of the analysis in previous chapters has depended on data available through official police, prosecution, and court records. In general, these data have been congruent with the feminist-conflict idea that evidence of nonconformist

behavior on the part of victims reduces the severity of outcomes for rape defendants and suspects. Thus, we saw in
Chapter 4 that no cases in which police alleged nonconformist
victim behavior resulted in arrest. Similarly, we saw in Chapter 5 that when victim nonconformity was alleged, guilty verdicts and convictions were less likely. However, although
these data are useful, they have some important limitations
for the study of how the gender-role behavior of rape victims
affects the processing of their cases. First, my analysis of official records lacked any data on the characteristics and attitudes of the processing agents involved in decision making.
For example, it seems reasonable to assume that evidence
of victim nonconformity may have differential effects, depending on whether officials hold traditional or less traditional views of women. Second, the argument that rape victims' nontraditional behavior affects the processing of their
cases assumes that effects are still present, controlling for evidential differences between cases. However, although the
official records included a great deal of information on evidence available in cases (especially in later stages of processing), the validity of evidence measures nonetheless must ultimately depend on the veracity, diligence, and interpretations
of the legal agents responsible for creating the records. The
limitations of official records for the study of legal decision
making encouraged me and my colleagues to undertake a
more in-depth study of the processing of rape cases that did
not depend on records. For several reasons, we decided to concentrate on the trial jury.

USING JURIES TO STUDY
SEXUAL ASSAULT CASES

Although jury systems have existed in nations as diverse
as Czarist Russia and contemporary Australia, the jury in the
twentieth century has been especially important in North
America. The founders of the United States included guarantees to a trial by jury in the third article of the Constitution
and strengthened these guarantees in the Fifth, Sixth, and
Seventh Amendments. The individual states followed the federal government's lead: each of the state constitutions also
guarantees the right to a trial by jury. In their classic study,

The American Jury, Harry Kalven and Hans Zeisel (1966, p. 13) estimate that more than 80 percent of the criminal jury trials *in the world* are held in the United States (see also Hans and Vidmar, 1986).

Jury trials have several characteristics that make them especially relevant for studies of how law is applied in sexual-assault cases. Although only a small proportion of reported sexual assaults are adjudicated by jury (5.5 percent of those reported to Indianapolis police in 1970, 1973, and 1975), expectations about how jurors are likely to respond to cases, as we have seen in earlier chapters, influence decisions throughout the criminal-selection process. Thus, expectations about what is likely to happen if a case goes to trial influence victims' decisions to report cases and to cooperate with police and prosecutors, influence police arrest and charging decisions, and influence prosecutors' decisions to press charges and the seriousness of the charges that are filed.

Moreover, jury verdicts are perhaps the purest example in our society of public decision making that actually defines the boundaries of criminal behavior. For example, when a jury returns a guilty verdict in a rape trial, it also contributes to the ongoing social process of defining rape. In addition, the jury verdict is final, and jurors are not held either professionally or legally responsible for the decisions they render. Clearly, much of the importance of rape laws is lost if jurors remain unwilling to apply the legal standards mandated. Hence, in a very real sense, rape is whatever a jury says it is.

Regardless of how interesting juries might be, studying them is not easy. A 1956 federal law (in response to the jury study that eventually resulted in Kalven and Zeisel's 1966 book, *The American Jury*) prohibits researchers from observing jury deliberations. To overcome this obstacle, researchers since then have relied mostly on studies of simulated juries. Early jury-simulation studies tended to be too simple and unrealistic. College students were often used as mock jurors and were simply asked to read and respond to case descriptions. Although recent studies of mock juries (for reviews, see Gerbasi, Zuckerman, and Reis, 1977; Visher, 1985) have become more methodologically sophisticated, it is my position that simulations, no matter how carefully designed, remain less compelling than real trials—a difference of particular importance in cases involving especially violent, personal crimes like rape.

A STUDY OF SEXUAL-ASSAULT TRIALS

Between July 1978 and September 1980, my colleagues and I studied all 38 jury trials of forcible-sexual-assault* cases held in Marion County (Indianapolis).† Our research team examined only trials in which the complainant was a female at least 12 years old. Three of the trials involved more than one defendant. Because guilt is a separate issue for each defendant, we treated each separately in the analysis, producing a total of 41 verdicts. Two observers were present at each trial, and both completed a lengthy, structured data-collection form. Observational data included information on defendants' and victims' characteristics and behavior prior to and at the time of the reported sexual assault, as well as their testimony and courtroom behavior. Observers also collected detailed information on the nature of evidence presented by the prosecution and the defense, including witnesses, exhibits, and general tactics. Observers independently coded each trial. At the conclusion of the trial, they compared their evaluations and resolved any discrepancies through a review of their observational notes and a reexamination of court records when necessary.

In addition to these observational data, we completed 90-minute post-trial interviews with 331 of the 456 jurors (70.4 percent) who served in the sexual-assault trials.** In

*Forcible sexual assaults included all completed and attempted rape and sodomy charges. Charges against defendants in 34 cases included rape or attempted rape. In four cases, charges included either sodomy or attempted sodomy. Eight cases involved both rape and sodomy charges.

†Professor Barbara Reskin and I were the co-principal investigators of this project, which was funded for three years by the National Institute of Mental Health. During some phases of our investigation the project included as many as 25 staff members and part-time interviewers. For a detailed description of the study and its results, see Reskin and LaFree (1981) and LaFree, Reskin, and Visher (1985).

**Respondents did not differ significantly in age, sex, or race from jurors who declined to be interviewed. Comparisons between the respondents and a sample of "nonrespondents" who consented to a brief telephone interview showed no systematic differences on a wide range of variables.

the three trials involving more than one defendant, we asked jurors to evaluate two defendants. The addition of these three cases yielded a total of 360 juror interviews. These interviews include data on jurors' background characteristics, their attitudes about sex roles, crime, and rape, and their reactions to victims and defendants. To maximize the validity of the interviews, we matched interviewers and juror-respondents for both race and sex.

We also collected post-trial questionnaires from the judges who presided over each of the rape trials in the study. These questionnaires asked judges for the verdicts they would have rendered on each of the charges and for evaluations of the evidence, the counsel for each side, and the legal complexity of cases. These three data sources were supplemented by court records. In addition, we completed unstructured interviews with judges, prosecutors, and defense attorneys who were frequently involved in the processing of rape cases.

Indianapolis Rape Trials

Well-established rules control the order in which trial events unfold. The major stages in the criminal trials we observed were (1) voir dire (jury selection), (2) counsel's opening statements, (3) presentation of the prosecution's case, (4) presentation of the defense's case, (5) presentation of any rebuttal witnesses, and (6) closing arguments. About half the trials in our study were concluded in a day. Fourteen (36.8 percent) lasted two days; four lasted three days; and only one required four days. The major official participants in rape trials, as in criminal trials in general, are all lawyers: judges, prosecutors, and defense attorneys. Indianapolis had four criminal courts, which were responsible for handling the trials in our study. According to official policy, criminal cases were randomly assigned to one of these four courts. However, the actual distribution of cases among the four courts makes it appear unlikely that cases were in fact randomly assigned. One male judge presided over only one trial. In contrast, the only woman judge in the criminal courts presided over 14 (36.8 percent) of the trials. In nine trials (23.7 percent), a judge other than one of the regular criminal-court judges heard the case.

Most often a single attorney represented the prosecution

and another the defense. However, in five trials (13.2 percent) there was more than one defense attorney. Two of these multiple-attorney cases involved more than one defendant. In 12 cases (31.6 percent) two prosecuting attorneys were present. The prosecutor's office sometimes paired an experienced prosecuting attorney with a novice to provide the newer attorney with trial experience. Because of the heavy case load in this jurisdiction, the prosecutor served mostly as a manager and rarely appeared in the courtroom. During the three years of our study, the prosecutor joined one of his deputies in the prosecution of a sexual assault case on only two occasions. Given the fact that public awareness of sexual assault as a social problem was very high during this period, the prosecutor no doubt appeared in these cases in part for the favorable media exposure.

As public pressure for reform of sexual assault prosecution increased in the 1970s, one response of the Indianapolis prosecutor's office was to assign more women attorneys to sexual assault cases. Women prosecuted 18 (43.9 percent) of the cases included in our study, and in an additional five cases (12.2 percent) the prosecution included a woman on a male–female prosecution team. Most of the female prosecutors I interviewed claimed that the experience of prosecuting sexual assault cases personally affected them. One woman prosecutor told me:

> I couldn't disassociate myself from the victim when I first started. . . . I never used to have any fear to walk the streets of Indianapolis by myself, but I do now.

Other women who were veterans of sexual assault prosecution told me that they disliked it. The following comment is typical:

> I don't like to do them. When I first started I felt sorry for the victims and wanted to do the best I could in court. After awhile my distaste for the whole thing [pauses]—I just didn't want to try them.

Jury Selection.   Jury selection is commonly referred to by the French expression voir dire, meaning literally "look-speak." In general, voir dire is more important and extensive in the United States than in other countries that have jury systems. In Canada and England, for example, questioning potential jurors about their beliefs and prejudices is forbidden unless the trial judge is persuaded by independent evidence that prospective jurors may be biased. In Indianapolis, as in most jurisdictions in the United States, 12 jurors are chosen for criminal cases.* In the Indianapolis trials we observed, one or two alternate jurors were frequently selected, especially if it appeared likely that the trial would last more than one day.

Panels of prospective jurors, called venires, are randomly selected from lists of registered voters. To register to vote in Indianapolis, individuals had to be at least 18 years old, a continuous resident of their township for 60 days, and living at the address given at least 30 days prior to the coming election. These requirements did not seem to have the effect of reducing the participation of blacks on juries. In fact, although blacks represented 13.5 percent of the population of Marion County in 1980, black men accounted for 6.5 percent and black women for 10.5 percent of the people interviewed for the juries in our study—a total of 17 percent. By comparison, white men constituted 41.2 percent and white women 41.7 percent of those examined for jury duty.

A prospective juror can be excluded for legal reasons if the judge, prosecution, or defense can demonstrate that the venireman has characteristics that would jeopardize her or his ability to serve impartially. For example, a potential juror may be related to or acquainted with one of the trial participants or may have particularly strong feelings about some aspect of the case. Courtroom rules in Indianapolis also allow each attorney 10 *peremptory challenges*. Attorneys may use peremptory challenges to remove potential jurors without providing a justification. The number of veniremen interviewed to arrive at a trial jury in the trials included in the study ranged from 15 to 41. The average number of potential jurors called was 25.

Sex and race ratios for persons selected as jurors were

---

*In *Williams* v. *Florida* (1970), the U.S. Supreme Court held for the first time that a 6-person jury did not undermine the jury's essential functions. However, 6-person juries are still rare in criminal cases. All the sexual-assault trials included in this study were heard by 12-person juries.

similar to the ratios of those examined as jurors. Thus, white women were most likely to appear as potential jurors as well as actual jurors, while black men were least likely to appear as potential or actual jurors. White women constituted 41.4 percent of all the jurors in the trials in our study, white men accounted for 40.1 percent, black women for 12.9 percent, and black men for the remaining 5.5 percent. The relatively small number of blacks in Indianapolis had obvious consequences for both the proportion of blacks on juries and the number of juries that altogether excluded black women, men, or both. On the average, each jury included five white women and five white men. By contrast, 6 trials (15.8 percent) included no black women, and 20 trials (52.6 percent) included no black men. In 13 trials, only one black woman was on the jury, and in 12 trials only one black man served.

Participation of blacks on juries stood in stark contrast with their courtroom participation as crime victims and defendants. Thirty-nine percent of the victims and 44 percent of the defendants in these trials were black.

After the official jury is impaneled, and potential jurors who were not selected are cleared from the courtroom, the judge reads the trial instructions. These instructions vary, but in the trials we observed they typically included definitions of key legal concepts like "reasonable doubt," a general summary of the jury's responsibility in criminal cases, and specialized information requested by the prosecution or defense, such as the admonition that the U.S. legal system does not require the defendant to testify and that jurors should not hold it against the defendant if he does not. It is difficult to estimate the impact of these instructions on the jury. However, for the trials we observed, the judge frequently read through the instructions so rapidly that they were difficult even for our veteran trial observers to follow, suggesting to us that the instructions probably had a minimal impact on these cases.

Opening Statements. Following the judge's instructions to the jury, first the prosecutor and then the defense attorney make their opening statements. In some cases, judges in the trials we observed limited the total length of each side's opening statement—usually to 20 minutes. Prosecution and defense attorneys generally used the opening statement to preview their cases. Often attorneys mentioned key witnesses and evidence and what they hoped to prove. One common strategy we observed in the opening statement was for the prosecution or defense to mention information that the other side was planning to introduce in the trial—a strategy aimed at reducing the impact of this information on the jury when it was later presented in open court.

Case Presentation. Following the opening statements, the actual presentation of each case begins. The prosecution always goes first. In the cases we studied, the victim was usually the prosecution's first witness. In six (15.8 percent) of the trials, victims were on the stand less than 30 minutes. By contrast, one victim testified for more than two and one-half hours. In about 75 percent of the cases, however, the victim's testimony lasted from 30 to 90 minutes.

The order of questioning for both prosecution and defense witnesses passes from one side to the other. The original questioning of a witness is called *direct examination*. The opposing side is then allowed to *cross-examine* the witness. The side that called the witness may then do a *redirect examination*, and the opposing side may in turn do a *recross-examination*.

Besides the victim, the number of other witnesses called by the prosecution in these trials ranged from 1 to 15. The average number was 4.5, and the modal number was 5. At least one police officer testified for the prosecution in every case we observed. As noted in Chapter 4, police play an important role in the selection of criminal defendants from start to finish. In 34 (82.9 percent) of the cases, the prosecution introduced a witness who testified about the victim's condition following the incident. Medical doctors testified in 21 (51.2 percent) of the cases—usually about their examination of the victim following the assault. Other types of prosecution witnesses included eyewitnesses, other women who had allegedly been assaulted by the defendant, and various types of experts (e.g., ballistics specialists, polygraph examiners).

Exhibits are introduced by both sides through the testimony of witnesses. The number of exhibits introduced by the prosecution in these cases ranged from zero to 60. The average number was 9.1 exhibits. The most common type of prosecution exhibit was photographs of the victim, introduced in 19 (46.3 percent) of the cases. Given the fact that the time between the incident and the trial was typically 6 to 18 months, photographs were often important for providing a record of the severity of injury to the victim. Police lineup photographs of the defendant were introduced in 37 percent of the cases and other defendant photographs in 34 percent of the cases. The latter were most often used to demonstrate that the defendant did not look the same in the courtroom as he had earlier, presumably to suggest that the defendant was trying to present himself in a more favorable light in the courtroom. Recovered weapons, results of medical exams, and various types of physical evidence (e.g., torn clothing, defendants' possessions recovered at the scene) were each introduced in about one-third of the cases. Other types of prosecution evidence included maps and diagrams of the crime scene, official police reports, and grand jury testimony. In contrast to the Hollywood image of police as scientific crime fighters employing a full range of high-technology methods, specialized laboratory tests and sophisticated crime-scene analyses were rare. Even fingerprints, long a staple of police television shows, were introduced in only one case during the three years of our trial observations. Defense attorneys, playing on expectations from television, frequently used this fact to suggest that the state's case was weak or halfheartedly prepared.

After the prosecution rests, the defense begins its case. A major difference between prosecution and defense presentations is that the defendant, unlike the victim, does not always testify. The defendant's protection against self-incrimination is guaranteed by the Fifth Amendment to the Constitution. Nonetheless, 31 (75.6 percent) of the defendants charged in these cases took the stand in their own defense. The average length of the defendant's testimony was shorter than that of victims. Of those defendants who testified, 17 (57 percent) were on the stand for less than 30 minutes; 10 defendants were on the stand for 30 to 60 minutes and only 3 were examined for more than 60 minutes. These facts—that defendants do not always testify in rape trials and that when they do testify, their testimony tends to be shorter than that of the victim—reinforce the courtroom impression that it is the victim rather than the offender who is really on trial.

Another difference between victims and felony defendants is that many of the defendants are in custody awaiting trial. Twenty-seven (65.9 percent) of the defendants in our study were being held in jail at the time of the trial.

In general, the defense in our cases presented fewer witnesses than the prosecution. This reflects the differing burden of proof for the prosecution and the defense in criminal cases. It is the prosecution's job to build a case, whereas the defense generally concentrates on refuting the case that is built. In seven (17.1 percent) of the cases, the defense presented no witnesses. The average number of defense witnesses was 4.2, but the modal number was only one. The most common type of defense witness was a relative or friend of the defendant. Spouses or girlfriends were included as defense witnesses in 15 (36.6 percent) of the cases and relatives other than the spouse in 23 (56.1 percent). These witnesses most often testified about the defendant's whereabouts at the time of the incident, his condition following the incident, or his moral character in general. In addition to the testimony of relatives and friends, nine witnesses were included by the defense as character witnesses and nine as alibi witnesses. In nine cases, the defense included a witness who saw the victim and defendant together socially or suggested that they had had sexual relations prior to the assault. Police were called to testify by the defense in seven cases.

On the average, the defense also presented fewer exhibits than the prosecution. In 24 (58.5 percent) of the cases, the defense presented no exhibits. The average number was 1.7 exhibits. The most common type of defense evidence presented was official transcripts from police incident reports or grand jury testimony. These exhibits were most often used to demonstrate inconsistencies between the courtroom testimony of prosecution witnesses and their earlier official statements. The defense introduced transcripts as evidence in seven (17.1 percent) of the cases. Other defense exhibits included photographs of the scene where the defendant was arrested, results of the medical examination of the victim, and signed statements by the defendant indicating that he had been elsewhere at the time of the offense.

After the defense rests its case, the prosecution and then the defense are allowed to call any *rebuttal* witnesses—

witnesses introduced to explain, contradict, or disprove facts given in evidence by the other side. In most cases neither side offered any rebuttal witnesses, and in the few remaining cases only one rebuttal witness was typically presented.

Closing Arguments. Trials are concluded with the closing arguments of the prosecution and defense. The prosecution always presents its argument first and in most states, including Indiana, is allowed a rebuttal statement following the defense's closing argument. Prosecuting attorneys frequently tell jurors that the reason the prosecution gets the last word in criminal trials is that their burden of proof is greater than that of the defense. Final arguments usually summarize each side's perceptions of the evidence, what it has demonstrated about the case, and what the other side has failed to demonstrate about the case. Because this is the last opportunity for both sides to influence the outcome, closing arguments often include the most carefully worded and eloquently delivered parts of the trial. Following the closing arguments, the judge issues a set of final instructions to the jury, and they are then charged with reaching a verdict.

THE STRUCTURE OF INDIANAPOLIS RAPE TRIALS: TWO CASE STUDIES

To better illustrate the sequence of courtroom events in rape cases, in this section I summarize in some detail two rape cases that are part of our Indianapolis jury data. While using fictitious names, I have tried to remain as faithful as possible to actual courtroom events. The summaries are based on detailed notes taken in the courtroom by myself and another observer. The case summaries should also serve as a reminder that issues and theories in criminology ultimately describe the experiences of real victims, suspects, and legal agents. As you read through these two cases, pay particular attention to differences in what happens in the two trials: questions asked, evidence presented, types of witnesses who testify, strategies used by prosecution and defense. Also remember that things unsaid or undone may also be important. For example, what types of questions are asked in one trial but *not* asked in the other? What types of witnesses appear in one trial but *not* in the other?

The Case of Wendy Yates

Crime Setting and Major Trial Participants.   Wendy Yates was an 18-year-old white woman. She was picked up one night by two men while hitchhiking home from her boyfriend's house. She later identified the men as 35-year-old Lester Wallace and 34-year-old George Hammond. Wallace was a single, white male, and Hammond was married and in the courtroom appeared to be Hispanic, although his actual ethnicity was never specifically mentioned. Wallace was charged with rape and criminal confinement and Hammond with criminal confinement only. Wallace was in jail at the time of the trial and Hammond was out on bail. During a recess, we learned from Hammond that Wallace had also been out on bail but had recently been rearrested on a theft charge.

The state was represented in the case by two men: a veteran deputy prosecutor and a law-student intern. The veteran wore a fashionable three-piece suit. He was tall and appeared to be comfortable in the courtroom. His intern seemed young—in his middle to late 20s. The intern was thin, had short hair and a mustache, and wore glasses in the courtroom. He frequently leaned over to whisper to the veteran prosecutor during the trial—apparently for advice. During a recess, the intern told us that he gets "scared shitless," but then "so does F. Lee Bailey." This was his first rape trial. In general, his attitude toward the prosecution of the case did not inspire much confidence. He told us that he was embarrassed to use words like "penetration" and "vagina" in public. He also told us that he preferred to get trial experience in the prosecutor's office rather than as a defense attorney because he didn't feel so bad if he lost cases as a prosecutor—at least his clients didn't go to jail. Despite his obvious lack of experience with rape prosecution, the intern handled most of the case. However, the veteran helped with jury selection and did the cross-examinations and the final rebuttal in closing. On the second day of the trial the veteran prosecutor was late, and the intern had to start without him.

Three defense attorneys were present for the entire trial—
one for Wallace and two for Hammond. Only one of Hammond's attorneys conducted all the examinations and courtroom presentations. Wallace's attorney was dressed in a three-
piece suit, was of medium height, and appeared well groomed.
Hammond's active attorney was in his late 50s and was wearing a conservative dark suit. He was balding, with no facial
hair; a short man, slightly paunchy. Both defense attorneys
seemed well prepared.

When the intern for the prosecution read his opening
statement, he appeared to be nervous and unsure of himself—
almost like a student reading a class paper. Opening statements by both the prosecution and the defense were brief.
The defense attorney for Wallace made it clear during his
opening statement that the defense would be that the victim
consented.

Testimony of Wendy Yates. Wendy Yates was the
first witness for the state. She had long, blonde hair and was
wearing a red leather jacket over a vest and shirt, open at the
neck. Both observers noted that she was "pretty." She spoke
with a slight southern accent and did not use slang, profani-
ties, or incorrect grammar in the courtroom. During the prosecutor's questioning, she stated that she was hitchhiking
from her boyfriend's house on the night of the incident. She
was offered a ride by the two defendants, who were driving a
pickup truck. She accepted their offer and climbed into the
middle of the truck's front seat, with one of the defendants on
either side of her.

She testified that shortly after she got into the truck,
Lester Wallace grabbed her thigh. She said that she tried to
get out the door but was pushed back by Hammond. The defendants told her that if she cooperated she would not get
hurt. The defendants drove her to the back of a bowling alley
in downtown Indianapolis and ordered her to take her boots
and pants off. She testified that the defendants were passing
a "silver object which resembled a knife" back and forth between them. The defendants next drove to an apartment complex. They had walkie-talkies in the truck. After parking the
truck, Hammond got out and Wallace forced her to have sexual intercourse. She said that while this was happening, she

started screaming and then "broke loose." She claimed, "I didn't care if they pulled my hair out. I was going to get away from them." She testified that the defendants then threw her clothing out the truck window. She ran to a nearby house and knocked on the door. When a man answered, she told him that she had been raped. She called the police, and an Officer Demaio arrived shortly afterward. When the police returned to the apartment complex where the incident had taken place, they found Lester Wallace still in the pickup truck. George Hammond had fled.

At this point the judge ordered a recess. While we were sitting in the courtroom, we overheard Yates telling the intern prosecutor that she was afraid of the defense attorney's cross-examination. The intern told her that the state had filed a motion under Indiana's rape shield law, which prohibits the defense from asking questions about her past sexual conduct. He also advised her to pause after each question to allow the prosecution time to object.

After the recess, the defense attorney's first question in the cross-examination was, "How do you usually get around town?" Yates answered, "Hitchhike, bus, cab, friends, or my grandfather." Then he asked her where her boyfriend was living at the time of the incident. She replied that her boyfriend lived seven miles away from her home and that she spent a lot of time at her boyfriend's house. On the day of the incident she had gone to his house while it was still daylight. She left between 11:00 P.M. and 1:00 A.M. and could not get a ride.

Defense attorney:

Was it common for you stay in your boyfriend's house overnight?

Yates:

When it was cold out.

Defense attorney:

Did you have any money on you this particular night?

Yates:

No, if I would have had any money, I would have taken a cab or a bus.

Defense attorney:

Did you use the normal hitchhiking method, your thumb?

Yates:

Yes.

The defense attorney then asked Yates at what point either defendant had started talking about sexual intercourse. Yates answered, "After he [Wallace] grabbed my leg." The defense attorney asked whether the defendant "bruised you when he grabbed your leg." She said, "No." The defense attorney introduced into evidence a map of the neighborhood where Yates lived with her grandparents. He asked whether she had ever asked the defendants to let her out at her house. She said she had not. He then asked her why she had not yelled or tried to get out when she was in the truck with the defendants in the back of the bowling alley. She said she had been too scared. The defense attorney then asked how long she has been dating her boyfriend. She said, "About a week — about a week or something like that."

Wendy Yates remained composed during the entire trial, unlike many of the other sexual assault victims we observed. She occasionally looked at a young man in the courtroom, who appeared to be her boyfriend. The young man had long hair, and one of our courtroom observers characterized him as a "loser." The only other spectator who seemed to be on Yates's side was an older woman, perhaps her grandmother. However, the older woman was present in the courtroom for only a few minutes during the second day of the trial. During a break in the defendant's testimony, Wendy Yates asked us what we were doing. When we told her that we were studying trials, she replied, "Good, I'm glad someone is getting something out of this." One of us responded, "You don't seem very hopeful." She answered, "I'm hopeful they'll get what they deserve."

After Wendy Yates's testimony George Hammond's mother asked us if it had been obvious that Yates was lying. Apparently it was obvious to her and she was searching for a more objective source to confirm her view. Hammond's mother said, "I raised that boy right. He wouldn't do something like that. If I ever thought he could treat a woman like that. . . ." She seemed very upset and walked away. A few minutes later, she appeared to be crying in the courtroom.

Other Prosecution Witnesses. The next prosecution witness was a doctor, a resident in gynecology-obstetrics who examined Wendy Yates after the incident. The medical examination had shown bruises on her neck and the presence of sperm in her vagina. During the cross-examination of this witness, the defense attorney showed that the medical exam had indicated no evidence of bruises on Yates's breasts or legs. He also established that she was on birth control pills at the time of the incident. He then asked the doctor if Yates "had been engaging in other sexual acts." The prosecutor objected to the question; the judge sustained the objection and admonished the jury to disregard it.

Defense attorney:

Was there any evidence that the vagina was ripped?

Doctor:

No, it was normal.

Defense attorney:

There were no tears in the cervix, is that right?

Doctor:

Yes.

Defense attorney:

You knew that she was claiming that there had been a sexual problem?

Doctor:

Yes.

The defense attorney was careful not to refer to the incident as "rape" during his cross-examination of Wendy Yates.

The prosecution next called the man from whose house Yates telephoned the police following the incident. He was a sales representative for a pharmaceutical company, married, with two children. He stated that on the night of the incident, he could tell that "whoever was knocking on the door was in trouble." He described Yates as wearing no socks, shoes, or coat and observed that her pants were unzipped—despite the fact that it was January in the Midwest—and noted that she was "crying and hysterical." He added, "I was stunned to the point where I could not react." He stated that she asked him if she could call the police. He let her in and then recovered her clothing from in front of his house. The police came shortly afterward.

In the cross-examination, the defense attorney pointed out that Yates's clothing was not recovered in the parking lot, as Yates had earlier testified, but from in front of this witness's house. The defense attorney then suggested that Yates's knock on the door did not awaken the witness's sleeping wife and that the witness had heard no screaming prior to Yates's knock on his door.

In the redirect examination, the prosecutor showed that the incident had indeed awakened the witness's wife and that it was the wife who had told the witness to let Yates in. The witness reiterated, "All I could get out of the conversation was that she had been raped, she was hysterical, and she asked to call the police."

The state's next witness was Deputy Sheriff Demaio, who was originally dispatched to investigate the case. He testified that:

> . . . she was extremely upset. Mascara was smeared all over her face. She was messed up to the point where she was almost incoherent.

When Demaio took Yates back to the scene of the crime, she saw Wallace and started screaming. Demaio testified that Yates told him that she had been hitchhiking and had been picked up by two men in a truck. When he arrived at the scene, Demaio observed a pickup truck and a man ducked down inside of it. Yates began yelling, "That's the truck!" He said that Yates was trying to lie down on the seat of the police car so that she could not be seen by the man in the truck and that she was hysterical.

The state's fourth witness was another deputy sheriff. He also responded to the police dispatch, although he was off duty at the time. When he searched the defendant's truck, he found two walkie-talkies. He found no knife at the scene.

The state's fifth witness was a sergeant for the Sheriff's Department, a large woman in her mid-30s. She talked to Yates at the hospital on the night of the incident. She was assigned to investigate the case and had testified in the grand jury hearing that led to the indictment. When she took Wendy

Yates's statement, she found out that the defendants were communicating with walkie-talkies during the assault.

The state's last witness identified himself as a "forensic serologist." He testified that the tests for sperm and seminal fluid were positive. In the cross-examination, the defense attorney established that sperm survive in the vagina for an average of three days. Thus, the sperm identified could have been from sexual intercourse that had taken place prior to the incident. The witness also testified that he had not tested for "fingernail scrapings" or "pubic markings" because he had not been asked to do so. After the testimony of this witness, the prosecution rested.

Defense Witnesses.   Defendant Lester Wallace was the first witness to testify for the defense. He was wearing a blue jean jacket and pants with an open shirt and no tie. He had medium-long hair, a beard, and a mustache. His actions in the courtroom seemed very slow, almost as if he were under the influence of tranquilizers. This impression was heightened by the fact that his eyelids appeared to be nearly closed during his testimony. Wallace claimed that when he and George Hammond offered Wendy Yates a ride, she told them that she was a "runaway" juvenile and that the police were looking for her. He said that he, Hammond, and Yates then began smoking marijuana together. He asked Yates whether she had a boyfriend, and she told him she didn't.

Defense attorney:

   Did you touch her?

Wallace:

   No, I didn't.

Wallace testified that they drove past Yates's house twice on the night of the incident and then went to a parking lot in back of a bowling alley.

Wallace:

   She had made it plain that she would go along with sex, [but] she did not want to have sex with both of us. She said that she did not like dark places. So we went to this bowling alley parking lot because it was lit.

Defense attorney:

Did she ever indicate that she wanted to get out of the truck?

Wallace:

No. I helped her remove her boots. She took her pants and pant-ies off. She used my coat for a pillow.

Wallace claimed that Yates never told him to stop after they began to have sexual intercourse, that he never held a knife on her, and that he never used a walkie-talkie to communicate with Hammond in the presence of Yates. He testified that when she did get out of the truck, she yelled, "Give me my clothes!" Wallace claimed that he never grabbed her and that when she fled, he noticed that his coat—which had his wallet in it—was missing. He claimed that by the time the police drove up, George Hammond had already left because he "didn't want to get involved." Wallace said that he was ducking down inside the truck when the police arrived because he was trying to hide "a bag of pot." When the de-fense attorney asked him why he didn't take Yates back to his apartment to have sex, he answered, "Because she was a runaway and I could not trust her." The only thing that he and Hammond passed back and forth was a "joint." He testified that there was no plan to rape Yates, that he "did not force himself on her," and that he did have an orgasm. Af-ter Wallace's testimony, the defense attorney looked at the jury and said, "I think the jury understands what happened" —implying that there could be no question about the validity of the testimony.

The jurors were clearly observing Wendy Yates through-out the trial, but especially during the testimony of the two defendants. It appeared that they were trying to gauge the credibility of the defendants' testimony by watching Yates's reactions to it.

In the cross-examination, the prosecutor asked Wallace how he knew that Wendy Yates wanted to have sex with him.

Wallace:

It's not so much what she said, but the way she was acting. She didn't say she wanted to have sex with me. [But] she was pretty agreeable about going home with me. George said it wasn't a good idea, that we shouldn't trust her. I can't remem-ber the conversation word for word after ten months. The apartments [i.e., the scene of the crime] were well lit—like she wanted.

The prosecutor then asked the defendant if he frequently picked up hitchhikers.

Wallace:

I pick up every hitchhiker I see.

Prosecutor:

Have you ever picked up a single woman who wanted to have sex before?

Wallace:

No.

Prosecutor:

Wasn't this a bit unusual?

Wallace:

Under the circumstances, I suppose so.

Prosecutor:

Did she ever touch you or fondle you?

Wallace:

No.

The prosecutor then asked how it happened that George Hammond came back to the truck just as Wallace was refastening his pants, if the two had not used walkie-talkies to communicate. Wallace answered that it was "just accidental."

George Hammond, the codefendant, was next to testify. He was wearing a shiny white and black shirt, open at the neck. He had shoulder-length black hair and no facial hair. He was unusually short. He never specifically stated his ethnicity, but at one point said that at times he had "been mistaken for a Hispanic." He claimed that when he had a beard (which he had had at the time of the incident), he "sometimes scares people." Hammond appeared to be working hard to answer questions. Several times he volunteered information without being asked a question. At these times the defense attorney asked him to be quiet.

Hammond claimed that he left work at 9:30 P.M. on the night of the incident. Lester Wallace was his employee, and they were both working at a job in Ohio installing floors. He was sleeping in the truck when Wallace stopped to give Wendy Yates a ride.

Hammond:

> She never told us which house she lived in. She never said she wanted out. She told us that she was a runaway and that she didn't want to go to juvenile [court]. She said that she wanted to have sex with Lester. She said that she was afraid of the dark, so we went to a bowling alley parking lot. We saw a security guard there, so we left and drove to the apartments. Wendy said, "How are we going to do this with all three in here?" So I got out of the truck and walked around for about a half-hour. When I came back to the truck, Wendy said "she had to pee" and asked me to take her to the bathroom. But when I started to do this, she screamed, "Give me my clothing!" and then ran. At no point from the time she got into the truck did I touch her in any way. After she left, I started the truck. I was scared. I didn't want to be in any trouble. Lester realized that his jacket was missing, and he went back to look for it. I walked to a friend's house, called my wife, and told her that I wouldn't be home that night. The next day I called the Sheriff's Department.

The defense attorney established that Hammond had called the police several times after the incident and had made no effort to leave town. Hammond also testified that he was a member of a CB (citizens' band) radio club that was affiliated with a local police department.

In the cross-examination, the prosecutor asked Hammond if he understood the charge against him and realized that he faced a prison term. He asked Hammond if he wanted to go to jail. He then asked him about his relationship with Wallace.

Hammond:

> Technically, he worked for me. I paid him wages.

Prosecutor:

> So, if you thought this was a bad idea, you could have told him so and gone home to your wife?

Hammond noted that he had "a wife and family and I've invested too many years to lose it on something like this." Hammond claimed that Yates ran because she was afraid of him—afraid that he wanted to have intercourse with her. But he said that he had had no such intention.

On redirect examination, the defense attorney asked:

Defense attorney:

Did you smoke marijuana?

Hammond:

Yes, all three of us did. She wanted to know if we could get her some cocaine. I don't mess with it. I don't know where to get it. Lester offered her pot.

In the recross-examination, the prosecutor asked:

Prosecutor:

If she wasn't going to get hurt, why did she jump out into the snow without any shoes on her feet?

Hammond:

I think she jumped out because she thought I wanted to have sex with her. She was not crying when she got out of the truck. . . . She had time to put her clothes on, I don't know why she didn't.

During a recess, we talked to defendant Hammond. He said that the veteran prosecutor in the case was really good. He told us that he was very scared, but had been more afraid "until I realized that nothing was going to be said but words." He said, "As long as I tell the truth, I will be all right." One of us asked Hammond how his family and friends had reacted when he was charged with the crime. He said that at first he didn't want anyone to know, but then decided to tell the truth. He said that his family and friends were supporting him.

The only other defense witness was a young woman who used to date Wallace. She testified that she had met Yates at a party at her house the night before the incident. She said that Yates's boyfriend was a relative of hers. The testimony was brief and established only that someone who knew one of the defendants had met Wendy Yates shortly before the incident.

Closing Arguments and the Verdict.   After a recess, the closing arguments began. The intern prosecutor presented the first argument, and the veteran presented the final rebuttal. The intern began by thanking the jurors for their attention. Most of his closing argument consisted of a summary of the elements of the crime and observations on the credibility of the witnesses.

Prosecutor:

> What does Wendy Yates have to gain? If she were going to lie, why didn't she say that George Hammond did more? This was no boyfriend–girlfriend spat. She was scared, she was afraid. She was hysterical.

The prosecutor described Yates as someone "who does dumb things because she is young."

The intern read most of his final statement and was obviously nervous. He did not seem professional, and it was difficult to keep in mind that he was describing a very serious crime. Near the end of his argument, several of the jurors appeared to be bored.

The two defense attorneys presented separate closing arguments. The attorney for Hammond went first. He emphasized to the jury that his client had to be considered separately from Wallace.

Defense attorney:

> George Hammond is a married man, a father of two children. He lives with and supports his wife. His wife is employed and has been for five years. The last six years he has been a subcontractor on his own. The only arrests the man has had have been for traffic tickets.

Wallace's attorney then gave his closing argument. He suggested that there were some things about the case that "we'll never know." For example, why had Wendy Yates hitchhiked home? What was the connection among Wendy Yates, Lester Wallace, and the defense witness who testified that she had dated Lester and had met Yates at a party? He claimed that Yates's story just didn't make sense. He argued that Hammond was not interested in sex with Yates because he was already married. He suggested that Yates stole Wallace's jacket and that was why she was scared.

Defense attorney:

> It was 12:00 at night, a 17-year-old girl is hitchhiking, she got into a truck. She had a boyfriend for all of one week. She was at his house. The whole thing was an escapade. They got together and decided that there was going to be sex that night.

There was nothing that Wallace or Hammond testified to to indicate that anything happened by force. There was nothing abnormal here. There was no physical force from that night. If there was a master plan of rape, why go to a bowling-alley parking lot? I can't believe anyone would be raped in a bowling-alley parking lot. Where did they park in the apartment complex? Way in the back? No way. Rape at knifepoint 30 feet from a major highway? Why didn't they take her back to their place? Why didn't Wendy Yates call her grandmother if she was so worried? She's a hitchhiker. Seventeen years old. Tuesday night. Twelve midnight and she is hitchhiking. I don't know what this means. Maybe when they smoked the marijuana cigarette they were feeling loose. They didn't force this girl to do anything she didn't want to do.

The rebuttal argument for the prosecution came next. The veteran prosecutor began by noting that either the victim or the defendants were lying and asked the jurors to "start from there." He noted that the deputy sheriff who saw the victim after the crime and the man from whose house she telephoned the police had both testified that she had been crying and hysterical. The prosecutor argued that although the victim was stupid for hitchhiking, this was no excuse for rape. He compared rape cases to robbery cases noting that a robbery victim is not expected to fight off the attacker.

The prosecutor specifically challenged several of the defense arguments. He pointed out that although there was no concrete evidence of force, a rape victim does not have to "get herself stabbed to demonstrate that force has been used." He noted that if Yates had really been free to get dressed, she would have done so, because it was extremely cold. The fact that the police had not found a knife did not mean that there had not been one. After all, the men installed flooring, and "how could they lay linoleum without a knife?"

Prosecutor:

Hitchhiking is not something you or I would do—but a 17-year-old may not have enough sense not to. I did foolish things when I was younger. Any woman has the right to say no—the wife of Eli Lilly [the pharmaceutical giant, whose headquarters is in Indianapolis] or a 17-year-old hitchhiker. You wouldn't let a burglar go free because the door was not locked. Don't let a rapist go free because a 17-year-old is too dumb not to make herself an easy mark.

The prosecutor's final argument was one of the most well reasoned and dramatic that we observed during the entire study. However, its effectiveness was probably marred by the fact that he ran out of time. The judge in this courtroom limited closing arguments to 20 minutes for each side. At one point the judge interrupted the prosecutor to tell him that he was "four minutes over time." This interruption seemed to make the prosecutor nervous, and he soon brought his summation to a close. The judge offered final instructions to the jury and ordered the bailiff to escort the jurors to the deliberation chamber. Less than 30 minutes later, the jury acquitted both defendants on all counts.

The Case of Kim Russell and Terry Chan

Crime Setting and Major Trial Participants. Kim Russell was a 35-year-old Asian-American woman. She moved to the United States in the early 1970s and spoke with a heavy accent. She was married, with two children—a 10-year-old daughter and a 7-year-old son. She had worked at a local restaurant, the Oriental Inn, for the past two years. Terry Chan was Kim Russell's 18-year-old niece. Terry had been living with the Russell family for four years. On the night of the incident, two friends of the Russell children were also spending the night. Kim Russell testified that she and her husband, Steve, were awakened early in the morning by two men wearing ski masks and gloves. They immediately bound her husband's hands and feet. One of the assailants forced Kim Russell to have sexual intercourse, and afterward the second forced her to have anal intercourse. One of the intruders then brought Terry Chan into the Russells' bedroom, and each of them had sexual intercourse with her. Terry Chan and Kim and Steve Russell all claimed in court that they recognized the voice of one of the assailants as belonging to the boyfriend of a sister of Kim Russell's best friend. The defendant, John Bates, was arrested shortly after the assault and charged with two counts of first-degree rape and one count of burglary. The victims were unable to identify the voice of the second assailant and no other defendants were ever arrested.

John Bates was a white male in his mid-20s. The police

arranged a voice identification lineup that included Bates and five other men. Terry Chan and Steve Russell picked out Bates's voice, but Kim Russell identified someone else. Bates claimed that he had been at home with his girlfriend, Cynthia Martin, and their baby at the time of the incident.

The state was represented at the trial by the chief prosecutor of Marion County and one of his deputies. Although the chief prosecutor sat at the prosecution table during most of the trial, his deputy presented the case. She was in her mid-40s, was well dressed, and seemed personally involved in the case. In her opening statement, she stressed that both the defendant and the state had the right to a fair trial. She explained to the jury that voice identification was going to be an important part of the state's case and emphasized that all three of the victims recognized the defendant's voice as the higher-pitched of the two assailants' voices. She noted that while Kim Russell had been unable to pick out the defendant's voice in the voice lineup, the other two victims had correctly identified the defendant. She concluded, "We are talking about someone breaking into a house and raping people in the presence of others."

The defense attorney claimed in his opening statement that at the time of the incident, John Bates, the defendant, had been at home with his girlfriend and their child.

Defense attorney:

> Of course what they say happened, and won't be challenged. It's a distasteful story . . . disgusting. It will move you—it has already moved you. You may have forgotten your oath for a minute. You may have looked at the defendant and thought: "How could he have done that?" That's only natural.

Testimony of Terry Chan and the Russells. Kim Russell was the first to testify for the state. She said that she was awakened early in the morning by two men wearing ski masks and gloves. One of them told her, "Don't make any noise." She testified that she and her husband were told to roll over on their stomachs. Then "the man with the higher voice" told her to "stand up beside me." He tied her hands, put tape across her eyes, and pushed something into her mouth as a gag. He told her to be quiet or he would hurt the kids. Russell could hear one of the defendants going through her bedroom cabinets. She testified that "the tall guy" then said, "I'll fuck you." After using this language in the courtroom, Russell apologized and began crying. She explained, "I was worried about my kids, so I didn't say anything." She said that the lower-voiced man climaxed and then the higher-voiced man walked to the bed and had anal intercourse with her. At one point the lower-voiced man asked the higher-voiced man if he had a knife. He said that he did. The lower-voiced man took the knife and cut off some of her pubic hair. After this happened, she heard someone else come into the bedroom crying, who at first she thought was her daughter or son but who was actually her niece. She then heard one of the assailants say, "Steve, hurry up," and one of the men asked her, "Where are your [car] keys?" She told the assailant that the keys were in her husband's pocket when they could not find them in her purse.

She testified that she heard the car leave and then untied herself. She asked her niece if she was all right and then untied her husband. She testified that she recognized the higher-voiced man as soon as he said, "Steve, be quiet." She thought, "Oh my God, he knows my husband." She stated that she had known the defendant—the higher-voiced man—for almost two years and explained that she worked at the Oriental Inn with his common-law wife. They had been at her house recently for a Thanksgiving party.

Russell had listened to six people in the lineup two or three times, but had not identified John Bates. She testified, "I wanted to listen one more time, but they said no."

The defense attorney then began his cross-examination.

Defense attorney:

Were you scared at the time of the incident?

Russell:

I was so scared, I almost peed in the bed.

The defense attorney asked her if she had correctly identified John Bates's voice in the lineup, and she repeated that she had not.

Defense attorney:

Did that surprise you?

Russell:

No—I had wanted to hear once more.

She testified that the man with the lower voice was the taller man. She said that John Bates's voice was different—he talked "smart." "He talks different than other people." The defense attorney pointed out that in Russell's original statement to the police, she had said that the voice of the assailant "sounded like John Bates"—not that "it was John Bates."

In the prosecutor's redirect examination, Russell testified that John Bates had spoken with her husband at a recent Thanksgiving party at her home. The prosecutor pointed out that the defendant had already been arrested for the crime before the lineup. Hence, Russell would have known he was in the lineup because she knew he had been arrested. This line of questioning was clearly an attempt by the prosecutor to counteract the defense's efforts to imply that there was something improper about a lineup in which the victim knew one of the suspects in advance, apart from the crime.

Terry Chan, Kim Russell's niece, was the second witness for the state. She testified that on the evening of the incident, she and her boyfriend had been at the Oriental Inn, where she worked with her aunt. She returned with her boyfriend to her aunt and uncle's home at about 11:00 P.M., and her boyfriend left the house at 1:00 A.M. She was awakened late at night by a man who told her to go to her "parents'" bedroom. The fact that the assailants did not know that Chan was not the Russells' daughter might suggest that they did not know the Russell family, but this issue was never raised in the courtroom. After entering her aunt and uncle's bedroom, Chan felt something metal against her neck. She could not see her assailant's face, but she testified that he was about 5 feet, 8 inches tall and weighed about 140 pounds. She was ordered to sit on the floor. The assailant put tape over her eyes and mouth and tied her hands behind her back. He then picked her up and took her inside a walk-in closet in the bedroom and removed her nightgown.

Chan:

He told me to be quiet, then he raped me.

Prosecutor:

What do you mean?

Chan:

> He put his penis in my vagina.

Prosecutor:

> Did he climax?

Chan:

> I think so.

At this point, Chan started shaking and crying. The prosecutor asked her if she "wanted the man to do what he did." Several seconds passed and she did not answer. The judge called a recess.

When testimony resumed, Chan stated that next the second assailant came to her, said, "Let me have it," and raped her. She testified that this man "had a higher voice." She then heard the higher-voiced man say, "I can't find the keys." Later, she heard the front door open and the screen door shut.

Chan:

> Then I untied myself and my aunt opened the door. The police took me to the hospital.

Chan stated that she recognized the voice of the higher-voiced man: "I was sure it was someone I knew."

Prosecutor:

> Are you certain that the voice was that of the defendant?

Chan:

> Yes, I'm positive.

She spoke this last sentence with determination, as though there was no doubt in her mind. She explained that she met the defendant, John Bates, through a girlfriend of hers. She had known him for "a year or so" and had seen him the week before the incident. She said that she often talked with him when he came to pick up his girlfriend at work because "he usually brought the baby and I like babies." She claimed that she had spoken with him about seven or eight times before the incident. She said, "I remember the voice of the person when I got raped and it was that voice."

During the cross-examination, the defense attorney asked Chan if the lower-voiced man's voice was lower than his own.

Chan:

Maybe lower, I don't remember.

Defense attorney:

Did the higher-voiced man have a voice higher than mine?

Chan:

Not high-pitched, but higher than yours.

Defense attorney:

Would you recognize the defendant's voice if he called on the phone?

Chan:

No.

Defense attorney:

If he were in the same room?

Chan:

Yes.

Defense attorney:

Have you ever heard the defendant's voice with something covering his mouth?

Chan:

No.

Defense attorney:

Were you scared?

Chan:

Yes.

The defense attorney's general strategy during this line of questioning appeared to be aimed at showing that Chan had simply picked out the voice of someone she had known prior to the incident.

The defense attorney next asked Chan how she judged the height of the assailant. She answered that the lower-voiced man was standing next to a bedroom dresser and she saw the higher-voiced man in the doorway. She could judge the height of the men by comparing them to the height of other objects in the room.

Defense attorney:

Are you sure about the heights of the men?

Chan:

Not positive.

The defense attorney noted that in her original police statement, Chan had given only a five-pound difference in weight between the two assailants.

The next prosecution witness was Steve Russell, Kim's husband. He was a high school graduate employed by the local Chrysler auto manufacturing plant. He appeared to be about 40 years old. He had short hair and was wearing a brown three-piece suit. As he walked to the witness stand, he took a deep breath; he seemed nervous. He testified that his name was not on the house or the mailbox—which is relevant to the prosecution, because the assailants used his name during the assault. He stated that the front door was locked on the night of the incident and that there was a dog in the front yard. His two children and their two friends went to bed around 10:30 P.M., and he and his wife retired shortly afterward. He said it was 4:00 in the morning when he was awakened by a flashlight shining in his eyes. He saw the time on the clock radio by the bed. A voice told him, "Steve, be quiet, you don't want to wake the kids."

He testified that his hands and feet were bound with ties and his eyes taped shut. One of the assailants said, "Where is your money?" He told them that if he had any, it would be in his trouser pockets. After looking through Steve Russell's wallet, the lower-voiced assailant said, "Only $10. They have to have more money than this." The intruders started "rummaging through drawers." They found a coin bank with $50 or $60 and savings bonds worth $1,500 and $2,000. They also asked Steve Russell if he had a gun, and he told them he did not. Then he was gagged. He testified that he could hear two distinct voices, one lower and one higher.

Steve Russell stated that after the assailants finished searching the room, he heard the lower-voiced man say to his wife, "Okay, we're going to fuck you. You don't want to wake the kids." Looking down as he testified, Steve Russell stated that the bed was moving "with a motion like sex." There was a pause as one of the intruders replaced the other, then the motion of the bed started again. He testified that the lower-voiced man asked the higher-voiced man if he had a knife, and the higher-voiced man said that he did. He did not hear his wife's niece being brought into the bedroom.

After the assailants fled, Steve Russell got one hand free and pulled the tape from his eyes. It was approximately 5:00 A.M. His wife eventually managed to get free of the bindings and then helped him get untied. He found that one of the telephone cords in the house had been cut. He called the police on another telephone, and they arrived in about 20 minutes. When he examined the room, he found that his savings bonds, a money bank, the money in his pants, his car keys, two packs of cigarettes, and a lighter were gone. The main entrance to the living room was open, and a screen had been removed from a front window.

Steve Russell testified that he recognized the voice of the higher-voiced man. He had known the man for about a year and a half and had seen him on about 10 occasions. He said that the defendant had been at his house for a Thanksgiving party about six months before the incident and that he had had a lengthy conversation with him.

Steve Russell:

> I recognized the voice, but I was trying to talk myself out of it. When the higher-voiced man made another statement, I knew who it was.

He was unable to describe the appearance of the assailants: "The flashlight was in my eyes, I was told to turn over and was bound immediately." In the voice-identification lineup, he heard six white males repeating phrases that the victims remembered from the night of the incident. He identified John Bates's voice.

Prosecutor:

> Do you have any doubt that John Bates was one of the intruders?

Steve Russell:

> No doubt at all.

In the cross-examination, the defense attorney asked Steve Russell about discrepancies between his testimony in court and his earlier statement to the sheriff. He had told the sheriff that he "only saw the one with the flashlight." Now he was saying that he meant that "he only saw the light." He explained that parts of his original statement were inaccurate because "I was shook up. The sheriff tried to get me to relax, but that is hard to do." The defense attorney commented, "So, you are explaining the discrepancy by saying that you were shook up?"

Steve Russell said that the lower-voiced intruder's voice was lower than the defense attorney's and the higher-voiced intruder's voice was higher. The higher-voiced man's voice was also "shaky—he may have been nervous."

Defense attorney:

Is there anything distinctive about John Bates's voice?

Steve Russell:

It's not high or low. I just recognize it when I talk to him.

Defense attorney:

When did you tell the sheriff that you were positive?

Steve Russell:

Between 7:00 and 8:00 A.M.

Steve Russell testified that four of the six voices in the lineup had been very similar in pitch. He said that he had not discussed the identity of the defendant with his wife or her niece before the voice-identification lineup. The defense attorney then asked why he had wanted to hear the voices twice— obviously trying to show that Steve Russell had not recognized the assailant's voice the first time through and was merely identifying the voice of someone that he had known prior to the incident. Counsel for the defense and the prosecution began arguing at this point; the prosecution apparently objected to the suggestion that Steve Russell had not recognized the voice the first time through. The judge banged her gavel and warned, "Both of you, please watch your mouths." After a couple of moments of uncomfortable silence, the defense attorney again asked Steve Russell why he had had to hear the voices twice.

Steve Russell:

I didn't change my pick.

Defense attorney:

You had to hear it twice.

Steve Russell:

> I heard it twice.

Defense attorney:

> Are you telling the jury that John Bates's voice is unlike any voice you've ever heard?

Prosecutor:

> I object.

Judge:

> Objection overruled.

Steve Russell:

> I'm saying that I recognized a voice in the lineup as the voice of the man in my house.

Defense attorney:

> You already knew the defendant's voice?

Steve Russell:

> Yes.

Defense attorney:

> You could separate that?

Steve Russell:

> I recognized his voice on the night that it happened.

Other Prosecution Witnesses. The state's next witness was a fingerprint expert who also took photographs of the Russells' home. He testified that Kim Russell's car was recovered at about 7:00 the following morning. He reported that he "dusted [the car] for latent fingerprints and found one." He found no latent fingerprints in the victims' residence. He also gathered the neckties used to bind the victims, the duct tape used on the victims' faces, and samples of hair found at the scene. In addition, he recovered duct tape from John Bates's car. However, none of this evidence—fingerprints, hair samples, or duct tape—linked John Bates to the scene of the crime. Near the end of his testimony the witness pointed out that it is impossible to get latent fingerprints from people who are wearing gloves.

The next state witness was a 19-year-old woman who testified that at the time of the incident she was living in a house with a group of people that included John Bates, his common-law wife Cynthia Martin, and their child. She had known the defendant for about three and a half years. His girlfriend worked at the Oriental Inn. The witness testified that on the night of the incident she went there with Bates to pick up Martin. They returned home at 12:30 A.M. Bates and Martin went to bed. The witness testified that she was in the room next to theirs. She said that sometime between 2:00 and 4:00 in the morning she heard a "loud car" coming from "either my house or across the street." She said that the neighbors later told her that they hadn't heard anyone leave her house. The defense attorney objected to this as "hearsay" because the neighbors referred to were not testifying. The judge sustained his objection. The witness said she heard noises coming from Bates's room: "It sounded like a sliding screen. It had to be their room." She said that she heard another car between 5:15 and 5:30 A.M. She noticed the car because it sounded like it had no muffler. That morning, Bates's alarm rang "longer than usual." When Bates left the house for work, "he didn't want coffee right away—he usually does." "He didn't look sleepy—his eyes are usually red when he gets up." The witness also testified that there was a window in the defendant's room large enough for a man to crawl through. She said she did not hear anyone coming in or going out the doors of the house on the night of the incident.

During the cross-examination, the defense attorney asked the witness whether she could hear very well with the stereo on and the fan in her room running.

Defense attorney:

Can you look at this jury and tell them it was John Bates's car?

Witness:

I never said that.

The attorney then asked her about the other noises she heard.

Witness:

I heard a noise that could have been a sliding screen. That was the only thing that would sound like that.

Defense attorney:

And if a window were being opened. . . .

Witness:

It would sound totally different.

The witness then acknowledged the possibility that Bates's apparent alertness on the morning after the assault could have been caused by a good night's sleep rather than by being up most of the night.

The next state witness was a woman who worked for an auto sales company that had sold a car to the defendant and his girlfriend shortly before the attack on Russell and Chan. When Bates and Martin missed some payments, the witness sent an agent out to repossess their car. Bates returned with the agent and made a $20 payment—the day after the assault and burglary. The state was clearly trying to provide a motive for the burglary here.

The next state witness was the investigating officer, a sergeant who had worked for the Indianapolis Police Department for 16 years. He said that when he arrived at the "crime scene," Kim Russell and her niece were at the hospital. He talked to the husband. He asked Steve Russell if he could make a positive identification of the assailants. Steve Russell told him that he could not, because they were wearing masks. However, he said, he recognized the voice of one of the men as the boyfriend of his wife's best friend's sister. This man had called him "Steve."

The detective stated that when he interviewed Kim Russell and Terry Chan, both said the assailants were wearing ski masks, dark clothes, baggy trousers, and gloves. Both women were "quite shaken," and he couldn't get them to give an exact height for either of the assailants. Both women said that they thought they knew one of the men by his voice.

The detective testified that at the voice-identification lineup, Steve Russell had identified John Bates. After Bates was moved to a different position in the lineup, Terry Chan had also identified him. Kim Russell had identified someone else, a man who was being held in jail in connection with another case.

The defense attorney next questioned the detective about tests done on the pubic-hair samples recovered at the scene. The detective said that because such a large quantity of hair had been recovered, it would not have been "practical" to test all of it, so no tests had been conducted. (Although it was never made clear, this may have been why the assailant cut off some of Kim Russell's pubic hair.)

The detective stated that he had driven the route from the Russells' house to where their car was recovered, to John Bates's house, and back to the Russells' house, taking into account the time necessary "to change cars." He estimated that it would have taken the defendant less than 25 minutes to make the round trip.

The detective had obtained permission to search the defendant's home from the defendant and the owner of the home. The window in the defendant's bedroom had a sliding screen. The detective, who was a big man with a large belly, told the jury, "Even I could fit through."

During the cross-examination, the defense attorney asked the detective if he had conducted any experiments to determine whether he could hear the screen window opening from the other bedroom.

Detective:

No. I don't think I knew that another witness had heard the screen slide.

Defense attorney:

What about hearing a car?

Detective:

If the music wasn't loud, there is no doubt that she could have heard.

After the testimony of the detective, the prosecution rested.

Defense Witnesses. The first witness for the defense was 40 years old, married, with a family. He owned a small business. He testified that he had known the defendant for about a year. He lent John Bates $20 dollars to make a car payment. He said that he would have been willing to lend Bates more, because Bates always paid him back. The defense was obviously introducing this witness to show that the defendant got money for his car payment from a friend and not from a burglary of the Russell home.

John Bates was next to take the stand. The defense attorney began with questions about Bates's background. Bates was 23 years old and unmarried, though at the time of the incident he was living with Cynthia Martin, the mother of his child. He explained that he "grew up in town," attended three high schools, and graduated in 1975. He served in the Army Reserve and, from 1975 to 1977, in the Army. He was employed at a local lumber yard until his arrest. He had been in jail for the past six months, awaiting trial. Bates said that he believed he was facing 60 years in jail for the charges against him. The deputy prosecutor objected. The defense attorney claimed that this answer was relevant to the defendant's credibility. The judge overruled the objection. During a recess, the deputy prosecutor told us, referring to Bates's statement about the length of prison time he was facing, "It doesn't go to his credibility, it just gives him more reason to lie."

John Bates said that he didn't know where Cynthia Martin and his baby were. He lost contact with them after he had been in jail for three weeks. He testified that he voluntarily turned over a knife he owned to the police when they asked for it and that he gave the police permission to search his car and house.

The prosecutor began her cross-examination with a question about Bates's girlfriend.

Prosecutor:

How long have you known Cynthia?

Bates:

Three years.

Prosecutor:

But you lost track of her while you were in jail?

Bates:

Yes.

Prosecutor:

Isn't that her in the last row [of the courtroom]?

Bates:

I can't be sure—it looks like her.

Prosecutor:

You're not sure? Stand up and take a look.

Bates:

(Standing up) Yes, that's her.

The prosecutor appeared to be trying a couple of things with this line of questioning. First, by having Bates suggest that he had lost track of his girlfriend and then showing that the girlfriend was in fact in the courtroom, she might have been trying to show that the defendant was not above stretching the facts. Second, the prosecutor also seemed to be trying to demonstrate that Cynthia Martin was still around and that there might have been some reason—damaging to the defense's case—for her not testifying on Bates's behalf.

The prosecutor next asked the defendant about his money problems. He testified that at the time of the incident, he owed $295 on his car. He said that he had borrowed $25 from a friend (the previous witness) for the remainder of the down payment. He claimed that the $20 dollars he paid for the down payment on his car came from his girlfriend's restaurant tips. (In fact, Bates's friend had testified earlier that he lent Bates $20 for the car—not $25. The discrepancy in amounts was never cleared up in court.) The prosecutor tried to demonstrate that the defendant was having serious financial problems at the time of the incident. Presumably, this strategy was aimed at providing a motive for the burglary of the Russell home. At a later point, the prosecutor claimed that Bates bribed the man who came to repossess his girlfriend's car and that Bates was a serious gambler. Bates responded that he only played "penny-ante poker" and never lost more than a dollar or two. He claimed that he and Martin spent their money on clothes or "going out"; they had "just gotten back together" and "wanted to have a good time." In a quick change in the direction of her questions, the prosecutor next asked Bates if he could fit through his bedroom window.

Bates:

I don't know, I never tried.

Prosecutor:

Do you understand that the penalty for these charges is 20 to 50 years?

Bates:

Yes.

Prosecutor:

And that the actual sentence is up to the judge?

Bates:

Yes.

Prosecutor:

Do you think this is a serious crime?

Bates:

Definitely.

The prosecutor next asked Bates about his relationship with the Russell family. He said that they were "casual acquaintances" and that he had been at their home once. He added that he bore no ill feelings toward them, even though they had identified him as the assailant.

Prosecutor:

Do you resent the fact that the Russells took care of your baby when you and Cynthia separated?

Bates:

No.

This last issue, about the Russells having taken care of Bates's baby, was never raised again. It seemed that the prosecutor raised this issue to try to demonstrate what an evil person Bates was: this was how he repaid people who had helped him out. But like many issues in trials, this one remained ambiguous.

The prosecutor's questioning of Bates was much different from her questioning of the other witnesses. She often asked him questions quickly and changed the line of questioning abruptly, apparently in an attempt to uncover a lie or a half-truth or to provoke some type of verbal misstep by the defendant. In rapid succession, the deputy prosecutor asked Bates about what type of car he drove, how loud it was, and what kind of uniform he wore at work. He described his car and the mechanical difficulty with it that accounted for its loudness. He described his work uniform as a pair of blue pants and a shirt. He added that his name and the name of the company were embroidered on the shirt.

As the prosecutor neared the end of her cross-examination of the defendant, she began to ask even faster, shorter questions, and she appeared to be angry:

Prosecutor:

Isn't it a fact that, not content with robbing that family, you raped Mrs. Russell?

Bates:

No.

Prosecutor:

Oh, that's right. It was the lower-voiced assailant who raped her. You only tried anal sodomy.

Bates:

I wasn't there. I was home.

Prosecutor:

With Cynthia—your lover.

Bates:

Yes.

After the cross-examination of the defendant, the defense rested its case and the judge ordered a short recess. Out in the hallway, we heard one of the defendant's female relatives say that she would have been scared had someone talked to her like the deputy prosecutor had talked to Bates. Her companion, another relative of the defendant, said, "I hope she [i.e., the prosecutor] can't sleep at night." And the first relative responded, "Well, that's her job."

Closing Arguments and the Verdict. Following the recess, the prosecution presented its closing argument. The deputy prosecutor began by thanking the jurors for their attentiveness—a standard remark in the closing arguments we observed. She then reviewed all three of the charges against the defendant and summarized what she considered to be the evidence supporting each charge. She mentioned the measures the Russell family had taken to secure their home. She stressed that the victims were asleep in their own house. She described vividly to the jurors the horrifying experience of Steve Russell, who could "feel the movement of the bed," but was unable to do anything to help. As she continued, Kim

Russell—who was in the courtroom—began crying. Her husband handed her a tissue. The prosecutor swung toward the jury box and continued:

> Next, Terry Chan is told to go to her aunt's room. She sees a man 5 feet, 8 inches to 5 feet, 10 inches tall, wearing dark clothes and gloves and carrying a weapon. At the time, Mrs. Russell thinks that the assailants have her 10-year-old daughter.

By the time the prosecutor finished this part of her closing arguments, both Kim Russell and Terry Chan were sobbing uncontrollably, and they both rose and left the courtroom. The prosecutor paused a moment while the two women walked toward the exit and then picked up Kim Russell's nightgown, recovered from the night of the assault. Wheeling toward the jury, she said, "This is the nightgown that was violently ripped off." In her hands she had a plain flannel gown, with an obvious rip below the zipper. She continued:

> John Bates then said, "Let me have it." What could she do but "let him have it?" She was in fear for her life.

At this point, it is evident that Steve Russell is also quietly crying at the prosecution table.

The prosecutor continued:

> At first, Mr. Russell did not want to believe that it was John Bates, someone he knew, doing this to them. Terry Chan told police that she knew who it was but was afraid to say anything. Terry and Mr. and Mrs. Russell were taken to a police lineup. Not a normal one, but a hearing lineup. The cops never told them that John Bates was in this lineup. The husband picked him out. Terry picked him out. Mrs. Russell didn't pick him out. You heard her difficulty with the English language. They wouldn't let her hear the lineup again. Would you recognize the voice of someone speaking a foreign language?
>
> You heard the testimony of the woman who lived with John Bates and his girlfriend. She lives in Texas now, but came up here to testify. She knew the routines in that house. She heard a car and she heard the baby. She was so concerned about the baby that she went to the door. She heard the muffler again and she heard the alarm clock. She told you that it was unusual that Bates was so wide-awake in the morning. Usually

he is sleepy and wants coffee. But he had been up. This woman has no reason to lie. If she were going to come from Texas to lie, she would have given a better story.

Everybody recognized Bates's voice—they said it was shaky. Did you notice his voice on the stand? It was shaky. The defendant says he is 5 feet, 7 inches tall and weighs 130 pounds. That's pretty close. It's hard to judge under those conditions.

The prosecutor then said, "We don't know the other man because Bates won't tell." The defense attorney jumped up to object to this statement. The judge said, "Your objection is noted." The prosecutor concluded:

There is no question that these things happened. The thing we hold most sacred is the privacy of our own home, and especially our own bodies. You said in voir dire that you could convict on voice identification alone. These three people are sure. You said you would convict. It is your duty to say, "No. We will not tolerate an activity like this which violates us to the bone."

After the prosecutor finished her closing argument, the defense attorney rose from his seat and began by emphasizing that he too believed that the crime occurred and that it was truly despicable:

There is no doubt that these crimes occurred. No one wants his worst enemy subjected to something like that. These are absolutely disgusting crimes. I believe the crimes happened. That is not the issue. You have to decide who did these things. You have to decide if the state proved its case beyond a reasonable doubt. I know you feel sorry for the victims. I feel sorry for these people, too. I have a job to do. I am defending John Bates. As one of you said during voir dire, that is part of our criminal-justice system. You know that the defendant is presumed innocent until proven guilty. He doesn't have to prove it. We have done everything that is required by law, which is only for the defendant to show where he was at the time of the incident.

The defense attorney attempted to refute the state's case point by point. He focused especially on the voice identification of the defendant:

Let's look at the voice identification. First ask yourself, did the evidence indicate that the victims were in distress? Decide for yourselves how that would affect their ability to identify someone. It is my understanding that studies show people subjected to stress are less able to make accurate identifications. The identification of the assailant's voice was made under these conditions. The voice could have been distorted—he was wearing a mask. In their original statements, no one told the police that they knew it was the defendant's voice for sure. Mrs. Russell said that it was "not just like the defendant's voice." Mr. Russell said that "it sounded like a fellow named John Bates." Terry Chan said nothing about the identity of the assailants in her statement.

So then they arrest John Bates and have a lineup. You have to get into the victims' minds. They already know John Bates's voice. Mr. Russell said that he recognized the voice when the assailant had said, "Steve, be quiet." In the lineup, the defendant is asked to say, "Steve, be quiet." But Mr. Russell doesn't immediately identify him. Why didn't he immediately identify him, like he said he could? As to Mrs. Russell, if she hadn't been told that she identified someone else's voice, she would still think she had identified the defendant. And Terry Chan identified John Bates, but she had the least opportunity to hear the assailant. She was in the closet in a most stressful situation. It is unfair of me to use that against her, but it's true.

The defense attorney next claimed that the state witness who used to live in the same house as John Bates and Cynthia Martin and testified about the noises she heard on the night of the incident was "biased" and was trying "to manipulate the jury":

> The state brought her up from Texas. In her original statement, she only said that she heard a loud noise—she never said that she heard the scream. She wants you to believe that she just remembered, but that is preposterous.

The defense attorney argued that the defendant was not the kind of person who would have committed these terrible crimes. He asked the jury, "Did you hear anything which suggests that he is capable of these terrible acts? Does he have a record of prior convictions for anything?"

The defense attorney also challenged the prosecutor's argument about the significance of the defendant's "shaky" voice while testifying:

> You've observed differences in my voice, too. It's natural, due to tension.

The defense attorney claimed that the only real evidence was the voice identification. He said that the police lab tests were negative, or the state would have introduced them. He said:

> The prosecutor will try to convince you otherwise. She wants to believe she's right—it makes her job easier. She will come at you hard. She wants you to believe that John Bates did it. She will be sincere—you may be swayed. I never wanted to prosecute. People think it is because I'm a knee-jerk liberal, but that's not true. I wouldn't want to be a prosecutor because I would someday have to prosecute a case like this one.

The defense attorney then reminded the jurors of a recent local case in which a priest was put on trial for a crime committed by someone who resembled the priest:

> Five people identified him—they were sure. Where would he be today if the guilty man hadn't confessed? This isn't TV—people don't confess.

The defense attorney's last words were a plea:

> Think of the most important decision you've ever made—a life-and-death situation. Think about the things you've done in the last 20 years—the joys and even the sorrows. All those life experiences could be taken away from John Bates. The evidence demands acquittal.

The deputy prosecutor then presented her final rebuttal. She argued that "the defense attorney is making a big deal out of discrepancies in height and weight, but no one measures the man who is raping them." She claimed that the state did produce a description that provided a "ballpark figure" for the assailant's height and weight. She reiterated that the victims were absolutely sure that they recognized the defendant and that two of the three were able to pick him out of the voice-identification lineup. She concluded:

> What do we have? The voice identification. I wish we had more. But the victims know it was John Bates. . . . They identified Bates because he did it. No one is asking you to convict an innocent man. Consider the nature of the crime and the horrendous pain and hurt that this family will have to live with all their lives.

After brief instructions by the judge, the jury was sent off to reach a verdict. After four hours of deliberation, they found the defendant guilty on all three counts: two rape charges and one burglary charge. In a hearing two weeks later, John Bates was sentenced to 30 years in the state penitentiary.

Evaluating the Cases

I began this chapter with a discussion of the conflict-theory argument that legal agents use the law in rape cases to control the behavior of women who have behaved nontraditionally. Wendy Yates is a clear example of a woman whose gender-role behavior affected courtroom proceedings. She is young and unmarried. There are allegations that she drinks, uses drugs, and has sexual relations with her boyfriend. The alleged assault happens after she hitchhikes and accepts a ride from two men. The assault occurs late at night and away from her residence. Note that a good deal of Yates's testimony, especially on cross-examination, is really about her life-style and behavior.

By contrast, Kim Russell is 35 years old, married, with two children. There are no allegations that she drinks excessively, uses drugs, or engages in extramarital sexual relations. She is assaulted in her own home by strangers. Her niece, Terry Chan, is the same age as Wendy Yates. However, no evidence is introduced to show that she drinks, uses drugs, or is sexually active.

Despite the fact that the defendants in the two trials face similar charges, the cases are completely different in terms of the focus of courtroom events. Compared to the Russell/Chan case, the Yates case includes much more testimony directed at the characteristics and behavior of the victim. For example, the defense attorney in the Yates case claims that Yates had sex with other men, that she was using birth control at the time of the incident, and that she led the defendants to think that she wanted to have sex. The defense also claims that she is a drug user and leads a hedonistic and largely unsupervised life. In recognition of the probable importance of the victim's prior behavior to the case, the prosecution files the rape shield law in the Yates case. And like the defense, the prosecution tends to focus on Wendy Yates rather than on the defendants, arguing that Yates was foolish for hitch-hiking and that, like many young people, she does some crazy things.

No such allegations are made about the victims in the Russell/Chan case. In fact, the only portion of the defense that deals directly with the behavior of the victims concerns the adequacy of their identification of the defendant. In this context, the defense argues that the victims could not see the assailants well enough to identify them and that they had made an honest mistake in the voice-identification lineup. The prosecution does not file the rape shield law in this case and asks few questions about the victims' background characteristics, behavior, or life-styles.

After these two cases are examined closely, it seems safe to conclude that what *doesn't* get said in the courtroom is as important as what does get said. Throughout the trial in the Russell/Chan case, the underlying issue for both the defense and prosecution appears to be the identification of the defendant. There is no direct testimony about the victims' behavior or moral character. By contrast, throughout the trial in the Wendy Yates case, the underlying issue appears to be the victim's moral character and the implications it has for her credibility.

The two trials also have more general implications for the longstanding debate in criminology about the nature of crime. Recall that one of the arguments against labeling explanations of crime is that there is widespread societal agreement that mala in se crimes like rape are serious offenses requiring punishment. But how useful was this fact to you in evaluating these two rape cases? Did you find that all the issues in the trials were satisfactorily resolved? Or did you find yourself developing your own "theories" of what really happened in the two cases? If you were examining statistics on rape from this jurisdiction, would it make sense to exclude the Yates case? Was Wendy Yates a victim of rape? According to police statistics, she was. The police apprehended a suspect and cleared the case. According to court statistics, however, she was not. The jury acquitted the defendants. Are you convinced that the correct man was identified in the Russell/Chan case? Was John Bates a rapist? Would it make sense to include John Bates but exclude George Hammond and Lester Wallace in a study of criminal etiology?

If you feel uncertain about these questions, you are not alone. The presiding judges in both cases disagreed with the verdict reached. The judge in the Wendy Yates case claimed that he would have convicted the defendants if he had heard the case as a bench trial. He further told us that the case was easy to comprehend, and he thought the jurors had let their sentiments about the victim enter into their verdict. By contrast, the judge in the Russell/Chan case said that she would have acquitted the defendant if she had heard the case as a bench trial. After voir dire, we overheard the judge telling the deputy prosecutor that she was surprised that many of the potential jurors said they were willing to convict on the basis of voice identification alone. Following the trial, the judge told us that a voice identification alone was "simply not sufficient" for a guilty verdict.

While detailed case studies are useful for illustrating the complexity of cases, they do not permit us to reliably identify more general patterns in the processing of cases. In the next chapter, I consider in detail the legal differences between the jury trials in our study and I examine the variables that the jurors used in arriving at their verdicts.

CHAPTER 8

Jurors' Responses to Victims' Behavior in Rape Trials

Rape is something awful that happens to females: it is the dark at the top of the stairs, the undefinable abyss that is just around the corner, and unless we watch our step it might become our destiny.

Susan Brownmiller, *Against Our Will.*

In cases where identification is not an issue, consent becomes important. These cases are reasonably easy. The parties will have known each other—will have been together, drinking, dancing. I try to point out to the jury that even if she did change her mind, it was in the middle of the act.

Indianapolis defense attorney.

Modern psychiatrists have amply studied the behavior of errant young girls and the women coming before the courts in all sorts of cases. Their psychic complexes are multifarious and distorted. . . . One form taken by these complexes is that of contriving false charges of sexual offenses by men. The unchaste mind finds incidental but direct expression in the narration of imaginary sex incidents of which the narrator is the heroine or the victim. . . . The real victim, however, too often in such cases is the innocent man; for the respect and sympathy naturally felt by any tribunal for a wronged female helps to give easy credit to such a plausible tale. . . .

John Henry Wigmore, *Evidence at Trials at Common Law.*

Comparisons of the Wendy Yates and Russell/Chan cases in the last chapter suggested that allegations about the moral character and background characteristics of rape victims can have major effects on jurors' verdicts. Feminists and conflict theorists have argued that rape laws are applied to punish women who violate traditional gender-role norms. In this chapter I use the Indianapolis jury data described in Chapter 7 to examine this argument more systematically. I begin by looking at the relationships between rape victims' behavior and jury verdicts and then consider the reactions of individual jurors to rape cases.

VICTIMS' BEHAVIOR AND CHARACTERISTICS AND JURY VERDICTS

A necessary starting point in an analysis of how rape victims' gender-role behavior affects verdicts is to develop operational definitions of traditional and nontraditional behavior. My colleagues and I developed a list of nontraditional behavior inductively, after observing many rape trials. Our list included (1) drinking, either in general or at the time of the incident, (2) using drugs in general or at the time of the incident, (3) engaging in sexual activity outside of marriage, (4) having illegitimate children, and (5) having a reputation as a "partier," a "pleasure seeker," or someone who stays out late at night. Our courtroom observers coded these types of behavior whenever testimony made it "highly probable" in the minds of both observers that they applied to the victim. We were not interested in proving conclusively that the rape victims in our study had engaged in any of these particular types of behavior, but rather in establishing that courtroom testimony had suggested it as very likely. At least one of these behaviors was attributed to women in 24 (58.5 percent) of the trials.

Table 8.1 summarizes relationships among allegations of victims' nontraditional behavior, trial outcomes, and selected victim and case characteristics. Compared to other cases, women in cases in which nontraditional victim behavior was alleged were likely to be younger (under 21 years old) and unmarried. A majority of the rapes against women who had allegedly engaged in nontraditional behavior took place at night (8:30 P.M. to 6:30 A.M.), away from the victim's residence. By contrast, relatively few of the cases in which the

TABLE 8.1   Victim Behavior with Trial Outcome and Victim and Case Characteristics

| | Victim Behavior | | | | |
| | Traditional (N = 17) | | Nontraditional (N = 24) | | |
Variables	N	%	N	%	Sig.[a]
Victim < 21 years old	2	11.8	10	41.7	.073
Black victim	7	41.2	9	37.5	NS
Marital status					
Married, widowed	8	47.0	1	4.2	
Divorced	3	17.6	6	25.0	
Not married	6	35.3	16	66.7	.006
Victim, offender acquainted	9	52.9	10	41.7	NS
Time and place of assault					
Night (8:30 P.M.–					
6:29 A.M.), at home	8	47.0	4	16.7	
Night, away from home	3	17.6	16	66.7	
Day (6:30 A.M.–8:29 P.M.)	6	35.3	4	16.7	.008
Assault included a weapon	14	82.3	12	50.0	.073
Defendant testified	9	52.9	22	91.7	.013
Eyewitness testimony	5	29.4	1[b]	4.5	.092
Rape shield law invoked	1	5.9	12	50.0	.008
Guilty verdict	14	82.3	12	50.0	.073
Length of sentence (in months)	$\bar{x}$ = 43.38[c]		$\bar{x}$ = 27.83		.048

[a] Chi-square statistics are reported for all variables except length of sentence, which reports a means-difference test. Two-by-two tables were corrected for discontinuity.
[b] Data were missing for two cases.
[c] N = 14 because of acquittals.

victim was classified as traditional took place at night, away from her home.

Compared to other cases, cases in which the victim was alleged to have engaged in nontraditional behavior tended to be lacking several important types of evidence. For example, Table 8.1 shows that recovered weapons and eyewitnesses were both less common in cases where victim nontraditional behavior was alleged. Kalven and Zeisel (1966, p. 165) argue that in cases in which the evidence is weak, jurors may be "liberated" from following the evidence. They conclude that many of the disagreements between judges and juries about the verdicts in their study could be explained by this process. Thus, disagreement between judge and jury results because jurors' doubts about the conclusiveness of the evidence allow them to disregard the evidence and decide the case on the basis more of their personal values than of the facts. In a related part of our Indianapolis jury project, sociologists Barbara Reskin and Christy Visher (1986) applied this "liberation hypothesis" to the data on rape juries. In support of Kalven and Zeisel's findings, they conclude (p. 437) that in cases with weak evidence, jurors turn to other factors, such as the defendant's physical appearance or the victim's life-style, in reaching decisions.

In contrast to the other measures of victim and case characteristics, there was no significant difference between traditional and nontraditional victims with regard to the race of the victim or the victim–offender relationship. The finding of no relationship between victim's race and allegations of nontraditional behavior is important, given analysis from earlier chapters showing that sexual assaults against black women resulted in less serious punishment for offenders. The finding of no association between victim–offender relationship and victim's behavior may be explained here by the fact that several of the cases in which no allegations about the victim's behavior were made involved charges against family members of the victim. Because the defense cannot realistically argue that the victim consented in these cases, the cases generally include less information about the gender-role behavior of the victim.

Indiana's rape shield law was passed in 1975, before our study of Indianapolis rape trials began. Table 8.1 shows that the law's use was strongly dependent on allegations about the victim's gender-role behavior. Of the 13 times the rape shield act was invoked in these cases, 12 (92.3 percent) involved women who had allegedly engaged in nontraditional behavior. Somewhat paradoxically, these results also tell us something about the success of the rape shield law in keeping information about the victim's nontraditional behavior out of the courtroom. Recall that we recorded only evidence of nontraditional behavior that was presented in the courtroom within the hearing of the jury. Thus, another way to interpret these results is that the jury still heard testimony about the victim's nontraditional gender-role behavior in 12 of the 13 trials in which the rape shield law was invoked—including the Wendy Yates case reviewed in the last chapter.

Criminologists William Chambliss and Robert Seidman (1982, p. 315) describe *symbolic law* as a technique used by powerful groups to placate dissident groups who challenge the status quo (see also Edelman, 1964). The law is symbolic because it appears to be responding to a particular demand, but does not actually change the behavior it was meant to regulate. Of course, I have no way of knowing whether other information about the complainant's gender-role behavior—perhaps even more damaging—was effectively excluded by the rape shield law in Indianapolis. However, to the extent that the Indiana rape shield law was designed to keep any evidence of rape victims' nontraditional gender-role behavior out of the courtroom, it seems to be consistent here with the idea of symbolic law described by Chambliss and Seidman.*

The last two entries in Table 8.1 compare verdicts and sentences by victim behavior. Differences between victims portrayed as either traditional or nontraditional are not limited to case characteristics. Acquittals were more common and final sentences were shorter when nontraditional victim behavior was alleged.

LEGAL DEFENSES IN RAPE TRIALS

The Wendy Yates and the Russell/Chan cases summarized in Chapter 7 illustrated how different rape trials can be, depending on whether the behavior of the victim is a major issue in the trial. These considerations are central to the type

---

*Michigan's criminal sexual conduct law, passed in 1974, has probably been more exhaustively studied than any other statute prohibiting evidence of the victim's sexual history from being introduced in rape trials. In general, evaluations of the Michigan law (e.g., Marsh, Geist, and Caplan, 1982; Caringella-MacDonald, 1985, 1988) conclude that there were some important changes, especially in the nature of the victim's interaction with the criminal-justice system and the breadth of rape definitions, but, at the same time, more basic attitudes about rape and the position of women in society remained fundamentally unchanged.

of defense pursued in the trial. In general, the types of defenses available in rape cases are relatively few. To convict a defendant of a forcible-sex offense, the state's burden (Dow, 1985, pp. 134–141) is to show that (1) a *sexual act* occurred or was attempted, (2) the victim did not *consent* but submitted under force or imminent threat of force, and (3) the person charged is the perpetrator (i.e., correct *identification*). For acquittal, the defense must successfully counter at least one of these elements. Its only other recourse is to acknowledge the sexual assault but show that because of insanity or intoxication, the assailant legally has *diminished responsibility* for his act.

We may use the Yates and Russell/Chan cases here to illustrate. In both cases, the defense acknowledged that a sexual act had taken place and did not allege the defendant's diminished responsibility in either case. The key difference between the two cases involved the issues of consent and identification. In the Yates case, the defense conceded that the correct men had been identified, but claimed that the victim had consented. In the Russell/Chan case, the defense conceded that the incident was nonconsensual, but claimed that the wrong man had been identified.

Comparing cases like that of Wendy Yates and Kim Russell and Terry Chan raises more general questions about the relationship between the victim's gender-role behavior and the type of defense pursued. In the Yates case, where consent was an issue, nontraditional gender-role behavior on the part of the victim was alleged. In contrast, in the Russell/Chan case, where identification was the main issue, there were no allegations of victim nontraditional behavior. The relationship between the victim's nontraditional behavior and major defense for all the trials in the study is shown in Table 8.2.* Most strikingly, allegations about the victim's nontraditional behavior were *always* made when the major legal issue in the trial was consent and were *never* made when the major legal issue was the defendant's diminished responsibility. Allegations about victims' nontraditional behavior were about

---

*In six cases the defense disputed more than one case element. We classified these cases according to the element the defense emphasized.

TABLE 8.2   Victim's Behavior with Type of Defense

	Traditional	Nontraditional	
Type of Defense	N	N	%
Consent	0	12	100.0
Identification	7	8	53.3
No intercourse	3	4	57.1
Diminished responsibility	7	0	.0
Total	17	24	58.5

Chi square = 18.5; p = .0003.

equally likely in the no-intercourse and identification types of defenses: 57.1 percent for the former and 53.3 percent for the latter.

While these data show a clear relationship between which type of defense is used and whether the victim is portrayed as gender-role nontraditional, they do not permit us to determine which variable causes the other. That is, do attorneys choose a consent defense because of the victim's nontraditional behavior, or do they highlight the victim's nontraditional behavior in the courtroom only when the main issue is consent? My hunch, based on my observations of the processing of rape cases, is that both processes are at work. Thus, in general, women who behave in nontraditional ways are more likely to be in social situations in which a consent rape defense is a viable option. For example, given her age, family situation, and life-style, Wendy Yates was undoubtedly more likely than Kim Russell to be involved in a rape prosecution in which consent was the major defense strategy. To cite the obvious, not many 35-year-old married women with two children hitchhike.

However, once a defense strategy is selected, it definitely affects the information presented in the courtroom. For example, consider how the jury might have reacted to Wendy Yates if she had been raped under the circumstances described by Kim Russell. It seems less likely that the defense attorney would have attempted a consent defense, regardless of the victim's moral character or background. Indeed, as we observed in the trial in the Russell/Chan identification case, the attorneys asked few questions about the victims' background and moral character. Recall that Terry Chan testified that she had spent several hours late at night at home with her boyfriend prior to the assault. However, neither prosecution nor defense questioned her about this behavior. Nonetheless, it is easy to imagine a much different line of questioning had the major issue in the Russell/Chan case been consent.

In the final analysis, the most important issue in the trial—for the victim as well as the defendant—is the verdict. Hence the importance of the association between the victim's behavior and the type of defense has more practical significance if there is also a link between type of defense and verdict. Table 8.3 compares verdict and major defense for the rape trials in our study. The results show clearly that there is such a link. According to the table, 73.3 percent of the cases in which identification was the chief issue resulted in guilty verdicts, and 100 percent of the cases in which diminished responsibility was the major issue resulted in guilty verdicts. In contrast, 57.1 percent of the no-intercourse cases and only 33.3 percent of the consent cases resulted in guilty verdicts. Note that the relationship between victim's behavior and type of defense (in Table 8.2) closely parallels the relationship between verdict and type of defense. Consent defenses were most likely to include allegations of nontraditional victim behavior and were least likely to result in guilty verdicts. Diminished-responsibility defenses were least likely to in-

TABLE 8.3 Verdicts with Type of Defense

| | | Verdict | |
| | Not Guilty | Guilty | |
Type of Defense	N	N	%
Consent	8	4	33.3
Identification	4	11	73.3
No intercourse	3	4	57.1
Diminished responsibility	0	7	100.0
Total	15	26	63.4

Chi square = 2.6; p = .02.

clude allegations of victims' nontraditional behavior and were most likely to result in guilty verdicts. Identification and no-intercourse cases were between the other two defense types both in terms of the proportion that included allegations of nontraditional victim behavior and the proportion that resulted in guilty verdicts.

JURORS' EVALUATIONS OF RAPE CASES

So far my analysis in this chapter has been limited to data on entire juries. However, our study of rape trials in Indianapolis also included post-trial interviews with 360 jurors. These data on individual jurors allow us to examine in more detail the argument that victims' gender-role behavior affects official reactions to rape cases.

After observing many rape trials over several years, we came to realize that the four rape defenses identified above could be combined into two groups. Consent and no-sex cases are similar in that the major issue in both is the complainant's status as a victim. Thus, in the Yates trial, where consent is the major issue, most of the defense questions centered on Yates's credibility as a rape victim—that is, had she really been raped? Similarly, at the beginning of Chapter 1 of this book, I summarized the case of George and Frank Davis, who were charged with raping George Davis's stepdaughters, Sheila and Rachel. In this case the defense was that nothing had happened. However, as with the Yates case, the main issue in the courtroom was whether the two girls had actually been raped.

In contrast, whether or not the complainant is really a rape victim is seldom a serious issue in cases in which identification or diminished responsibility is the major defense.* Recall that neither prosecution nor defense in the Russell/Chan identification case ever questioned whether the complainants were rape victims. Instead, the defense centered on

---

*This division also distinguishes forcible-sex offenses from other felonies. While mistaken identification and diminished responsibility are routine defenses in other felonies, consent and no-intercourse defenses are unique to forcible-sex-offense cases.

whether the correct man had been identified. Similarly, in the Lloyd Jeffries insanity-defense case, summarized in Chapter 1, the defense attorney conceded that something terrible had happened to Martha Jones, but argued that Jeffries was insane at the time of the offense.

Differences in type of defense appeared to be so fundamental to actual courtroom events that we decided to explicitly include these distinctions in our analysis of jury verdicts. Hence, we did a separate analysis for those cases in which the defense questioned whether the complainant had been victimized (consent and no-sexual-contact cases) and those in which the defense acknowledged the victimization (identification and diminished-responsibility cases). To control for type of defense within the two analyses, we included a binary variable (coded 0 or 1) to distinguish consent from no-sex cases and identification from diminished-responsibility cases. As in earlier chapters, in order to determine what variables affected official decisions, we developed statistical models. In the next section I describe the variables included in these models.

Dependent and Independent Variables

The general goal in selecting variables for this part of the analysis was to include measures of victims' behavior and characteristics as well as variables shown by prior research to be important in official evaluations of rape. The variables are summarized in Table 8.4. The dependent variable is an individual juror's assessment of a defendant's guilt. Our questionnaire allowed jurors, in evaluating a defendant's guilt, to choose between more or less certainly innocent or guilty with a four-category dependent variable.

Jurors' Characteristics and Attitudes.   At the outset, we hypothesized that decisions in rape cases may depend on both victims' characteristics and legal agents' subjective reactions to cases. The latter vary in their acceptance of conservative gender-role norms, and researchers (e.g., Holmstrom and Burgess, 1978; Stanko, 1981–1982) have argued that agents' attitudes affect their reactions in rape cases. However, most research testing this presumption has been based on experimental subjects (Feild, 1978; Borgida and Brekke, 1985) or

TABLE 8.4 Variables, Coding, and Frequencies for Analysis of Indianapolis Rape Trials

Variables	Coding	Distribution N^e	Percent
Dependent Variable			
Juror's perception of defendant's guilt prior to deliberations	1 = Certainly innocent	47	13.8
	2 = Probably innocent	44	12.9
	3 = Probably guilty	119	35.0
	4 = Certainly guilty	130	38.2
Jurors' Characteristics and Attitudes			
Sex	0 = Male	159	46.8
	1 = Female	181	53.2
Race	0 = White	287	84.4
	1 = Black[a]	53	15.6
Age		Range = 20–74	
		Median = 42.14	
Occupational prestige	Hodge-Siegel-Rossi occupational prestige score	Range = 12–78 Median = 44.95	
Education		Range = 0–22 years Median = 12.62	
Prior jury service in last three months	0 = no	229	67.4
	1 = yes	111	32.6
Women's sex-role scale (see Appendix 8.1)		Mean = .21 SD = .41	
Women's social-sexual freedom scale (see Appendix 8.1)	High factor score indicates conservative sex-role attitudes	Mean = .28 SD = .45	

	High factor score indicates	Mean = .00[c] SD = .80
Anti-crime scale (see Appendix 8.1)	anti-crime attitude	
Victims' Characteristics and Behavior		
Race	0 = White[b]	222 (23)[c] 65.3
	1 = Black	118 (15) 34.7 (39.5)
Marital status	0 = Not mentioned or not married	273 (30) 80.3 (78.9)
	1 = Married	67 (8) 19.7 (21.1)
Drinks, uses drugs	0 = No or not mentioned	198 (24) 58.2 (64.9)
	1 = Mentioned in court	142 (13) 41.8 (35.1)
Sexual activity outside marriage or illegitimate children	0 = No or not mentioned	195 (23) 57.4 (60.5)
	1 = Mentioned in court	145 (15) 42.6 (39.5)
Defendants' Characteristics and Behavior		
Race	0 = White	208 (23) 61.2 (56.1)
	1 = Black	132 (18) 38.8 (43.9)
Criminal record	0 = No prior record or none mentioned	232 (22) 68.2 (53.6)
	1 = Prior record mentioned	108 (19) 31.8 (46.3)
Character (few ties, negative impression on jurors; see Appendix 8.2)	High factor score indicates few social ties, negative impressions	Mean = .01 SD = .80
Evidence and Case Characteristics		
Victim–defendant[d] relationship	0 = Acquaintance	176 (23) 51.8 (56.1)
	1 = Stranger	164 (18) 48.2 (43.9)

TABLE 8.4 (continued)

Variables	Coding	Distribution N^e	Percent
Weapon	0 = No	138 (15)	40.6 (39.5)
	1 = Yes	202 (23)	59.4 (60.5)
Eyewitness	0 = No	288 (32)	84.7 (84.2)
	1 = Yes	52 (6)	15.3 (15.8)
Number of criminal charges		Range = 1–8	
		Median = 2.08	
Victim injury	0 = No	177 (17)	52.1 (44.7)
	1 = Yes	163 (21)	47.9 (55.3)

[a] We coded the only juror who was neither white nor black as white.

[b] One victim was Japanese. Prior research (Chambliss and Nagasawa, 1969) has shown that officials react more favorably to delinquent Japanese students than to similar black students. Our courtroom observations suggested that this racial pattern was also probable with respect to rape victims. Because we expected reactions to the Japanese victim to be more similar to those for white than black victims, we coded this victim's race as white.

[c] Values in parentheses are frequencies or percentages of the 38 trials, except for the defendant-related variables, which are based on all 41 defendants to whom jurors responded. (Three trials had more than one defendant.)

[d] This variable is coded differently in consent and no-intercourse than in identification and diminished-responsibility cases in view of the differing implications of victim's acquaintance with defendant. In the latter cases, any acquaintance at all is coded 1, since any acquaintance is presumably sufficient to enhance the victim's ability to identify her assailant correctly. In the former cases, victim–defendant relationship was coded 1 when the victim and the defendant had met shortly before the assault only if they had spent some time together and could be said to be acquainted at the time the assault allegedly occurred.

[e] Because of missing data, analyses are based on 340 cases.

SOURCE: LaFree, Reskin, and Visher, 1985, pp. 394–395. © 1985 by the Society for the Study of Social Problems, Inc. Original version appeared in *Social Problems* 32:4 (1985). Used by permission.

general samples (J. Williams, 1979; Burt, 1980) rather than on actual participants in the criminal-justice system. While some researchers have directly examined the effects of respondents' attitudes (Feild, 1978; J. Williams, 1979; Acock and Ireland, 1981), others, perhaps on the assumption that personal characteristics ultimately influence attitudes, have looked at the effects of gender (Scroggs, 1976; Borgida and White, 1978; Feild, 1978), age (Scroggs, 1976; Calhoun et al., 1978), education (Feild, 1978; J. Williams, 1979), and occupational prestige (Sealy and Cornish, 1973; Feild, 1978). In general, results have suggested that jurors' gender-role attitudes are more important than their personal characteristics for understanding their perceptions of rape. For example, Kristen Williams (1976) has reported that the more gender-role-conservative white respondents are, the less likely they are to define vignettes as rape, and Hubert Feild (1978) has found that respondents who believe that women precipitate rape are less likely than others to characterize vignettes as rape.

Few researchers have examined the possibility that legal agents' gender-role attitudes come into play only if the victim violated gender-role norms to which agents subscribe. An exception is research by Alan Acock and Nancy Ireland (1981), in which they simultaneously examined both experimental subjects' gender-role attitudes and hypothetical rape victims' conformity to traditional gender-role expectations. The authors found no relationship between subjects' attitudes and victims' behavior, but their sample was composed of undergraduate college students and the range of victims' gender-role violations was relatively limited, so the findings may not apply to real jurors.

Based on juror responses to questions about their gender-role attitudes and attitudes toward crime, we created three scales (shown in Appendix 8.1 at the end of this chapter). The first two focus on related aspects of women's gender roles, which we construed as ranging from more conservative to more liberal. For example, jurors who strongly agreed with the statement "Although women hold many important jobs, their proper place is still in the home" were considered to be more gender-role-conservative. We included a measure of juror's attitudes toward crime to control for the possibility that general anti-crime attitudes rather than responses specific to sexual-assault cases were responsible for the results.

Victims' Characteristics and Behavior. As we have seen in earlier chapters, some theorists have argued that because women have been and are socially defined as men's sexual property, rape was originally and may continue to be construed as a property crime against men (e.g., Brownmiller, 1975; Clark and Lewis, 1977; MacKinnon, 1987) and that the responses of the criminal-justice system to rape defendants are influenced by the alleged victims' sexual-property status and value.* Hence, they predict more serious sanctions for men accused of raping married women and virgins. Historically, the law of torts allowed men to seek payment for sexual "trespass" against their wives (MacKinnon, 1979, pp. 169–171). However, research has shown both positive (Jones and Aronson, 1973; Feldman-Summers and Lindner, 1976) and negative (Sebba and Cahan, 1975, p. 33) effects of a victim's being married on the severity of the sanctions received by alleged assailants.†

A central concern in this chapter is to determine whether measures of the victim's gender-role conformity affect verdicts. We used two variables to measure the victim's confor-

---

*The assumption that society will sanction women who jeopardize their sexual-property value to their present or future husbands by overstepping traditional female gender roles links the sexual-property thesis to women's gender-role behavior. But no a priori bases exist to determine whether any effects of gender-role-nontraditional behavior result from sexual-property considerations or simply from a tendency for officials to treat as less serious those cases in which men are accused of raping women whose behavior violates conservative gender roles.

†Others (e.g., Clark and Lewis, 1977) have operationalized women's sexual-property value in terms of sexual desirability (measured by age and virginity) and social status (measured by economic class and race). Findings for a sexual-desirability effect are mixed (Jones and Aronson, 1973; K. Williams, 1976; Feldman-Summers and Lindner, 1976; Seligman, Brickman, and Koulack, 1977; Holmstrom and Burgess, 1978; Calhoun et al., 1978). Moreover, these findings can be interpreted without specifically invoking the sexual-property thesis (for example, people may simply view rape as more traumatic for teenage victims or virgins) and may not be specific to rape victims or even women (such as bias against unattractive complainants).

mity to traditional gender roles: (1) whether testimony showed that the victim drank or used drugs either in general or at the time of the incident and (2) whether testimony indicated that the victim had been sexually active outside marriage or had illegitimate children.

Defendants' Characteristics. Defendants' characteristics included in this part of the analysis were race and criminal record. We also included a scale that measures defendants' ties to the community and courtroom appearance. Variables that made up this scale were being unmarried, being childless, being unemployed, lacking a sexual partner, and presenting a negative appearance to jurors (see Appendix 8.2).

Evidence and Case Characteristics. On the basis of prior research (K. Williams, 1978; Holmstrom and Burgess, 1978; LaFree, 1980a, 1980b, 1981), we included five measures of evidence and case characteristics: victim–defendant relationship, whether the assault involved a weapon, eyewitnesses, or victim injury, and the number of criminal charges against the defendant. Our main interest in these variables was to determine whether other measures had an effect, controlling for differential strength of the evidence.

Analytic Technique

The statistically significant variables for both types of cases are summarized in Table 8.5 (for the complete results, see Appendix 8.3). As in earlier analyses, the variables are rank-ordered by the size of their standardized regression coefficients—that is, beta weights. Recall that because beta weights are standardized, we can compare them directly within the same equation. Thus, Table 8.5 shows that the measure of defendant's character was the best predictor of jurors' evaluations of his guilt (beta = .37) in the consent and no-sex cases. Next most important was the measure of courtroom allegations that the victim was sexually active (beta = − .34). Moreover, for the consent and no-sex cases, allegations that the

TABLE 8.5 Best Predictors of Defendants' Guilt in Consent and No-Sex Cases and in Identification and Diminished-Responsibility Cases

Consent and No-Sex Cases (N = 172)		Identification and Diminished-Responsibility Cases (N = 165)	
Variable	Beta	Variable	Beta
1. Defendant character	.37	1. Eyewitness	.40
2. Victim sexually active	−.34	2. Weapon	.37
3. Defendant criminal record	.26	3. Defendant character	.31
4. Victim drank, used drugs	−.22	4. Diminished responsibility	.27
5. Victim and defendant acquainted	−.16	5. Number of charges	.27
6. Victim black	−.14	6. Victim and defendant acquainted	−.26
		7. Defendant criminal record	−.21
		8. Victim injured	.15
		9. Jurors' attitude toward crime	.12
		10. Victim drank, used drugs	−.12

Note: All variables are significant at $p = .05$ except number 10 for the identification and diminished-responsibility cases, which is significant at $p = .07$.

victim was sexually active are more than twice as important for predicting jurors' reactions than whether the victim and defendant were acquainted (beta = − .16).

CONSENT AND NO-SEXUAL-CONTACT CASES

Victim Gender-Role Behavior

Our first concern in this part of the analysis was to determine whether measures of victims' gender-role behavior and moral character affected jurors' verdicts. Table 8.5 shows that six variables had a significant ($p < .05$) effect on jurors' assessments of defendants' guilt in the consent and no-sex cases. Three of these variables—victim sexually active, victim drank or used drugs, and victim and defendant acquainted—were directly linked to jurors' evaluations of victims' gender-role behavior and moral character.

Jurors were less likely to believe in a defendant's guilt when the victim had reportedly engaged in sex outside marriage, drank or used drugs, or had been acquainted with the defendant—however briefly—prior to the assault. In contrast, note that none of the evidence measures—weapon, victim injury, number of charges, eyewitnesses—had a significant effect on verdicts in the consent and no-sex cases. Our interviews with jurors were full of comments about the impact —both negative and positive—of the victim's gender-role behavior on their evaluations of cases. One white female juror noted that the complainant "was on birth control pills. She was experienced." A white male told us that:

> Maybe she wouldn't [have had sexual intercourse] if she hadn't been drinking and smoking marijuana. I think she was more carefree after that and that she just let it happen. I don't think she was sober enough to care.

Evidence of a good moral character also swayed jurors. One white male noted that the victim was "a baby sitter, which speaks to her moral character. She liked kids." A white female juror was impressed by the fact that the victim did not say the word "penis" in the courtroom. She claimed that this convinced her of the victim's "good character."

Jurors frequently used testimony about a victim's behavior both in general and at the time of the incident to reach conclusions about her carelessness. For many jurors, carelessness was in turn linked to shared responsibility for the assault. One white female juror told us, "You don't get in a car at midnight with two complete strangers and not expect to do something." A black female told us that the victim "put herself in a position for it. She asked for it and got it. It's a poor man who turns down anything for free." Another white female told us, "She led him on. [She] accepted a ride in the middle of the night. [She] rode around with him for several hours."

Jurors' evaluations of a victim's moral character and behavior were also directly linked to their decisions about whether she had consented. One white male claimed that the complainant had "consented when she invited [sic] to take him home." A white female juror told us that the complainant in one case had "consented with her body language." As is evident in Table 8.5, for jurors the victim's moral character was even more important than medical evidence or victim injury. In one consent case, a black female juror noted that hospital records don't "mean it was rape. Abrasion of the vagina still doesn't mean rape—she might want that force."

Reactions to Defendants

The results also suggest that jurors formed stereotypes of a defendant, based especially on their evaluations of his character and evidence about his criminal record. Defendants who had few social ties and who presented a negative courtroom appearance (for scale construction, see Appendix 8.2) and those who had criminal records that were mentioned in court were significantly more likely than other defendants to be thought guilty by jurors. Impressions of the defendant's courtroom appearance seemed to be important for jurors in reaching verdicts. One black male juror said of one defendant, "With his eyes I could see some sense of good or truth. He did not seem to be the type of person who would rape." A white female told us that, "I wanted him [i.e., the defendant] to act either guilty or innocent." She then explained that the defendant's unresponsiveness in the courtroom "probably worked against him." Another white female claimed that she found the defendant "kind of frightening. He seemed to glare at you. I took it as a dare to convict him. [He had a] threatening [look] rather than a look of innocence."

Many of the jurors made comments about characteristics of defendants that either confirmed or disconfirmed their stereotypes about rapists and other criminals. One white female juror said that a defendant "looked to be the juvenile delinquent type. He looked like a troublemaker. An unsavory sort of person." A black female described a defendant as "a degenerate. He even looked like one. He stared every woman up and down who walked up to the stand, so you know what he had on his mind." A black male noted that a defendant "struck me as the kind of person who would take advantage of a woman if he got the chance." A white female described a defendant as a "mean, hard-looking person that gave us horrible looks. [He] put fear in you."

But in other cases, the defendant's courtroom appearance troubled jurors because it was contrary to their stereotypes of rapists. One white female juror told us that a defendant was:

> A nice-looking young fellow. Nice dressed, like a college boy. Neat haircut. I couldn't believe he would be capable of something like this.

A white male told us that a defendant:

> Didn't match the stereotype of rapist. Quiet. Looking at him, how could he commit crime? An average person intellectually. [He] looked like a stock boy at the local grocery store.

Victim's Race

Table 8.5 shows that the victim's race was also an important predictor of jurors' case evaluations. Jurors were less likely to believe in a defendant's guilt when the victim was black.* Our interviews with jurors suggested that part of the

---

*As we saw in Chapter 6, race composition of the victim–offender dyad is often more important than individual measures of defendant's and victim's race in explaining processing decisions. Because of its theoretical importance, we experimented with using a measure of the race composition of the victim–offender dyad rather than measures of victim and offender race in the

explanation for this effect was that jurors—many of whom were middle-class whites—were influenced by stereotypes of black women as more likely to consent to sex or as more sexually experienced and hence less harmed by the assault.* In a case involving the rape of a young black girl, one juror argued for acquittal on the grounds that a girl her age from "that kind of neighborhood" probably wasn't a virgin anyway. Other jurors were simply less willing to believe the testimony of black complainants. One white juror told us:

> Negroes have a way of not telling the truth. They've a knack for coloring the story. So you know you can't believe everything they say.

IDENTIFICATION AND DIMINISHED-RESPONSIBILITY CASES

The right side of Table 8.5 summarizes the results for the identification and diminished-responsibility analysis—the cases in which the defense acknowledged the sexual assault but claimed that the defendant was not the assailant or that his responsibility was mitigated by insanity or drug or alcohol use. These cases resemble nonsexual felony cases in that the victim's behavior and character have no direct bearing on the legal issues being disputed. A priori testimony and evidence about the assailant's identity should be most important to the identification cases, and testimony about the defendant's behavior at the time of the assault and his past history should be most relevant to the diminished-responsibility cases. Thus, we might expect evidence measures, and perhaps the defendant's characteristics, to be paramount in these cases. However, the perspective we are examining in this chapter—that the law is applied to control

---

analysis. The results showed that for the analysis of verdicts, victim's race was a more important determinant than the race composition of the victim–offender dyad. However, this conclusion is no doubt due in part to the fact that there were very few cases of interracial rape in the data; of 38 trials, none involved white offenders and black victims and only two involved black offenders and white victims.

*This interpretation also receives support in the criminology literature (e.g., Bohmer, 1974, p. 307; Swigert and Farrell, 1977; Walsh, 1987).

the behavior of women who behave nontraditionally—has not distinguished cases on the basis of type of legal defense. It simply suggests that the victim's character affects verdicts regardless of the legal issue disputed. The results in Table 8.5 do not provide much support for this claim.

Measures of Evidence

In contrast to the consent and no-sex cases, measures of evidence were very important predictors of jurors' reactions in the identification and diminished-responsibility cases. Jurors were more certain that the defendant was guilty when there was eyewitness testimony, evidence of a weapon, more charges against the defendant, and evidence of physical injury to the victim. The value of eyewitnesses in identification cases is obvious; in diminished-responsibility cases, they provide information about the defendant's behavior and, possibly, his state of mind at the time of the assault. While force is not legally at issue in these cases, evidence that a weapon was used or the victim injured probably increases the jurors' sense of the seriousness of the crime.

Type of Defense

Although identification and diminished-responsibility cases are similar in that the victim's character is not at issue, differences between them are still important. When the defense argues diminished responsibility, it acknowledges that the defendant attempted to assault or did assault the victim, but must prove that the defendant did not intend and was not responsible for his actions. We found this to be a generally unpopular defense with jurors, and the defense attorneys we observed avoided it unless their case was very strong or the facts permitted no tenable alternative. Recall that none of the cases in which diminished responsibility was a major defense resulted in acquittals (Table 8.3). The comments of this juror were typical:

> I didn't like the plea of insanity. Well, I think in a few instances it's probably true, but in the vast majority of instances it's just an excuse. It seems strange in a trial of rape. It's not a

split-second decision. It's complicated, and you have to make so many decisions it seems a person would have to be rational to do it.

Victim and Case Characteristics

In strong contrast to the consent and no-sex cases, only one victim characteristic even approached statistical significance in the identification and diminished-responsibility cases. The tenth most important variable (in terms of the size of the standardized coefficients) for the diminished-responsibility and identification cases was whether there were allegations that the victim drank or used drugs (significant at the $p = .07$ level). Allegations about the victim's sexual activity had no effect on these cases.

However, the victim–defendant relationship did have a significant effect on jurors' evaluations. As with the consent and no-sex cases, any prior relationship between the victim and the defendant reduced the chances that jurors would consider the defendant guilty. This is a particularly interesting finding for the identification cases, because it would seem plausible that previously knowing an assailant would make the case stronger when the key issue was identification. However, the negative impact of the victim–defendant relationship also remained in a separate analysis in which we included only identification cases. Apparently, the tendency for jurors to favor acquittal in cases involving a prior acquaintance applies even when the prior relationship between victim and defendant would presumably strengthen the evidence relevant to the major legal issue being disputed.

Defendant's Characteristics

Not surprisingly, measures of a defendant's background and character also affected outcomes. As with the consent and no-sex cases, defendants who lacked stable family or work ties and who made a poor impression in court were more likely than other defendants to be judged guilty. However, unlike the results for the consent and no-sex cases, jurors were less likely to believe guilty those defendants who had a criminal record. One possible explanation for this is that the measure of criminal record used here—any testimony indicating a prior felony record—was not sensitive enough. Recall that our analysis in Chapter 5 showed that jurors' verdicts were affected by evidence of prior record for sex offenses, but not for felonies in general.

Jurors' Characteristics and Attitudes

Contrary to some studies of simulated juries (e.g., Jones and Aronson, 1973; Stephan, 1974), jurors' characteristics —sex, race, age, occupational prestige, education, and recent jury experience—had no significant effect on their judgments of defendants' guilt in either the consent and no-sex cases or the identification and diminished-responsibility cases. Experimental studies may overestimate the importance of jurors' characteristics by omitting variables that are important in actual trials. Moreover, experimental studies of juries rarely include a realistic approximation of jury selection. Voir dire allows attorneys to eliminate prospective jurors whose characteristics or attitudes might make them strongly sympathetic to one side. Defense attorneys in these rape cases frequently challenged jurors who espoused what might be construed as feminist viewpoints. Likewise, prosecuting attorneys eliminated jurors who expressed skepticism about rape complainants. Jurors who are ultimately seated represent neither the general population nor the panel of prospective jurors. In addition, voir dire helps to educate jurors about their proper role and to encourage them to suppress personal feelings in arriving at verdicts. Thus, jury selection may weaken any relationships that exist in the larger population among persons' characteristics, gender-role attitudes, and a propensity to blame or exonerate rape defendants.

As with the consent and no-sex cases, our measures of the jurors' gender-role attitudes had no effect on their evaluations of cases. However, jurors who were "tough on crime" were more likely to favor conviction, although this attitude was much less important than many other variables. The fact that jurors' gender-role attitudes had no direct effect on their judgments of defendants' guilt in the analysis led us to wonder whether the relationship between jurors' attitudes and their judgments might in turn be related to the characteristics of the victim. After all, case characteristics, including the victim's behavior, do not exist in a social vacuum. They must be interpreted by the legal agents who evaluate and process cases. Is it possible that gender-role-conservative jurors are influenced more than liberal jurors by a victim's failure to conform to behavioral norms?

JURORS' GENDER-ROLE ATTITUDES AND VICTIMS' GENDER-ROLE BEHAVIOR

Our data allow us to test this possibility by comparing the impact of victims' character on jurors with varying gender-role attitudes. We did the analysis for consent and no-sex cases and identification and diminished-responsibility cases a second time, including "product terms"—the same technique used to test for differences before and after the creation of the Sex Offense Unit described in Chapter 4. This time we created product terms by multiplying each of the two measures of jurors' gender-role attitudes by each of the measures of victims' gender-role behavior (which produces a total of four new variables). For example, we included a variable that was the product of multiplying one of the jurors' gender-role-attitude measures by whether the victim was allegedly drinking or using drugs. If this variable is statistically significant in the analysis, it tells us that jurors' gender-role conservatism affects their judgments only when there is evidence that the victim was nontraditional. We introduced each of the four product terms, one at a time, into the two analyses (complete results are shown in Appendix 8.3, equations 2 and 4).*

For the consent and no-sex cases, each of the four product terms had a significant statistical effect when added to the equation. Thus, when a victim allegedly drank or used drugs or was alleged to be sexually active outside of marriage, gender-role-conservative jurors were less likely to believe

---

*We experimented with including more than one product term at a time in each equation. However, because the four product terms are products of the two juror-attitude and the two victim-behavior scales, each term shares a common component with two other terms. The resulting multicollinearity yielded unreliable and uninterpretable estimates when more than one product term was included.

in the defendants' guilt. Although the results for the identification and diminished-responsibility cases were more complex,* we again found that when there was evidence that a victim used drugs or drank, jurors' adherence to traditional gender-role attitudes led them to believe in the defendant's innocence.

Again, our interviews with jurors were consistent with the conclusion that their gender-role attitudes affected their judgements in rape cases. In fact, a representative sample of jurors' comments about rape reflects many of the attitudes that led feminists and others to seek reforms in the 1970s. For example, many jurors claimed that through their clothing and behavior women often "ask" to be raped. One white female juror told us, "Sometimes it [i.e., rape] is asked for. Women go to taverns and get drunk and leave with strangers." A black male noted, "Some women put themselves on men. It is the way that they dress. It is in the clothes." Another white female juror said, "Women may tempt them [i.e., men] by too short or seductive attire or skin-tight pants." The idea that an unwilling woman cannot be raped also surfaced. One white male juror told us:

> I don't think a woman can be raped. . . . I ask why are they out at that time of the night? What did they do to provoke it? . . . A judge over in Ohio told me that a woman can run faster with her pants down than a man, and I believe that. . . . If you want to say rape, then she must be unconscious. She can scream and kick if she's awake and doesn't want it.

While attitudes like these were common, they were by no means universal. For example, one white male juror concluded, "Even a prostitute has the right to say yes or no." A white female juror told us, "Rape is a crime of violence, not

---

*The direction of the interaction effect was reversed for the effect of jurors' commitment to women's social and sexual equality. Here, more conservative jurors were more likely to believe in the guilt of defendants accused of assaulting women who allegedly drank or used drugs. This counterintuitive finding is probably due to the high correlations among the relevant variables. The two attitude scales are highly correlated ($r = .75$ for the identification and diminished-responsibility cases), and each product term is highly correlated with victims' drug or alcohol use. Thus, the results with more than one product term included may be unstable.

sexual gratification. It is a violent crime." Another white woman told our interviewer that she was "disturbed" by her fellow jurors because one of them "felt the girl got what she deserved because of her life-style." In fact, the attitudes of the jurors in these Indianapolis rape cases were probably a fair representation of the mixture of traditional and more contemporary attitudes toward rape that characterizes much of the population of the United States today.

CONCLUSIONS: WOMEN'S BEHAVIOR AND OFFICIAL REACTIONS TO RAPE

Conflict theorists have argued that law is generally applied so as to maintain the power of dominant groups and that individuals who challenge these groups often find themselves outside the law's protection. Feminists have applied similar reasoning to rape cases, arguing that women in our society who behave nontraditionally are less likely to receive justice from the criminal-justice system if they are rape victims. Are jurors less likely to believe defendants in rape trials are guilty when there is evidence that the victim has behaved nontraditionally? In part. Consistent with feminist-conflict views, jurors in consent and no-sex cases were clearly influenced by testimony about victims' life-styles. Any evidence of drinking, drug use, or sexual activity outside marriage led jurors to doubt defendants' guilt, as did any prior acquaintance between victim and defendant.* In fact, in the consent and no-sex cases, measures of victims' gender-role behavior were more important than measures of physical evidence and seriousness of offense in predicting jurors' case evaluations. The results clearly suggest that women who have engaged in extramarital sexual behavior or who are depicted as regular alcohol or drug users are likely to be seen by jurors as careless and as at least partly, if not totally, to blame for the reported sexual assault.

---

*According to Indiana law, prior sexual involvement between an alleged victim and defendant is legally relevant, but in only two of the 13 consent cases in which the two parties were acquainted did the defense allege prior sexual involvement.

However, contrary to the conflict proposition with which we began, our measures of victims' gender-role behavior had little effect on jurors' judgments when the major legal issue was identification or the defendant's diminished responsibility. The Russell/Chan case is typical. Questions asked in the trial revealed very little about the previous behavior or moral character of the victims. Possible indications of nontraditional behavior—such as Terry Chan's inviting her boyfriend to her home late at night—were simply not explored. In fact, in this case, jurors were so offended by the crime that they returned a guilty verdict based on a voice identification, which, at least in the off-the-record opinion of the presiding judge, was insufficient to sustain a conviction.

Even in the consent and no-sex cases, the impact of the victim's gender-role behavior on trials was complex. Jurors did not directly observe the alleged criminal behavior. Seldom were there reliable eyewitnesses. In many cases, there was little physical evidence. It appears likely that in cases where the evidence was inconclusive, jurors relied heavily on their interpretations of the victims' credibility. But how could jurors realistically weigh the credibility of a witness whom they did not know, testifying about an incident that they did not see, in the context of contradictory courtroom testimony? To the extent that jurors weighed such behaviors as drinking, using drugs, and being sexually active outside of marriage as indicators of a victim's *credibility*, their concern with such factors is arguably a permissible one. However, to the extent that jurors used such factors as evidence of a victim's *character*, such inferences were improper. Common sense, as well as our interviews with jurors, suggest that they were no doubt weighing the behavior of the rape victims we studied in both senses.

If the preceding analysis suggests that reactions to rape cases are conditioned by the legal issues disputed, the results are also a powerful reminder that the sanctioning power of the law may be withheld from individuals who do not conform to traditional behaviors. Jurors in the consent and no-sex cases were clearly influenced by measures of victims' gender-role behavior. Perhaps such results do not justify Susan Brownmiller's extremely cynical view of rape as "a conscious process of intimidation by which *all men* keep *all women* in a state of fear" (1975, p. 15), but they do support the proposition that criminal sanctions are based in part on definitions constructed through social interaction and the corollary argument that these definitions are closely linked to the characteristics of the people involved.

The final chapter is the place to take stock. In Chapter 9, I consider the labeling and conflict arguments with which I started in light of the data I have presented, and I then draw some conclusions about the application of law in rape cases.

APPENDIX 8.1 Jurors' Attitude Scales

Jurors' Attitudes	SA	A	D	SD	Factor 1	Factor 2
A. Women's Sex Roles[a]						
1. One of the most important things a mother can do for her daughter is to prepare her for being a wife and mother.[b]	33.1%	52.1%	13.4%	1.4%	.576	−.038
2. Women should worry less about their rights and more about being good wives and mothers.[b]	9.5	39.5	40.1	10.9	.756	.060
3. Although women hold many important jobs, their proper place is still in the home.[b] Reliability (standardized alpha) = .74	8.2	37.0	42.7	12.1	.713	.054
B. Women's Social-Sexual Freedom						
1. Women should be able to go to the same places and have the same freedom to move around as men have.	31.6%	51.7%	15.5%	1.1%	.173	.505
2. A woman should be able to go to a bar alone if she wants to.	9.8	67.4	19.1	3.7	.115	.623
3. Women should have as much sexual freedom as men. Reliability (standardized alpha) = .68	11.0	69.5	17.8	1.7	−.101	.706

APPENDIX 8.1 (continued)

Jurors' Attitudes	SA	A	D	SD	Factor 1	Factor 2
C. Attitudes Toward Crime						
1. Capital punishment should be abolished for all crimes.	3.9%	8.4%	58.4%	29.2%	.334	
2. If judges gave harsher sentences, there would be fewer crimes.[b]	17.8	57.9	23.2	1.1	.739	
3. Everyone worries about criminals' rights, but people have forgotten about victims' rights.[b]	27.2	58.4	13.8	0.6	.464	

	Not Effective			Very Effective		Factor 1	Factor 2
	1	2	3	4	5		
4. How effective would harsher punishment for convicted rapists be?[c]	4.8%	8.4%	11.2%	18.5%	57.0%	.512	
5. How effective would stricter laws against rape be?[c]	5.6	8.5	17.2	19.5	49.2		

Reliability (standardized alpha) = .59

[a] Both of the two sex-role-attitude scales are based on oblique rotation principle component factor analysis.

[b] We reversed the order of the response categories before scaling so that high scores on these indicate traditional sex-role attitudes or strong anti-crime attitudes.

[c] Items 4 and 5 were first standardized and then summed to create one measure.

SOURCE: LaFree, Reskin, and Visher, 1985, p. 405. © 1985 by the Society for the Study of Social Problems, Inc. Original version appeared in *Social Problems* 32:4 (1985). Used by permission.

APPENDIX 8.2 Defendants' Behavior and Appearance Scale[a]

	Coding, Distribution	Factor 1	Factor 2
1. Defendant's intelligence according to jurors	Intelligent 1 2 3 4 5 Unintelligent — 9.7% 15.0 42.5 21.1 9.2	.444	−.042
2. Socioeconomic status	1 = middle, upper-middle — 6.7% 2 = lower-middle, working — 52.8 3 = lower — 40.5	440	−.030
3. Four items were combined[b] to form a score for social ties: married, access to a sexual partner, any children, employed (1 = mentioned in court; 0 = not mentioned)	0 = low integration — 20.0% 1 — 17.2 2 — 23.1 3 — 15.0 4 = high integration — 24.7	.577	.020
4. Two items were combined to form a score for jurors' impression of defendant: Did defendant present a negative appearance Mention of general negative reaction to defendant by jurors Reliability (standardized alpha) = .59	0 = neither mentioned — 41.7% 1 = negative appearance or negative reaction — 34.7 2 = both negative appearance and negative reaction — 23.6	591	035

[a] Defendant behavior and appearance scale based on orthogonal rotation principle component factor analysis.
[b] These four measures were summed to create a 0–4 scale and then recoded so that high values mean fewer social ties (i.e., not married, no sexual partner, etc.).

SOURCE: LaFree, Reskin, and Visher, 1985, p. 406. © 1985 by the Society for the Study of Social Problems, Inc. Original version appeared in *Social Problems* 32:4 (1985). Used by permission.

APPENDIX 8.3 Regression Coefficients and Standards Errors for Predictors of Defendants' Guilt in Consent and No-Sex Cases and in Identification and Diminished-Responsibility Cases

| Independent Variables | Consent and No Sex-Cases (N = 172) | | | | | | Identification and Diminished-Responsibility Cases (N = 165) | | | | | |
| | Equation 1 | | | Equation 2 | | | Equation 3 | | | Equation 4 | | |
	b	SE	B	b	SE	B	b	SE	B	b	SE	B
Consent	−.35	.32	−.15	−.37	.33	−.16	—	—	—	—	—	—
Diminished responsibility	—	—	—	—	—	—	.44*	.15	.27	.46*	.15	.28
Number of charges	.11	.09	.09	.11	.09	.09	.14*	.06	.27	.12*	.06	.24
Eyewitness	—	—	—	—	—	—	.67*	.18	.40	.67*	.18	.40
Weapon	−.19	.22	−.09	−.21	.22	−.09	.73*	.15	.37	.71*	.15	.36
Victim injured	.12	.22	.02	.12	.22	.05	.27*	.15	.15	.25*	.15	.14
Victim sexually active	−.75*	.21	−.34	−.73*	.21	−.33	−.06	.16	−.03	−.05	.16	−.03
Victim drank, used drugs	−.51*	.31	−.22	−.47*	.31	−.20	−.24**	.16	−.12	−.15	.16	−.07
Victim black	−.35*	.21	−.14	−.28	.21	−.11	−.08	.15	−.05	−.14	.15	−.09
Victim and defendant acquainted	−.35*	.16	−.16	−.32*	.16	−.14	−.42*	.19	−.26	−.43*	.19	−.26

Defendant character	.50*	.12	.37	.48*	.12	.35	.31*	.10	.31	.30*	.10	.30
Defendant criminal record	.58*	.17	.26	.56*	.17	.25	−.32*	.13	−.21	−.28*	.13	−.18
Jurors' attitude toward crime	.11	.09	.08	.14*	.10	.10	.11*	.06	.12	.12	.07	.13
Jurors' sex-role attitude	—	—	—	.09	.16	.07	—	—	—	−.02	.10	.02
Jurors' sexual/social-freedom attitude	—	—	—	—	—	—	—	—	—	−.13	.11	−.14
Product Terms												
Victim drank, drugs x jurors' sex-role attitude	—	—	—	−.29*	.18	−.19	—	—	—	−.46**	.28	−.18
Victim drank, drugs x jurors' sexual/social-freedom attitude	—	—	—	—	—	—	—	—	—	.83*	—	—
Y-intercept	3.49			3.43			2.25			2.32		
R^2	.30*			.31*			.26*			.29*		

*$p < .05$; ** $.05 < p < .10$; R-square adjusted for small sample size.

SOURCE: LaFree, Reskin, and Visher, 1985, p. 398. © 1985 by the Society for the Study of Social Problems, Inc. Original version appeared in *Social Problems* 32:4 (1985). Used by permission.

CHAPTER 9

Constructing Rape: Conclusions and Implications

The continuum in which we live is not the kind of place in which middles can be unambiguously excluded.

Reuben Abel, "Pragmatism and the Outlook of Modern Science."

Reality is an activity of the most august imagination.

Wallace Stevens, *Opus Posthumous.*

We have now examined some of the dynamics of legal decision making in rape cases. In this final chapter I summarize the findings and consider their implications for the labeling and conflict propositions with which I began, for future research, and for social policy.

THE SOCIAL CONSTRUCTION OF RAPE

Beginning in the 1960s, labeling theory became a major theoretical force in criminology. Perhaps the single most influential labeling proposition is that crime is not an objective property of certain behavior, but a definition constructed through social interaction. In contrast with mainstream criminology in the United States, labeling theorists argue that, far from being based on neutral legal standards, criminal labels result from the typifications of those involved in official decision making. Like the symbolic-interaction theory, to which it is most closely related, the labeling perspective interprets the social world as relatively fluid and flexible rather than fixed and unchanging. Thus, labeling theory asserts that definitions of crime change over time and across locations, that there is limited agreement about the severity of crime and deviance, and that the criminal-selection process bears little or no relationship to the actual commission of criminal acts.

This image of crime and the legal system has had an enormous impact on both criminology and social policy. Labeling theory suggests that criminological research should abandon its traditional emphasis on criminal etiology and instead redirect its attention to the processes by which criminal offenders are selected. Labeling theory was used to justify movements aimed at legalizing behavior over which there was a great deal of societal ambivalence (e.g., marijuana use, juvenile "status offenses," and homosexuality), keeping as many offenders out of prisons and mental institutions as possible, and avoiding altogether the official labeling of those who committed less serious forms of deviance.

Labeling-theory ideas were already well established in the late 1960s, when the feminist movement began to argue that rape was a major social problem and that legal treatment of rape cases was badly in need of reform. However, a connection between labeling theory and a new interest in the reform of the official processing of rape cases was not immediately obvious. First, the major interests of labeling theorists and feminists were to some extent opposed on the issue of rape. Criminological research based on labeling perspectives had been most often concerned with poor and minority-group offenders and defendants, the majority of whom were men. In contrast, the primary goal of feminists was to improve women's position in society. Thus, while the first inclination of labeling theorists interested in rape research was to look for evidence that men charged with rape were being unfairly processed, the first concern of feminists was with the treatment of rape victims, including the factors that affected official reactions to their cases. Moreover, the labeling assertion that there is typically little consensus in societies about law was more obvious in the case of mala prohibita crimes than in the case of mala in se crimes like rape.

However, the labeling idea that legal-classification decisions are not necessarily the direct result of actual behavior but represent the typifications of legal agents is equally applicable to rape victims and offenders. Moreover, as I have argued in earlier chapters, there can be a great deal of agreement about the fact that rape is a serious crime that must be harshly punished and, at the same time, a great deal of disagreement about whether a particular case is really rape. Thus, the observation that all contemporary societies prohibit rape or that virtually all persons in a society agree about its severity does not necessarily preclude the labeling-theory concern with the processes by which legal agents determine whether a rape happened in a given case.

The labeling proposition I have explored in this book can be divided into two related parts: first, that criminal selection is generally independent of criminal behavior and, second, that criminal selection instead represents the typifications of legal agents. Perhaps the most direct evidence for the first part of this proposition is found in the case-attrition data presented in Chapter 4. Of 881 rape cases reported to police, 12 percent eventually resulted in conviction. If the crime of rape is an objective property of specific behavior, then by definition the other 88 percent of the reported rape cases did not exhibit the behavior legally defined as rape. This is clearly nonsense, even if we disregard the fact that these 881 reported cases no doubt represent only a fraction of all rapes that actually occurred in Indianapolis during the years of my study. Moreover, it is possible (and even probable) that one or more of the 104 men who were convicted of rape in these cases were in fact innocent.

The second part of the labeling proposition is that criminal categories are based on the typifications of legal agents. Again, the support for this proposition was substantial. Evidence from victims, police, prosecutors, judges, and juries supports the idea that widely held stereotypes about rape affect the processing of cases. Like many ideas that have extremely broad implications, this observation borders on being trite. After all, legal agents, no less than other human beings, must actively construct their own perceptual world. This world is always at least one step away from the world "as it really is." But the distance between perception and reality is likely to be especially great in the case of the criminal-selection process, because legal agents most often respond to events that they did not actually observe. Thus, from the very beginning of legal processing, officials must depend on interpretations, stereotypes, definitions, and accounts at least one step removed from the actual events they describe. In fact, it is these accounts, colored in turn by the typifications of the agents themselves, that are the reality of criminal processing—not the events on which these presentations are based. Hence, beginning with the victim herself, those who interpret and process cases are often as concerned about how the case will be interpreted by others as they are with what "really" happened.

But here I must add that I am not contending that the criminal-selection process is based entirely on discriminatory or legally irrelevant factors. In fact, decision making in these cases was clearly influenced by measures of the seriousness of the criminal behavior alleged. Thus, the labeling proposition is correct to the extent that a great deal of behavior that was objectively definable as rape did not result in legal processing and conviction. The labeling proposition is incorrect to the extent that the label "rapist" is not independent of the behavior defined as rape by the legal system. The ongoing challenge for criminologists is to determine more precisely what factors influence legal decision making, how these factors relate to broader social forces, and how they vary depending on the crime, the jurisdiction, and the time period. This is a fundamental task of the sociology of law.

RAPE AND THE SOCIAL CONTROL OF BLACKS

Although conflict theory has a long and distinguished history in the development of social thought, it first became a major source for research and policy in the United States in the 1970s. Earlier conflict ideas were reinvestigated, extended, and modified, so that by the mid-1970s a more or less cohesive perspective had emerged. This perspective has continued to evolve in recent years. Despite the breadth and complexity of conflict theory, at the most general level all versions of the theory assert that law is applied to control the behavior of individuals who threaten the power of dominant social groups.

Applying conflict theory to the legal processing of blacks

is fairly obvious, given the sad history of race relations in the United States. For many years, criminologists in the United States have attempted to determine whether black and white defendants received similar treatment in the criminal-justice system. Until the early 1970s, most of this research concluded that there was ample evidence of discrimination against black defendants. Although blacks were still much more likely than whites to be arrested, tried, convicted, and imprisoned in the United States, conclusions about how to interpret these facts began to change in the early 1970s. Part of this change may be due to corollary changes in the research methods favored by criminologists in the late 1960s and the 1970s. Increasingly, researchers began to test for racial discrimination by including the defendant's race in statistical models that attempted to control for legal differences between cases. This new generation of research has generally found either no evidence of discrimination against black defendants or only qualified evidence.

These general trends also apply in the specific case of rape. My main concern with prior research showing little or no difference by race in the treatment of rape defendants was that in most cases it did not take into account the race composition of the victim–offender dyad. Sexual-property rules provide a link between the application of the law and the races of the victim and the offender in the case of rape. Like other scarce resources, sexual access is determined by power relationships in a stratified market. In the past, white men have clearly controlled this market. To the extent that white men still control sexual-property relations, conflict theory suggests they will use all the mechanisms available to them to maintain their favorable position. From this point of view, the criminal law is simply another resource available to those with the most power to apply it.

Rape violates sexual-property rules by taking away the control of the male sexual-property owner. It is clearly the case that in the past, the severity of official reactions to rape depended in large part on the relative statuses of the victim and the defendant. As we have seen, prior to the Civil War some of these distinctions were actually written into law. But even when there were no explicit differences in the written law, white men were rarely prosecuted for the rape of black women, while black men were frequently prosecuted and severely punished for the rape of white women.

My data from the official processing of rape cases in Indianapolis provides evidence that contemporary legal systems still contain vestiges of an older sexual-stratification system that punishes men accused of rape according to the race composition of the victim–offender dyad. Cases involving black offenders and white victims were treated the most seriously, while black intraracial cases were treated the least seriously. At the same time, the race composition of the victim–offender dyad was not the most important and certainly not the only predictor of case dispositions. In general, structural versions of conflict theory seem to be more useful in explaining the results than instrumental, conspiracy-based versions. The more severe treatment of black offenders who rape white women (or, for that matter, the milder treatment of black offenders who rape black women) is probably best explained in terms of racial discrimination within a broader context of continuing social and physical segregation between blacks and whites.

RAPE AND THE SOCIAL CONTROL OF WOMEN

As with the application of conflict theory to race relations, its application to gender relations is also obvious—although it required the feminist movement to firmly establish conflict interpretations of male–female relationships in criminological research. As feminists began to target rape as a problem requiring major social changes, the possibility that the processing of rape cases by the legal system sometimes serves as a mechanism for social control became an increasingly common theme in the rape literature. The main form this argument has taken is that if women who violate traditional gender roles and are raped are unable to obtain justice through the legal system, then the law is serving as an institutional arrangement that reinforces women's gender-role conformity. We tested this argument with data from jury-tried rape cases in Indianapolis. The most common types of nontraditional behavior alleged in these cases were drinking or using drugs either in general or at the time of the incident, engaging in sexual activity outside of marriage, having illegitimate children, and having a reputation as a "partier," a "pleasure seeker," or someone who stays out late at night.

Consistent with the feminist-conflict argument, jurors were less likely to convict in cases in which there was evidence of nontraditional behavior by the victim. In one of the analyses, victims' nontraditional behavior was more important in predicting verdicts than any of the evidence or crime-severity measures. However, our results showed that allegations of nontraditional victim behavior were also associated with important legal considerations. Notably, nontraditional victim behavior was most often alleged in cases in which the major legal defense was either consent or no-intercourse. Such allegations were less likely when the major defense was either identification or the defendant's diminished responsibility. The extremes were consent and diminished-responsibility defenses. In the former, victims were always portrayed as gender-role nontraditional; in the latter, they never were.

When we analyzed cases separately, depending on whether the legal defense challenged the victim's status as a victim, we found important differences. In general, the feminist-conflict argument was strongly supported for the consent and no-sex cases and was only weakly supported for the identification and diminished-responsibility cases. In short, the actual effect of victims' nontraditional behavior on jurors' reactions to these rape cases appeared to fall somewhere between the claim that jurors in rape cases are motivated solely by legal considerations and the early feminist assumption that rape victims' behavior predicts verdicts regardless of legal considerations.

SOME FINAL OBSERVATIONS

The positivist model in criminology and other social sciences, adopted from our physical science cousins, is to formulate hypotheses, provide data relevant to these hypotheses, and then either reject or fail to reject the hypotheses being tested. If I had to follow this model, I would now conclude that the hypotheses considered in this book cannot be rejected. Officials do use stereotypes about rape to decide cases, black men charged with raping white women are punished more harshly, and women who have allegedly engaged in nontraditional behavior are less likely to see their rape complaints result in the conviction and punishment of their assailants. However, such conclusions, without further refinements, would not be the most accurate depiction of the results and would miss some of the major implications of the research.

Throughout the analysis, I found support for the labeling and conflict themes that I identified—but it was qualified support in each case. Processing decisions in rape cases are clearly based in part on the typifications of rape held by processing agents. At the same time, the rape cases I studied were also influenced strongly by considerations that most observers would interpret as justified. Thus, while black offenders charged with raping white women consistently received harsher punishments than other offenders, race composition was not the only, or even the most important, predictor of outcomes in the data examined. Similarly, while evidence that rape victims had allegedly engaged in nontraditional behavior was very important in jury-tried rape cases, it was mostly important when the major disputed issue involved whether the complainant was in fact a rape victim. These conclusions have implications for the official processing of rape cases, for criminological research, and for social policy in general.

In terms of the official processing of rape cases, the results suggest that legal agents were not always either insensitive sexists or unbiased professionals—although I found clear examples of both. Real social change is no doubt part of the reason that the reactions of most of these legal agents to rape, the race composition of the victim–defendant dyad, and the nontraditional behavior of rape victims fell between these two extremes. We can debate whether changes in laws against rape have made the treatment of rape victims identical to the treatment of other victims of violent crime and whether the fundamental attitudes of legal agents toward men, women, and the proper roles of each have actually changed in fundamental ways. What is clearly not debatable is the fact that in recent years, rape laws in virtually all states have been extensively modified, communities have added special counseling and medical services for rape victims, police departments have formed rape-investigation units, and many prosecutor's offices have developed special rape-prosecution teams. Whether these trends will continue, regress, or stabilize is, of course, a question for future research.

The kind of research described in this book is frequently

used by criminologists to reach conclusions about whether the field should focus on criminal etiology or on the sociology of law. With the emergence of labeling theory in criminology in the 1960s, criminology's traditional emphasis on etiology was greatly reduced. In fact, during the 1960s and 1970s, criminology produced few new etiological ideas. However, the emphasis in criminological research seems to be shifting back to an etiological focus. Indeed, much of the criminological research of the late 1970s and 1980s has focused primarily on the behavior of the alleged offender, including research on theories of deterrence (e.g., Tittle, 1980; Sherman and Berk, 1984), social control (e.g., Meier, 1982; Matsueda, 1982; Hagan, Simpson, and Gillis, 1987), crime victimization (e.g., Cohen and Felson, 1979; Cohen, Felson, and Land, 1980), economic inequality, poverty, and stress (e.g., Berk, Lenihan, and Rossi, 1980; Cohen, Kluegel, and Land, 1981; Blau and Blau, 1982; Currie, 1985; Fiala and LaFree, 1988), and a variety of biological and psychological factors (e.g., Hirschi and Hindelang, 1977; Wilson and Herrnstein, 1985). It is not yet clear how complete this shift will be. Nonetheless, my interpretation of the data presented here is that an understanding of crime—including mala in se crime like rape—also requires an understanding of the decision-making processes of legal agents.

In short, the findings suggest that the rape cases examined were neither the totally objective phenomena that positivists have sometimes assumed, nor were they the totally subjective phenomena sometimes implied by labeling and conflict theorists. Insisting that crime must be one or the other may actually hinder our understanding of crime and its treatment. In a book on common fallacies in reasoning, historian David Hackett Fischer describes the "black and white fallacy" (1970, p. 276), in which researchers insist on portraying phenomena as dichotomous; for example:

> There is no firm and fixed criterion for distinguishing between hot and cold, no sharp line which separates these two words, but an area of doubt between them.

Fischer points out that an insistence on drawing an arbitrary line between concepts like hot and cold can be misleading in two ways. Some researchers rigidify the arbitrary line, transforming dark gray into black and light gray into white. Thus, in criminology, the same differences in sentencing by race may be construed as evidence for wholesale racism or impartial decision making, depending on the philosophical outlook of the researcher. Other researchers may incorrectly interpret the fact that a distinct categorization of issues is impossible as evidence that no real distinction between categories of issues exists. For example, while labeling theorists correctly criticized etiological theories for assuming that official statistics perfectly separate criminals from noncriminals, some labeling theorists incorrectly concluded from this criticism that there are no differences between criminals and noncriminals.

Although this book has examined only rape cases, the quotation from philosopher Reuben Abel at the beginning of this chapter suggests that social experience can often be characterized as standing midway between objectivity and subjectivity. This does not mean that our conclusions about crime are unrelated to reality; nor does it mean that they totally depict reality. Rather, we are stuck somewhere in between.

Beginning in the 1960s, labeling and conflict theorists reminded criminologists and policymakers that the study of how laws are written and applied should be an integral part of criminological research and the focus of major social-reform efforts. However, in their more extreme forms, labeling theory and conflict theory have either implied or actually argued that studying street crimes like rape, and certainly attempting to control crime, should be outside the scope of criminology—that our efforts should be directed solely at determining who benefits by the law and its application. This is nonsense. Rape and other forms of criminal violence are a pervasive, brutal reality that sometimes strikes at the very heart of civilized social life. Fear of crime changes the lives of most of us in myriad ways. It is especially likely to affect the lives of women and the elderly. Clearly, criminology cannot abandon efforts to understand the cause of rape and other violent street crimes.

And, in fact, the continuing high rates of street crime in recent years have probably served to move criminologists back to the study of criminal etiology. But now the possibility of overreaction—of abandoning a research interest in the processes by which legal agents make decisions and the consequences of this decision making for those being processed—seems to be a real one. This book is an argument against such a development. Instead, criminology needs to encourage researchers to follow both paths. Even better, we need to seek ways of synthesizing these questions in our research. Criminology should not abandon the study of etiology; nor can it neglect the dynamics of official decision making. Rape and the processing of rape cases demonstrate why both concerns must remain central to criminology.

References

Abel, Reuben
    1966 Pragmatism and the outlook of modern science. *Philosophy and Phenomenological Research* 27:45–54.

Acock, Alan C., and Nancy Ireland
    1981 "Attribution of blame in rape cases: The impact of norm violation, gender, and sex-role attitude." Paper presented at the annual meeting of the American Sociological Association, Toronto.

Akers, Ronald L.
    1977 *Deviant behavior: A social learning approach.* Belmont, Calif.: Wadsworth.

Amir, Menachem
    1971 *Patterns in forcible rape.* Chicago: University of Chicago Press.
    1967 Patterns of forcible rape. In *Criminal behavior systems*, edited by M. B. Clinard and R. Quinney, 60–74. New York: Holt, Rinehart and Winston.

Bart, Pauline B.
    1975 Rape doesn't end with a kiss. *Viva* 11:39–42, 100–101.

Bart, Pauline B., and Patricia O'Brien
    1985 *Stopping rape: Successful survival strategies.* Elmsford, N.Y.: Pergamon Press.

Becker, Howard S.
    1963 *Outsiders: Studies in the sociology of deviance.* Glencoe, Ill.: Free Press.

Beirne, Piers
    1979 Empiricism and the critique of Marxism on law and crime. *Social Problems* 26:373–85.

Berger, Peter L., and Thomas Luckmann
    1967 *The social construction of reality.* Garden City, N.Y.: Anchor Books.

Berk, Richard A., Harold Brackman, and Selma Lesser
1977 *A measure of justice: An empirical study of changes in the California Penal Code, 1955–1971*. New York: Academic Press.

Berk, Richard A., Kenneth J. Lenihan, and Peter H. Rossi
1980 Crime and poverty: Some experimental evidence from ex-offenders. *American Sociological Review* 45:766–86.

Bernard, Thomas J.
1983 *The consensus–conflict debate: Form and content in social theories*. New York: Columbia University Press.

Bernstein, Ilene Nagel, William R. Kelly, and Patricia A. Doyle
1977 Societal reaction to deviants: The case of criminal defendants. *American Sociological Review* 42:743–55.

Bernstein, Ilene Nagel, Edward Kick, Jan T. Leung, and Barbara Schultz
1977 Charge reduction: An intermediary stage in the process of labelling criminal defendants. *Social Forces* 56:362–84.

Bierstedt, Robert
1974 *Power and progress: Essays on sociological theory*. New York: McGraw-Hill.

Black, Donald
1971 The social organization of arrest. *Stanford Law Review* 23:1087–1110.

Blalock, Hubert M.
1979 *Social statistics*. 2d ed. New York: McGraw-Hill.

Blanchard, W. H.
1959 The group process in gang rape. *Journal of Social Psychology* 49:259–66.

Blau, Judith R., and Peter M. Blau
1982 The cost of inequality: Metropolitan structure and violent crime. *American Sociological Review* 47:114–28.

Blau, Peter M.
1977 *Inequality and heterogeneity: A primitive theory of social structure*. New York: Free Press.

Blumer, Herbert
1969 *Symbolic interactionism*. Englewood Cliffs, N.J.: Prentice-Hall.

Bohannan, Paul
1967 The differing realms of law. In *Law and Warfare*, edited by P. Bohannan, 43–56. New York: Natural History Press.

Bohmer, Carol
1974 Judicial attitudes toward rape victims. In *Forcible rape: The crime, the victim and the offender*, edited by D. Chappell, R.

Geis, and G. Geis, 161–69. New York: Columbia University Press.

Bonger, William Adriaan
1916 *Criminality and economic conditions*, trans. by H. P. Horton. London: Heinemann.

Borgida, Eugene
1981 Legal reform of rape laws. In *Applied social psychology annual*, vol. 2, edited by L. Bickman, 211–41. Beverly Hills, Calif.: Sage.

Borgida, E., and N. Brekke
1985 Psychological research on rape trials. In *Rape and sexual assault*, edited by A. Burgess, 313–42. New York: Garland.

Borgida, E., and P. White
1978 Social perception of rape victims. *Law and Human Behavior* 2:339–51.

Bowers, William
1974 *Executions in America*. Lexington, Mass.: D. C. Heath.

Braungart, Margaret, Richard Braungart, and William Hoyer
1980 Age, sex, and social factors in fear of crime. *Sociological Focus* 13:55–66.

Brereton, David, and Jonathan D. Casper
1981–1982 Does it pay to plead guilty? Differential sentencing and the functioning of criminal courts. *Law and Society Review* 16:45–70.

Broverman, I. K., S. R. Vogel, D. M. Broverman, F. E. Clarkson, and P. S. Rosenkrantz
1972 Sex-role stereotypes: A current appraisal. *Journal of Social Issues* 28:59–78.

Brown, Edward J., Timothy J. Flanagan, and Maureen McLeod (eds.)
1984 *Sourcebook of criminal justice statistics—1983*. U.S. Department of Justice, Bureau of Justice Statistics. Washington, D.C.: U.S. Government Printing Office.

Brownmiller, Susan
1975 *Against our will: Men, women, and rape*. New York: Simon and Schuster.

Bullock, Henry
1961 Significance of the social factor in the length of prison sentences. *Journal of Criminal Law, Criminology, and Police Science* 52:411–17.

Burt, Martha R.
1980 Cultural myths and supports for rape. *Journal of Personality and Social Psychology* 38:217–30.

Burt, Martha R., and Rochelle Albin
1981 Rape myths, rape definitions, and probability of conviction. *Journal of Applied Social Psychology* 11:212–30.

Calhoun, Lawrence G., J. W. Selby, A. Cann, and G. T. Keller
1978 The effects of victim physical attractiveness and sex of respondent on social reactions to victims of rape. *Journal of Social and Clinical Psychology* 17:191–92.

Cameron, Mary Owen
1964 *The booster and the snitch.* New York: Free Press.

Caringella-MacDonald, Susan
1988 Marxist and feminist interpretation of the aftermath of rape reforms. *Contemporary Crises*, 12:125–44.
1985 The comparability in sexual and nonsexual assault case treatment: Did statute change meet the objective? *Crime and Delinquency* 31:206–22.

Chambliss, William J.
1979 On law-making. *British Journal of Law and Society* 6:149–71.
1975 *Criminal law in action.* New York: Wiley.
1964 A sociological analysis of the law of vagrancy. *Social Problems* 12:67–77.

Chambliss, William J., and Richard H. Nagasawa
1969 On the validity of statistics: A comparative study of white, black and Japanese high school boys. *Journal of Research in Crime and Delinquency* 6:71–77.

Chambliss, William J., and Robert Seidman
1971 *Law, order and power.* Reading, Mass.: Addison-Wesley.

Chappell, Duncan, Gilbert Geis, Stephen Schafer, and Larry Siegel
1971 Forcible rape: a comparative study of offenses known to the police in Boston and Los Angeles. In *Studies in the sociology of sex*, edited by J. M. Henslin, 169–90. New York: Appleton-Century-Crofts.

Chappell, Duncan, Robley Geis, and Gilbert Geis (eds.)
1977 *Forcible rape: The crime, the victim, and the offender.* New York: Columbia University Press.

Check, James V. P., and Neil M. Malamuth
1983 Sex role stereotyping and reactions to depictions of stranger versus acquaintance rape. *Journal of Personality and Social Psychology* 45:344–56.

Chilton, Roland, and Jan DeAmicis
1975 Overcriminalization and the measurement of consensus. *Sociology and Social Research* 59:318–29.

Chiricos, Theodore G., and Gordon P. Waldo
1975 Socioeconomic status and criminal sentencing: An empirical assessment of a conflict proposition. *American Sociological Review* 40:753–72.

Clark, Lorenne, and Debra Lewis
1977 *Rape: The price of coercive sexuality.* Toronto: The Women's Press.

Cobb, Thomas Read Rootes
1851 *A digest of the statute laws of the state of Georgia.* Athens, Ga. Christy, Kelsea, and Burke.

Cohen, Lawrence E., and Marcus Felson
1979 Social change and crime rate trends: A routine activity approach. *American Sociological Review* 44:588–608.

Cohen, Lawrence E., Marcus Felson, and Kenneth C. Land
1980 Property crime rates in the United States: A macrodynamic analysis 1947–1977 with *ex ante* forecasts for the mid-1980's. *American Journal of Sociology* 86:90–118.

Cohen, Lawrence E., James R. Kleugel, and Kenneth C. Land
1981 Social inequality and criminal victimization. *American Sociological Review* 46:505–24.

Collins, Randall
1975 *Conflict sociology.* New York: Academic Press.

Condran, John G.
1979 Changes in white attitudes toward blacks: 1963–1977. *Public Opinion Quarterly* 43:463–76.

Currie, Elliott
1985 *Confronting crime: An American challenge.* New York: Pantheon.

Curtis, Lynn A.
1975 *Violence, rape, and culture.* Lexington, Mass.: D. C. Heath.

Dahrendorf, Ralf
1958 Toward a theory of social conflict. *Journal of Conflict Resolution* 2:170–83.

Davis, Kingsley
1949 *Human society.* New York: Macmillan.

Deming, Mary Beard, and Ali Eppy
1981 The sociology of rape. *Sociology and Social Research* 65:357–80.

de Sade, Marquis
1966 *The complete Justine, philosophy in the bedroom and other writings,* trans. by Richard Seaver and Austry N. Wainhouse. New York: Grove Press.

Domhoff, G. William
1978 *The powers that be: Processes of ruling class domination in America*. New York: Random House.

Dostoevsky, Fyodor
1971 *The house of the dead*, trans. by Constance Garnett. London: Heinemann. (First published in English in 1911.)

Dow, Paul E.
1985 *Criminal law*. Monterey, Calif.: Brooks/Cole.

Drass, Kriss A., and J. William Spencer
1987 Accounting for pre-sentencing recommendations: Typologies and probation officers' theory of office. *Social Problems* 34:277–93.

Durkheim, Emile
1933 *Division of labor in society*. New York: Macmillan.

Edelman, Jacob Murray
1964 *The symbolic use of politics*. Urbana: University of Illinois Press.

Emerson, Robert M., and Sheldon L. Messinger
1977 The micro-politics of trouble. *Social Problems* 25:121–34.

Engels, Friedrich
1972 *The origin of the family, private property, and the state*, introduction and notes by E. B. Leacock. New York: International Publishers. (First published in English in 1902.)

Erikson, Kai T.
1964 Notes on the sociology of deviance. In *The other side: Perspectives on deviance*, edited by H. S. Becker, 9–22. New York: Free Press.
1966 *The wayward Puritans*. New York: Wiley.

Erskine, Hazel
1973 The polls: Interracial socializing. *Public Opinion Quarterly* 2:283–94.

Estrich, Susan
1987 *Real rape*. Cambridge, Mass.: Harvard University Press.

Etzioni, Amitai
1972 Human beings are not very easy to change after all. *Saturday Review* 3:45–48.

Farrell, Ronald A., and Victoria L. Swigert
1978 Prior offense as a self-fulfilling prophecy. *Law and Society Review* 12:437–53.

Feild, Hubert S.
1978 Attitudes toward rape: A comparative analysis of police, rap-

ists, crisis counselors, and citizens. *Journal of Personality and Social Psychology* 36:156–79.

Feild, Hubert S., and Leigh Buchanan Bienen
1980 *Jurors and rape.* Lexington, Mass.: Lexington Books.

Feldman-Summers, Shirley, and Clark D. Ashworth
1981 Factors related to intentions to report a rape. *Journal of Social Issues* 37:53–70.

Feldman-Summers, Shirley, and Karen Lindner
1976 Perceptions of victims and defendants in criminal assault cases. *Criminal Justice Behavior* 3:135–50.

Fiala, Robert, and Gary LaFree
1988 Cross-national determinants of child homicide. *American Sociological Review* 53:432–445.

Finkelhor, David, and Kersti Yllo
1982 Forced sex in marriage: A preliminary report. *Crime and Delinquency* 28:459–78.

Fischer, David Hackett
1970 *Historians' fallacies.* New York: Harper & Row.

Foucault, Michel
1971 *The order of things.* New York: Pantheon.

Frieze, Irene Hanson
1983 Investigating the causes and consequences of marital rape. *Signs* 8:532–53.

Galvin, Jim
1985 Rape: A decade of reform. *Crime and Delinquency* 31:163–68.

Galvin, Jim, and Kenneth Polk
1983 Attrition in case processing: Is rape unique? *Journal of Research in Crime and Delinquency* 20:126–54.

Garber, Steven, Steven Klepper, and Daniel Nagin
1982 *The role of extralegal factors in determining criminal case dispositions: Toward more reliable statistical inference.* Pittsburgh: Carnegie-Mellon University Press.

Garfinkel, Harold
1956 Conditions of successful degradation ceremonies. *American Journal of Sociology* 61:420–24.

Geis, Gilbert
1977 Forcible rape: An introduction. In *Forcible rape: The crime, the victim, and the offender,* edited by D. Chappell, R. Geis, and G. Geis, 1–44. New York: Columbia University Press.

Gerbasi, Kathleen C., Miron Zuckerman, and Henry T. Reis
1977 Justice needs a new blindfold: A review of mock jury research. *Psychological Bulletin* 84:323–45.

Goffman, Erving
1959 The moral career of the mental patient. *Psychiatry: Journal for the Study of Interpersonal Processes* 22:123–35.

Gold, David A., Clarence Y. H. Lo, and Erik Olin Wright
1975 Recent developments in Marxist theories of the capitalist state. *Monthly Review* 27:29–43.

Goode, William J.
1971 Force and violence in the family. *Journal of Marriage and the Family* 33:624–36.

Gornick, Janet, Martha R. Burt, and Karen J. Pittman
1985 Structure and activities of rape crisis centers in the early 1980s. *Crime and Delinquency* 31:247–68.

Gove, Walter
1980 The labeling perspective: An overview. In *The labeling of deviance*, edited by W. R. Gove, 9–32. Beverly Hills, Calif.: Sage.

Graham, James M.
1972 Amphetamine politics on Capitol Hill. *Transaction* (January):14–72.

Greenberg, David F.
1981 *Crime and capitalism*. New York: Mayfield.
1976 On one-dimensional criminology. *Theory and Society* 3:610–21.

Groth, A. Nicholas
1979 *Men who rape: The psychology of the offender*. New York: Plenum Press.

Gusfield, Joseph R.
1967 *Symbolic crusade: Status politics and the American temperance movement*. Urbana: University of Illinois Press.

Guttmacher, Manfred S., and Henry Weihofen
1952 *Psychiatry and the law*. New York: W. W. Norton.

Hagan, John
1974 Extra-legal attributes and criminal sentencing: An assessment of a sociological viewpoint. *Law and Society Review* 8:857–84.

Hagan, John, and Kristen Bumiller
1983 Making sense of sentencing: A review and critique of sentencing research. In *Research in sentencing: The search for re-*

form, vol. 2, edited by A. Blumstein, J. Cohen, S. Martin, and M. Tonry, 1–54. Washington, D.C.: National Academy Press.

Hagan, John, and Jeffrey Leon
1977 Rediscovering delinquency: Social history, political ideology, and the sociology of law. *American Sociological Review* 42:587–98.

Hagan, John, John Simpson, and A. R. Gillis
1987 Class in the household: A power-control theory of gender and delinquency. *American Journal of Sociology* 92:788–816.

Hall, Jerome
1935 *Theft, law, and society*. Boston: Little, Brown.

Hamilton, D. L.
1979 A cognitive-attributional analysis of stereotyping. In *Advances in experimental social psychology*, vol. 12, edited by L. Berkowitz, 53–84. New York: Academic Press.

Hans, Valerie P., and Neil Vidmar
1986 *Judging the jury*. New York: Plenum Press.

Hanushek, Eric A., and John E. Jackson
1977 *Statistical methods for social scientists*. New York: Academic Press.

Hart, H. L. A.
1961 *The concept of law*. Oxford, England: Clarendon Press.

Hernton, Calvin C.
1965 *Sex and racism in America*. New York: Grove Press.

Heumann, Milton
1978 *Plea bargaining: The experiences of prosecutors, judges, and defense attorneys*. Chicago: University of Chicago Press.

Hinch, Ronald
1983 Marxist criminology in the 1970s: Clarifying the clutter. *Crime and Social Justice* (Summer): 65–71.

Hindelang, Michael J.
1978 Race and involvement in crime. *American Sociological Review* 43:93–109.

Hindelang, Michael J., and Bruce Davis
1977 Forcible rape in the United States: A statistical profile. In *Forcible rape*, edited by D. Chappell, R. Geis, and G. Geis, Chapter 4. New York: Columbia University Press.

Hindelang, Michael J., Michael Gottfredson, and Timothy Flanagan (eds.)
1981 *Sourcebook of Criminal Justice Statistics, 1980*. Washington, D.C.: U.S. Government Printing Office.

Hindelang, Michael J., Michael Gottfredson, and James Garofalo
  1978 *The victims of personal crime.* Cambridge, Mass.: Ballinger.

Hirschi, Travis, and Michael J. Hindelang
  1977 Intelligence and delinquency: A revisionist review. *American Sociological Review* 42:571–87.

Hirschi, Travis, and David Rudisill
  1976 The great American search: Causes of crime 1876–1976. *The Annals of the American Academy for Political and Social Science* 423:14–30.

Hirst, Paul Q.
  1975 Marx and Engels on law, crime, and morality. In *Critical criminology*, edited by I. Taylor, P. Walton, and J. Young, 203–321. London: Routledge & Kegan Paul.

Hoebel, E. Adamson
  1954 *The law of primitive man.* Cambridge, Mass.: Harvard University Press.

Holmstrom, Lynda L., and Ann W. Burgess
  1978 *The victim of rape: Institutional reactions.* New York: Wiley-Interscience.

Horney, Julie, and Cassia Spohn
  1987 The impact of rape reform legislation. Paper presented at the meeting of the American Society of Criminology, Montreal.

Hostika, Carl J.
  1979 "We don't care about what happened, we only care about what is going to happen": Lawyer–client negotiations of reality. *Social Problems* 26:599–610.

Johnson, Elmer
  1957 Selective factors in capital punishment. *Social Forces* 36:165–69.

Jones, C., and E. Aronson
  1973 Attribution of fault to a rape victim as a function of respectability of the victim. *Journal of Personality and Social Psychology* 26:415–19.

Kairys, David (ed.)
  1982 *The politics of law: A progressive critique.* New York: Pantheon.

Kalven, Harry, and Hans Zeisel
  1966 *The American jury.* Boston: Little, Brown.

Kanin, Eugene J.
  1967 Reference groups and sex conduct norm violation. *Sociological Quarterly* 8:495–504.

Karpman, Benjamin
1954 *The sexual offender and his offenses*. New York: Julian Press.

Kerlinger, Fred N., and Elazar J. Pedhazur
1973 *Multiple regression in behavioral research*. New York: Holt, Rinehart and Winston.

Kitsuse, John I.
1975 The new conception of deviance and its critics. In *The labelling of deviance: Evaluating a perspective*, edited by W. R. Gove, 381–92. New York: Sage Publications.
1962 Societal reaction to deviant behavior: Problems of theory and method. *Social Problems* 9:247–57.

Kleck, Gary
1981 Racial discrimination in criminal sentencing. *American Sociological Review* 46:783–804.

Koeninger, R.
1969 Capital punishment in Texas, 1924–1968. *Crime and Delinquency* 15:132–41.

Koss, Mary P., and Kenneth E. Leonard
1984 Sexually aggressive men: Empirical findings and theoretical implications. In *Pornography and sexual aggression*, edited by N. Malamuth and E. Donnerstein, 213–32. Orlando, Fla.: Academic Press.

LaFree, Gary
1985a Official reactions to Hispanic defendants in the Southwest. *Journal of Research in Crime and Delinquency* 22:213–37.
1985b Adversarial and nonadversarial justice: A comparison of guilty pleas and trials. *Criminology* 23:289–312.
1982 Male power and female victimization: Toward a theory of interracial rape. *American Journal of Sociology* 88:311–28.
1981 Official reactions to social problems: Police decisions in sexual assault cases. *Social Problems* 28:582–94.
1980a Variables affecting guilty pleas and convictions in rape cases: Toward a social theory of rape processing. *Social Forces* 58:833–50.
1980b The effect of sexual stratification by race on official reactions to rape. *American Sociological Review* 45:842–54.
1979 *Determinants of police, prosecution, and court decisions in forcible rape cases*. Unpublished Ph.D. dissertation, Indiana University.

LaFree, Gary, Barbara Reskin, and Christy Visher
1985 Jurors' responses to victims' behavior and legal issues in sexual assault trials. *Social Problems* 32:389–407.

LaPiere, Richard T.
  1936 Type-rationalizations of group antipathy. *Social Forces* 15: 232–37.

Largen, Mary Ann
  1976 History of the women's movement in changing attitudes, laws, and treatment toward rape victims. In *Sexual assault*, edited by M. J. Walker and S. L. Brodsky, 69–73. Lexington, Mass.: D. C. Heath.

L'Armand, K., and A. Pepitone
  1982 Judgments of rape: A study of victim–rapist relationship and victim sexual history. *Personality and Social Psychology Bulletin* 8:134–39.

Lasswell, Harold Dwight
  1948 *Power and personality*. New York: W. W. Norton.

Lasswell, Harold Dwight, and Abraham Kaplan
  1950 *Power and society: A framework for political inquiry*. New Haven, Conn.: Yale University Press.

Laub, John H.
  1983 *Criminology in the making*. Boston: Northeastern University Press.

LeGrand, Camille E.
  1973 Rape and rape laws: Sexism in society and law. *California Law Review* 61:919–41.

Lemert, Edwin M.
  1951 *Social pathology*. New York: McGraw-Hill.

LeVine, Robert A.
  1959 Gusii sex offenses: A study in social control. *American Anthropologist* 61:965–90.

Lewis-Beck, Michael S.
  1980 *Applied regression: An introduction*. Beverly Hills, Calif.: Sage.

Lindesmith, Alfred R.
  1965 *The addict and the law*. New York: Vintage.

Lippmann, Walter
  1922 *Public opinion*. New York: Harcourt, Brace.

Lizotte, Alan J.
  1985 The uniqueness of rape: Reporting assaultive violence to the police. *Crime and Delinquency* 31:169–90.

Loh, Wallace D.
  1981 Q: What has reform of rape legislation wrought? A: Truth in criminal labelling. *Journal of Social Issues* 37:28–52.

1980 The impact of common law and reform rape statutes on prosecution. *Washington Law Review* 55:543–652.

Loseke, Donileen R., and Spencer E. Cahill
1984 The social construction of deviance: Experts on battered women. *Social Problems* 31:296–310.

Lundsgaarde, Henry P.
1977 *Murder in space city*. New York: Oxford University Press.

MacKinnon, Catherine A.
1987 *Feminism unmodified: Discourses on law and life*. Cambridge, Mass.: Harvard University Press.
1979 *Sexual harassment of working women*. New Haven, Conn.: Yale University Press.

Malinowski, Bronislaw
1926 *Crime and custom in savage society*. London: Routledge & Kegan Paul.

Marsh, Jeanne C., Alison Geist, and Nathan Caplan
1982 *Rape and the limits of law reform*. Boston: Auburn House.

Marshall, Donald S., and Robert Carl Suggs (eds.)
1971 *Human sexual behavior: Variations in the ethnographic spectrum*. New York: Basic Books.

Marx, Karl
1981 Theories of surplus value. In *Crime and Capitalism*, edited by David F. Greenberg, 52–53. Palo Alto, Calif. Mayfield.

Marx, Karl, and Friedrich Engels
1973 The communist manifesto. In *Marx/Engels Selected Works*, vol. 1, 98–137. Moscow: Progress Publishers. (First published in 1848.)

Mather, Lynn M.
1979 *Plea bargaining or trial? The process of criminal-case disposition*. Lexington, Mass.: Lexington Books.

Matsueda, Ross L.
1982 Testing control theory and differential association: A causal modeling approach. *American Sociological Review* 47:489–504.

Matza, David
1969 *Becoming deviant*. Englewood Cliffs, N.J.: Prentice-Hall.

Maynard, Douglas
1982 Defendant attributes in plea bargaining: Notes on the modeling of sentencing decisions. *Social Problems* 29:345–60.

McCauley, C., C. L. Stitt, and M. Segal
1980 Stereotyping: From prejudice to prediction. *Psychological Bulletin* 87:195–208.

McDonald, Lynn
1976 *The sociology of law and order*. Boulder, Colo.: Westview Press.

Meier, Robert F.
1982 Perspectives on the concept of social control. *Annual Review of Sociology* 8:35–55.

Messerschmidt, James W.
1986 *Capitalism, patriarchy, and crime: Toward a socialist-feminist criminology*. Totowa, N.J.: Rowman and Littlefield.

Michalowski, Raymond J., and Edward W. Bohlander
1976 Repression and criminal justice in capitalist America. *Sociological Inquiry* 46:95–106.

Miliband, Ralph
1969 *The State in Capitalist Society*. New York: Basic Books.

Mills, C. Wright
1956 *The power elite*. New York: Oxford University Press.

Mollenkopf, John H.
1975 Theories of the state and power structure research. *Insurgent Sociologist* 5:245–64.

Murchison, K.
1978 Toward a perspective on the death penalty cases. *Emory Law Journal* 27:469–556.

Myers, Martha A.
1979 Offended parties and official reactions: Victims and the sentencing of criminal defendants. *Sociological Quarterly* 20:529–40.

Myers, Martha A., and Gary LaFree
1982 The uniqueness of sexual assault: A comparison with other crimes. *Journal of Criminal Law and Criminology* 73:1282–1305.

Myrdal, Gunnar
1944 *An American dilemma: The Negro problem and modern democracy*. New York: Harper.

Nagel, Ilene H.
1983 The legal/extra-legal controversy: Judicial decisions in pretrial release. *Law and Society Review* 17:481–515.

Nagel, Ilene H., and John Hagan
1982 The sentencing of white-collar criminals in federal district court: A socio-legal exploration of disparity. *Michigan Law Review* 80:1427–1465.

National Institute of Law Enforcement and Criminal Justice
1977 *Forcible rape: A national survey of the response by police*, vol. 1. Law Enforcement Assistance Administration, U.S. Department of Justice. Washington, D.C.: U.S. Government Printing Office.

Nettler, Gwynn
1984 *Explaining crime.* 3rd ed. New York: McGraw-Hill.

The New York Times
1987 Suspect seized in rapes in town that fingerprinted blacks. Saturday, September 5, Section 1, p. 46.

Newman, Graeme R.
1976 *Comparative deviance: Perception and law in six cultures.* New York: Elsevier.

O'Brien, Robert M.
1987 The interracial nature of violent crimes: A reexamination. *American Journal of Sociology* 92:817–35.

Offe, Claus
1974 Political authority and class structure: An analysis of late capitalist societies. *International Journal of Social Sciences* 2: 73–108.

Orcutt, James D., and Rebecca Faison
1988 Sex-role attitude change and reporting of rape victimization. *Sociological Quarterly* 29, in press.

Oros, Cheryl J., Kenneth Leonard, and Mary P. Koss
1980 Factors related to a self-attribution of rape by victims. *Personality and Social Psychology Bulletin* 6:193–212.

Ortega, Suzanne T., and Jessie L. Myles
1987 Race and gender effects on fear of crime: An interactive model with age. *Criminology* 25:133–52.

Parsons, Talcott, and Robert F. Bales
1954 *Family socialization and interaction process.* Glencoe, Ill.: Free Press.

Partington, Donald H.
1965 The incidence of the death penalty for rape in Virginia. *Washington and Lee Law Review* 22:43–75.

Petersilia, Joan
1983 *Racial disparities in the criminal justice system.* Santa Monica, Calif.: Rand.

Peterson, Ruth D., and John Hagan
1984 Changing conceptions of race: Toward an account of anoma-

lous findings of sentencing research. *American Sociological Review* 49:56–70.

Platt, Anthony
1969 *The child-savers: The invention of delinquency.* Chicago: University of Chicago Press.

Polk, Kenneth
1985 Rape reform and criminal justice processing. *Crime and Delinquency* 31:191–205.

Pound, Roscoe
1943 A survey of social interests. *Harvard Law Review* 57:1–39.

Quinney, Richard
1973 *Critique of legal order.* Boston: Little, Brown.
1970 *The social reality of crime.* Boston: Little, Brown.

Quinney, Richard, and John Wildeman
1977 *The problem of crime.* 2d ed. New York: Harper & Row.

Reiman, Jeffrey H.
1984 *The rich get richer and the poor get prison.* 2d ed. New York: Wiley.

Reiss, Albert, Jr.
1967 Studies in crime and law enforcement in major metropolitan areas. In *Measurement of the nature and amount of crime*, field surveys III, vol. 1, section I. President's Commission on Law Enforcement and Administration of Justice. Washington, D.C.: U.S. Government Printing Office.

Reskin, Barbara F., and Gary LaFree
1981 Final report to National Institute of Mental Health on Grant No. R01MH29727. Unpublished.

Reskin, Barbara F., and Christy A. Visher
1986 The impact of evidence and extralegal factors in jurors' decisions. *Law and Society Review* 20:423–38.

Riger, Stephanie, Margaret Gordon, and Robert LeBailly
1978 Women's fear of crime: From blaming to restricting the victim. *Victimology* 3:274–84.

Robin, Gerald
1977 Forcible rape: Institutionalized sexism in the criminal justice system. *Crime and Delinquency* 23:136–53.

Roby, Pamela A.
1969 Politics and criminal law: Revision of the New York State penal law on prostitution. *Social Problems* 17:83–109.

Rose, Vicki McNickle
1977 Rape as a social problem: A by-product of the feminist movement. *Social Problems* 25:75–89.

Rossi, Peter, Emily Waite, Christine Bose, and Richard Berk
1974 Seriousness of crime: Normative structure and individual differences. *American Sociological Review* 39:224–37.

Russell, Bertrand
1949 *Authority and the individual.* New York: Simon and Schuster.

Russell, Diana E. H.
1982 *Rape in marriage.* New York: Macmillan.
1975 *The politics of rape.* New York: Stein and Day.

Sanday, Peggy R.
1981 *Female power and male dominance: On the origins of sexual inequality.* New York: Cambridge University Press.

Sanders, William B.
1980 *Rape and women's identity.* Beverly Hills, Calif.: Sage.

Scheff, Thomas J.
1974 The labelling theory of mental illness. *American Sociological Review* 39:444–52.

Schrag, Clarence
1971 *Crime and justice, American style.* Rockville, Md.: National Institute of Mental Health.

Schur, Edwin M.
1975 Comments. In *The labelling of deviance: Evaluating a perspective*, edited by W. R. Gove, 393–402. New York: Sage Publications.
1971 *Labelling deviant behavior.* New York: Harper & Row.

Schutz, Alfred
1970 *On phenomenology and social relations.* Chicago: University of Chicago Press.

Schwendinger, Julia R., and Herman Schwendinger
1983 *Rape and inequality.* Beverly Hills, Calif.: Sage.
1980 Rape victims and the false sense of guilt. *Crime and Social Justice* 13:4–17.

Scroggs, James R.
1976 Penalties for rape as a function of victim provocativeness, damage, and resistance. *Journal of Applied Social Psychology* 6:360–68.

Sealy, A. P., and W. R. Cornish
1973 Jurors and their verdicts. *Modern Law Review* 36:496–508.

Sebba, Leslie, and Sorel Cahan
1975 Sex offenses: The genuine and the doubted victim. In *Victimology: A new focus*, vol. 5, edited by I. Drapkin and E. Viano, 29–46. Lexington, Mass.: Lexington Books.

Seligman, C., J. Brickman, and D. Koulack
1977 Rape and physical attractiveness: Assigning responsibility to victims. *Journal of Personality* 45:554–63.

Sellin, Thorsten
1938 *Culture, conflict, and crime*. New York: Social Science Research Council.

Sellin, Thorsten, and Marvin E. Wolfgang
1964 *The measurement of delinquency*. New York: Wiley.

Sherman, Lawrence W., and Richard A. Berk
1984 The specific deterrent effects of arrest for domestic assault. *American Sociological Review* 49:261–72.

Shotland, R. Lance, and Lynne Goodstein
1983 "Just because she doesn't want to doesn't mean it's rape": An experimentally based causal model of the perception of rape in a dating situation. *Social Psychological Quarterly* 46:220–32.

Sinclair, Andrew
1964 *Era of excess: A social history of the prohibition movement*. New York: Harper & Row.

Skolnick, Jerome H., and J. Richard Woodworth
1967 Bureaucracy information and social control: A study of a morals detail. In *The police: Six sociological essays*, edited by D. Bordua. New York: Wiley.

Spitzer, Steven
1980 Leftwing criminology: An infantile disorder? In *Radical criminology*, edited by J. A. Inciardi, 169–90. Beverly Hills, Calif.: Sage.

Stanko, Elizabeth
1981–1982 The impact of victim assessments on prosecutor screening decisions. *Law and Society Review 16:225–39*.

Statsky, William
1985 *Legal thesaurus/dictionary*. St. Paul, Minn.: West.

Stember, Charles Herbert
1976 *Sexual racism: The emotional barrier to an integrated society*. New York: Elsevier.

Stephan, Cookie
1974 Sex prejudice in jury simulation. *Journal of Psychology* 88: 305–12.

Stevens, Wallace
1957 *Opus posthumous*, edited by S. F. Morse. New York: Knopf.

Strunk, William, Jr., and E. B. White
1959 *The elements of style*. 2d ed. New York: Macmillan.

Sudnow, David
1965 Normal crimes: Sociological features of the criminal code. *Social Problems* 12:255–70.

Sumner, William Graham
1906 *Folkways*. New York: Dover.

Sutherland, Edwin H.
1939 *Principles of criminology*. 3rd ed. Philadelphia: J. B. Lippincott.

Svalastoga, Kaare
1962 Rape and social structure. *Pacific Sociological Review* 5:48–53.

Swigert, Victoria Lynn, and Ronald A. Farrell
1977 Normal homicides and the law. *American Sociological Review* 42:16–32.

Tannenbaum, Frank
1938 *Crime and the community*. Boston: Ginn.

Tawney, R. H.
1971 *Equality*. London: Unwin Books. (First published in 1931.)

Taylor, D. Garth, Paul B. Sheatsley, and Andrew M. Greeley
1978 Attitudes toward racial integration. *Scientific American* 238:42–49.

Taylor, Ian, Paul Walton, and Jock Young
1973 *The new criminology: For a social theory of deviance*. New York: Harper & Row.

Thomson, Randall J., and Matthew T. Zingraff
1981 Detecting sentencing disparity: Some problems and evidence. *American Journal of Sociology* 86:869–80.

Tierney, Kathleen
1982 The battered women movement and the creation of the wife-beating problem. *Social Problems* 29:207–17.

Tittle, Charles R.
1980 *Sanctions and social deviance*. New York: Praeger.

Turk, Austin T.
1976 Law, conflict, and order: From theorizing toward theories. *Canadian Review of Sociology and Anthropology* 13:282–94.
1969 *Criminology and legal order*. Chicago: Rand McNally.

United States Bureau of the Census
   1987 *Statistical abstracts of the United States.* 107th ed. Washington, D.C.: U.S. Government Printing Office.

United States Department of Justice, Bureau of Justice Statistics
   1983 *Report to the nation on crime and justice.* Washington, D.C.: U.S. Government Printing Office.

United States Department of Justice, Bureau of Prisons
   1981 *Capital punishment, 1980.* Washington, D.C.: U.S. Government Printing Office.
   1971 National prisoner statistics. Bulletin No. 46 (August). *Capital punishment 1930–1970.* Washington, D.C.: U.S. Government Printing Office.

University of Pennsylvania Law Review
   1968 Police discretion and the judgment that a crime has been committed: Rape in Philadelphia. 117:227–322.

Unnever, James D.
   1982 Direct and organizational discrimination in the sentencing of drug offenders. *Social Problems* 30:212–25.

Velez-Diaz, A., and E. I. Megargee
   1970 An investigation of differences in value judgments between youthful offenders and nonoffenders in Puerto Rico. *Journal of Criminal Law, Criminology and Police Science* 61:549–53.

Visher, Christy
   1985 Research on juror decision making: Do experimental studies generalize? Unpublished. Washington, D.C.: National Research Council.

Vold, George B.
   1958 *Theoretical criminology.* New York: Oxford University Press.

Vold, George B., and Thomas J. Bernard
   1986 *Theoretical criminology.* 3rd ed. Oxford, England: Oxford University Press.

Walsh, Anthony
   1987 The sexual stratification hypothesis and sexual assault in light of the changing conceptions of race. *Criminology* 25:153–74.

Warr, Mark
   1985 Fear of rape among urban women. *Social Problems* 32:238–50.

Weber, Max
   1946 *From Max Weber: Essays in sociology,* trans. and edited by

H. H. Gerth and C. Wright Mills. New York: Oxford University Press.

Weis, Kurt, and Sandra Borges
1973 Victimology and rape: The case of the legitimate victim. *Issues in Criminology* 8:71–115.

Wellford, Charles
1975 Labelling theory and criminology: An assessment. *Social Problems* 22:332–45.

Whitt, Alan A.
1979 Class-dialectical model of power. *American Sociological Review* 44:81–99.

Wigmore, John Henry
1970 *Evidence at trials at common law*, vol. 3A, rev. ed., edited by J. C. Chadbourn. Boston: Little, Brown. (First published in 1904.)

Wilbanks, William
1987 *The myth of a racist criminal justice system*. Monterey, Calif.: Brooks/Cole.
1985 Is violent crime intraracial? *Crime and Delinquency* 31:117–28.

Williams, Joyce
1979 Sex-role stereotypes, women's liberation, and rape: A cross-cultural analysis of attitudes. *Sociological Symposium* 25:61–67.

Williams, Kristen M.
1981 Few convictions in rape cases: Empirical evidence concerning some alternative explanations. *Journal of Criminal Justice* 9: 29–39.
1978 *The role of the victim in the prosecution of violent crimes.* Washington, D.C.: Institute for Law and Social Research.
1976 The effects of victim characteristics on the prosecution of violent crimes. In *Criminal Justice and the Victim*, edited by W. F. McDonald, 177–226. Beverly Hills, Calif.: Sage.

Williams, Linda S.
1984 The classic rape: When do victims report? *Social Problems* 31:461–67.

Williams v. *Florida*
1970 Supreme Court of the United States. 339 U.S. 78, 90 S. Ct. 1893, 26 L. Ed. 2d 446.

Wilson, James Q., and Richard J. Herrnstein
1985 *Crime and human nature*. New York: Simon and Schuster.

Wolfgang, Marvin E.
  1958 *Patterns of criminal homicide.* Philadelphia: University of
    Pennsylvania Press.

Wolfgang, Marvin E., and Franco Ferracuti
  1967 *The subculture of violence: Toward an integrated theory in
    criminology.* London: Tavistock.

Wood, Pamela Lakes
  1973 The victim in a forcible rape case: A feminist view. *American
    Criminal Law Review* 11:335–54.

Zatz, Marjorie S.
  1984 Race, ethnicity, and determinate sentencing: A new dimen-
    sion to an old controversy. *Criminology* 22:141–71.

Zatz, Marjorie S., and Alan J. Lizotte
  1985 The timing of court processing: Towards linking theory and
    method. *Criminology* 23:313–35.

Index

ABOUT THE AUTHOR

GARY LAFREE is Associate Professor of Sociology at the University of New Mexico, where he specializes in criminology and the sociology of law. He is also the Director of the New Mexico Criminal Justice Statistics Center and a past member of the New Mexico Sentencing Guidelines Commission. He has recently been a visiting Associate Professor at the University of New Mexico law school and at the Center for Research on Crime and the Criminal Law, Universidad de los Andes, Venezuela. He has published numerous articles in law reviews and sociology and criminology journals on a wide range of topics, including the official processing of rape cases and discrimination in the application of criminal law. His current research includes a cross-national study of violent crime victims and an analysis of post-World War II trends in U.S. crime rates. He received his Ph.D in sociology in 1979 from Indiana University and has served as a consultant to lawyers and government in race, sex, and age discrimination cases.

A NOTE ON THE TYPE

The text of this book was set via computer-driven cathode-ray tube in 10/12 Century Schoolbook, a typeface based on a design drawn in 1894 by L. B. Benton and T. L. DeVinne for the *Century* magazine. Century Schoolbook is an excellent example of a refined Egyptian typeface. The Egyptian family of faces is characterized by thick slab serifs and little contrast between thick and thin strokes. The large x-height and simple letter forms of Century Schoolbook make it very legible.

Composed by Eastern Graphics

Printed and bound by R. R. Donnelley & Sons Company